Person-centred Counselling

Therapeutic and Spiritual Dimensions

The Whurr Counselling and Psychotherapy Series seeks to publish selected works of foremost experts in the field of counselling and psychotherapy. Each volume features the best of a key figures work, bringing together papers that have been published widely in the professional literature. In this way the work of leading counsellors and psychotherapists is being made accessible in single volumes.

Windy Dryden
Series editor

Previous printings of this book have contained a chapter entitled 'Beyond the Core Conditions'. This chapter has been withdrawn for personal and professional reasons at the joint request of the author and the client whose process is recorded in the chapter.

Person-centred Counselling

Therapeutic and Spiritual Dimensions

Brian Thorne
*Director of Student Counselling
University of East Anglia
and
Fellow of the College of Preceptors*

Counselling and Psychotherapy Series
Series Editor: Windy Dryden

W

WHURR PUBLISHERS
LONDON AND PHILADELPHIA

© 2000. This book is copyright. Copyright holders are indicated on the first page of each chapter. Where not named, the copyright rests with Whurr Publishers Ltd.

First published 1991 by

Whurr Publishers Limited
19b Compton Terrace
London N1 2UN

Reprinted 1993, 1994, 1996, 1997, 1998, 2000, 2001 and 2003

All rights reserved. This book is protected by copyright. No part of this book may be reproduced in any form or by any means, including photocopying, or utilised by any information storage or retrieval system without written permission from the copyright owner.

British Library Cataloguing in Publication Data
Thorne, Brian
Person-centred counselling: therapeutic and spiritual dimension. – (Counselling and psychotherapy series)
I. Title II. Series
253.5

ISBN 1-870332-87-3

Phototypset by J&L Composition Ltd, Filey, North Yorkshire
Printed in Great Britain by
Athenaeum Press Ltd, Gateshead, Tyne & Wear

Contents

Prologue	vii
Part I Self-exploration	1
Chapter 1	
The blessing and the curse of empathy	3
Chapter 2	
The God who comes: Good Friday 1946	19
Part II Theory and Practice	23
Chapter 3	
Person-centred therapy	25
Chapter 4	
The person-centred approach to large groups	50
Chapter 5	
The quality of tenderness	73
Part III Values and Meaning	83
Chapter 6	
In search of value and meaning	85
Chapter 7	
Ethical confrontation in counselling	93

Chapter 8	
Carl Rogers and the doctrine of Original Sin	102

Chapter 9	
Counselling and the grocer's shop on campus	111

Part IV Papers for Special Occasions	117
Chapter 10	
Intimacy	119

Chapter 11	
Counselling and community development	130

Chapter 12	
Conventional and unconventional relationships	136

Chapter 13	
Who hates the counsellor?	143

Chapter 14	
Carl Rogers: The legacy and the challenge	154

Postscript	166
Author index	167
Subject index	169

Prologue

It is a rare privilege to be given the opportunity to bring together, between the same covers, chapters, articles and lectures which span some 12 years of my professional life as a person-centred therapist. With one exception, I have largely excluded material from full-length books that I have written or edited but I sense that the exception may provide a clue to the underlying theme that permeates many of these pages. On Good Friday, 1946, not long after the end of the Second World War, I experienced as a boy of nine a mystical encounter which endowed me with a deep sense of my own unique worth and of my essential lovableness. I describe this experience in my latest book *Behold the Man* (1991) and the description is reproduced here as the second chapter of the present volume.

The significance of this encounter lies in its continuing power to uphold me even when I am feeling exhausted and inadequate or when I am assailed by massive doubt or paralysing guilt. It is as if what happened to me all those years ago opened up a channel to the core of my being where I recognised my own soul and knew that it was infinitely desirable and indissolubly linked to the souls of all my fellow human beings. It would seem that, once opened up, the channel has remained navigable ever since, despite the flotsam and jetsam of my far from perfect life and the polluting influences of my many fears and anxieties.

Fortunately, I was not quite arrogant enough, either at the time or later, to believe that my mystical experience made me some kind of special being. On the contrary, I assumed that if it were truly the case that I was of unique value and essentially lovable, then this must also be true of everyone else. It was only too apparent, however, that few people seemed from their words and actions to have grasped this somewhat amazing fact about themselves. I was deeply conscious throughout my later childhood and adolescence that, on the contrary, most people seemed to have a low opinion of themselves and that those who did not often found it necessary to denigrate others in order to preserve their own shaky self-esteem. It was particularly puzzling to discover that things were no different within the 'household of faith'. Indeed many of my fellow Christians seemed particularly prone to self-rejection; the fear of judgement (rather than the experience of unconditional love) often characterised the prevailing climate within the Church community. What was even more distressing was the discovery that, for many people outside it, the Church symbolised the baneful power of perpetual accusation, and its priests and people were feared as the sinister purveyors of insidious guilt. In such a situation it was scarcely surprising that the 'good news' fell on deaf ears, even on those rare occasions when it was accurately proclaimed.

For me, the discovery of client-centred therapy and the work of Carl Rogers was a revelation that illuminated the mystical encounter of my childhood and gave it a new and compelling significance. When I began my counsellor training in 1967 and read of the core conditions of acceptance, empathy and congruence, I knew instinctively that the climate of relationship which was being described in a psychotherapy textbook defined precisely the transforming and validating experience of welcoming intimacy that I had received as a totally unexpected and unmerited gift as a boy of nine. This realisation was almost too awesome to be borne for it suggested that to become a client-centred or person-centred therapist was an invitation to offer to others the kind of relationship which I had myself experienced in the presence of the source of all being – whom I call God. In short, under the guise of consellor training, I was embarking upon the imitation of divine love. I am sure that most of my fellow trainees of those days would be startled to hear their training programme described in these terms, and I am equally certain that most other person-centred therapists would have grave difficulty in labelling their therapeutic practice in this way. But this is how it was and is for me, and I have no wish to conceal the fact even if, in most of the chapters that follow, the reader will look in vain for any mention of God or of spirituality.

It is perhaps not surprising that for me the core conditions of acceptance, empathy and congruence have come over the years to have something of the same resonance as the monastic vows of chastity, poverty and obedience! They are the corner-stone of the person-centred therapist's way of being and constitute the central reference points for the rigorous discipline to which the therapist must submit if he or she is to offer a relationship with the power to transform. This discipline is unrelenting and its demands are great, because the person-centred therapist can have no recourse to a complex theory of personality development or to the subtle techniques of the psychological expert. Instead he or she must be continually attentive to the flow of his or her own inner experience and must constantly renew the will and the imagination to understand and to accept without prejudice or premature judgement. The comparison with the monastic life can be taken further, because just as the monk through his disciplined life may hope, from time to time at least, to experience the presence of God, so too the therapist may be

Prologue

privileged on rare occasions to find him- or herself swept up with the client into a current of healing of which he or she is merely the channel. Such moments are almost impossible to capture in words although the attentive reader will discover in the following pages, almost as a *leit motif*, a repeated paragraph in which I attempt to give expression to what is essentially a mystery of relationship that transcends time and space. It is this mystery that both sustains and challenges me in my work as a therapist. On the one hand, it provides me with the assurance that, on those occasions when my client and I feel most helpless and most stuck, there are resources readily available to us if only we can trust each other enough to allow them access. On the other hand, it challenges me to be in such a way that mutual trust of this awesome magnitude can be established between us. Nothing could be further removed from the role of the objective clinician. Instead I am required to be transparent and vulnerable as I surrender to the process of what I have come to recognise as disciplined intimacy.

The material in the book is arranged in four parts, each with its own brief introduction. I have attempted to give some intitial shape to the contents by starting with an autobiographical section which traces aspects of my own spiritual and vocational history over the years. This is followed by the longest section which presents my theoretical understanding and elaboration of the person-centred approach, together with detailed descriptions of key therapeutic relationships in which I have been involved. The third section focuses on issues of value and meaning and also tackles fundamental questions about human nature. The chapters in the fourth section revive for me many poignant memories. They are all the texts of special lectures given before invited audiences and reading them again has brought back many faces and forgotten fragments of the often heated discussions that followed the lectures when they were first delivered. Here, as in some of the other chapters, there are glimpses into the nightmarish psychological history of British higher education during the last decade and insights into the intensity of the university counsellor's day-to-day experience during a period in which the ethos of higher education has changed beyond recognition. I recall with sadness, too, that the published text of the lecture on 'Intimacy' which I gave to the Anglican clergy of the Norwich diocese was unobtainable from the Cathedral bookshop, although the Diocese's own Board for Social Responsibility had published it. Perhaps it will always be the case that yearning and fear will be locked in frozen conflict in the lives of many. Certainly, it has been my greatest privilege as a therapist to herald the advent of spring and sometimes to witness the gradual melting of the ice.

Brian Thorne
Norwich, 1991

To Windy Dryden, arch-facilitator of books and editor supreme.

Part I
Self-exploration

Introduction

The two chapters which make up the opening part of the book have been written from different perspectives and go some way, I hope, towards providing a comprehensive picture of my vocational development and my reasons for being a therapist. The first chapter was written in response to the direct request of Windy Dryden and Laurence Spurling who were simultaneously making the same request of several other therapists both in Britain and North America. Their resulting book, *On Becoming a Psychotherapist* (1989), offers a fascinating analysis of the complex factors that lead people to undertake the arduous work of the therapist. For me, the writing of this chapter (which I completed rapidly in the space of a week) came at a point when I was overworked and exhausted, and it had the surprising effect of putting me in touch with new energy. I suppose it was something to do with the rediscovery of meaning and the inescapable confrontation with the fact that my life has been filled with remarkable and loving people. In brief, this requested autobiographical review showed me that I had every reason to be immensely grateful for the affirmation that I had received from so many quarters throughout my life.

The second chapter goes to the core of my being and tells of the greatest affirmation of all which I received as a boy of nine. It was written as a preparatory piece for meditations on the Passion and Crucifixion of Christ which form the centre-piece of my most recent book *Behold the Man* (1991). Whereas the first chapter seeks to explain why I am a therapist, this second chapter traces the origins of my Christian commitment and goes some way towards explaining why, despite many struggles and conflicts and an almost permanent restlessness, I remain a member of the Church.

References

DRYDEN, W. and SPURLING, L. (1989). *On Becoming a Psychotherapist*. London: Tavistock Publications/Routledge.

THORNE, B. (1991). *Behold the Man*. London: Darton, Longman & Todd.

Chapter 1
The Blessing and the Curse of Empathy

Why did I become a Psychotherapist?

Whenever I think back to my childhood, I find my eyes filling with tears. This is not because my early days were particularly unhappy. The tears are of nostalgia for a time of extraordinary intimacy and intensity. I grew up during the Second World War (I was 2½ years old when war broke out) and my earliest memories are of scenes played out against a background of anxiety and uncertainty. I remember vividly the horror of the first major air-raid on the city of Bristol in 1940 when my parents and I (I was an only child) were trapped for half the night in the house of my paternal grandmother, on the far side of the city many miles from our home. I recall the long walk back through shattered streets still ablaze and the arrival at the pile of masonry which, only hours before, had been the home of my mother's parents. I still remember my mother's scream and the comforting neighbour with the brandy bottle who assured her that my grandparents were safe and that their newly errected air-raid shelter had stood the vital test.

In such a world and at such a time there was no room for pretence or superficiality. We all lived with the possibility of sudden death. On another occasion, for example, my mother and I missed a bus in the city only to learn that minutes later the vehicle had been destroyed in a freak afternoon air-raid. At school, lessons were often interrupted by the chilling sound of the sirens announcing the German Luftwaffe and we would be herded into long and dank concrete shelters in the playground. It was in this environment that I learned from a very early age to live with the deepest human emotions of love and fear and to witness the extreme limits of human courage and vulnerability, of hope and despair.

From *On Becoming a Psychotherapist*, 1989, edited by W. Dryden and L. Spurling, Tavistock/Routledge, London with permission.

The feelings of nostalgia are strongest when I recall my friends of those days. In an important way, the fact that I had no brothers and sisters made me more available to others. I was constantly invited into other children's houses and I suppose I grew accustomed to adapting myself to different life-styles and to changing emotional patterns. Children whose fathers were away from home in the Services would often talk of their anxiety (sometimes tragically justified by events) and their mothers, too, would speak openly to me of their fears and loneliness. As I write now I realise how much I loved them all and how very loved I felt, not only in my own home, but in the whole neighbourhood. Looking back on it, I think it would be fair to say that I grew up in a remarkably therapeutic community which was somehow learning to live creatively with the cruel vagaries of war.

I realised during my primary school days that I had an ability that seemed unusual and that was both a blessing and a curse. Today I would call it the capacity to empathise. At that time I simply experienced, with alarming frequency, the powerful sensation of knowing what it felt like to be in someone else's skin. In some ways this gave me exquisite satisfaction for it enabled me to come close to others (especially my own contemporaries) and to share a warmth of companionship which I know now was exceptional. Often, however, it would lead me into very painful situations where I felt helpless. The worst example of this was with a spinster teacher at my infants' school whom I knew to be desperately unhappy and who was ragged unmercifully by the other children. With 60 in a class there was little I could do to influence the environment and I would sit in misery as I watched this poor woman's gradual disintegration. She eventually put her head in the gas oven one summer's morning. I have never forgotten her and the occasion of her death was perhaps the first time I experienced a powerful resentment about my own nature. Then, and often since, I have raged against my own empathic ability and insightfulness. I have wanted to be preserved from the burden of my own understanding and have even felt moments of hatred for those who suffer and whose sufferings are so obvious to me but not apparently to others.

The spiritual event which undoubtedly determined the direction of my life was also in some ways the outcome of this empathic ability. I have described it at length elsewhere (Thorne, 1987a) but, in essence, it was the almost unbearable experience of glimpsing the nature of the Passion and Crucifixion of Christ (see also Chapter 2). This happened on Good Friday afternoon in 1946 and left me, after what seemed like hours of solitary weeping, exhausted and at peace. There is no doubt, I believe, that from that moment my journey towards becoming a psychotherapist was inevitable.

I was 28 before the idea took final shape. During the intervening years I had won a scholarship to a famous boys' public school (which provided yet another context of intensity and intimacy), served as a National Service Officer in Cyprus (where, again, sudden death was always a possibility), gone to Cambridge to read languages, trained to be a teacher in my own home city and taken my first post as a schoolmaster in a public school on the south coast.

I am not, I believe, a natural linguist but it gives me great pleasure to speak German, French and a smattering of other European languages. The decision to specialise in German (taken when I was 12) was clearly fired by my wartime experiences and my first trip abroad at the age of 16 was to Hamburg to stay with a German family where the father had died at the Russian front. Looking back on it, this too was a pivotal experience. Speaking a different language from my own enabled me to find parts of myself that had previously lain dormant and I drew on such a well of emotion that I wonder now how my new German friends coped with me. German and French literature also touched me deeply. In many ways the study of literature is a training in empathy and a profound challenge to the imagination. During my time both as a student and as a teacher, I realise that I lived in a world which was densely populated by novelists and poets, and by the fictitious characters of their creation. In such company it was impossible to feel parochial.

The same is true of my experience of the Church. Anglican by denomination and catholic in spirit, I have from an early age known something of the universality of the Church and of its existence outside time and space. I have talked with saints and heard angel choirs. In all this I was much encouraged by a series of remarkable priests whose influence on me was profound. Gerard Irvine, poet, writer, man of letters, and friend of writers and artists, befriended me when I was 10 years old and treated me as an equal. Stuart Tayler, former naval officer, skilled confessor and passionate lover of Italy, invited me to be his travelling companion when I was 17 and for the next 25 years opened up the treasures of European culture to me whilst showing me that the disciplined life and having fun are not incompatible. Hugh Montefiore, later Bishop of Birmingham, revealed to me while I was at Cambridge the fascination of theology and the beauty of intellectual and spiritual tolerance. Richard Eyre, now Dean of Exeter, allowed me to be his companion at the altar and in the daily offices of the Church, as we both struggled to make sense of our unlikely presences in the daily turmoil of the life of a public school at a time of educational change. All these men, through their friendship and their generosity of spirit, enabled me to live in depth and to experience myself as intelligent, insightful and loving.

It was perhaps not surprising that my experience as a schoolmaster provided the final impetus for my pilgrimage towards the therapeutic profession. A boarding school is full of wounded souls, many of them suffering from feelings of rejection or suppressed rage. It was not long before I was working well into the night as a constant stream of adolescents came to my door to pour out their misery or to seek support in their psychological pain. In 1965, one such young man was taxing me beyond the limits of my competence and energy and, although by now I had gained much in confidence through contact with local psychiatrists and through seminars at the Tavistock Institute, I knew I was out of my depth. It was about this time that I came to hear of George Lyward, the remarkable therapist who had established Finchden Manor in Tenterden, Kent as a therapeutic refuge for badly disturbed young men, many of whom were products of public schools. I knew little of the nature of Lyward's work but was increasingly awed by what I heard of its effectiveness and power. One night, in desperation, I telephoned him and told him something of myself and of my predicament with my unhappy student who seemed by now on the verge of psychosis. Within 48 hours I was sitting in Lyward's study at Finchden and my life's work for the next 20 years was determined.

George Lyward was a genius and this is not the place to attempt a description of what he achieved or of the methods he employed. For me his importance lies in the way he related to me that day and in the following years until his death in 1973. Within minutes, it seemed, I felt recognised, valued and seen through. This last aspect of the encounter was both disturbing and liberating. I felt totally exposed and yet, because there was no point in pretending, I was able to relax into being myself. This sense of my own authenticity was crucial for what followed because otherwise it was unlikely that I could have taken Lyward seriously. I should simply have assumed that his judgement was based on his imperfect knowledge of me or on my own successful play-acting. In the event, Lyward informed me that I was a therapist already and that clearly only I could see my client through the next part of his journey. He then said many helpful things about adolescence, allowed me to stay while he talked at length with several of his own young residents, served delicious Lapsang tea in beautiful china cups and asked me to come again when I wanted to do so.

After that meeting with Lyward I knew that my days as a teacher were numbered. There were more visits to Finchden, a deepening of many of the relationships I had with both boys and colleagues in the school, the falling in love with the woman who is still my wife and, finally, acceptance at one of the first counsellor training courses to be established in a university in Britain. In the autumn of 1967 I entered full-time study at the Guidance Unit of Reading University and began my training as a client-centred counsellor.

I have no doubt that at that stage I had many fantasies about the work of a therapist. In the first place, I did not envisage myself ever leaving the education scene. I suppose I thought of the therapist as a kind of teacher/priest. Certainly my image was of a somewhat patriarchal figure who would have wisdom to impart as a result of his training and experience. Secondly, I was fascinated by the mystery surrounding therapeutic encounters and I believe I was excited by the prospect of sharing many secrets and exercising a subtle power on the inner lives of others. I do not think I underestimated the hard work which would be involved. George Lyward maintained that he had been tired for most of his life and the depth of his dedication to the young men at Finchden left me in no doubt that the life of a therapist was a tough and demanding one. There were times when I suspected that I could not summon up such commitment and, having only recently married, I was also worried about the effect on my wife of this life of intimate relationships upon which I was now embarking. I feared that I might pay a high price for such 'promiscuity' and that my wife might pay an even higher one.

Some of my friends at that time made it clear to me that they were greatly alarmed at my apparent foolhardiness in subjecting a recent marriage to such a premature trial. There were those, too, who were opposed to my plans for a quite different reason. One of my own sixth-form pupils voiced clearly what others only hinted at. 'You're being a traitor to your vocation. You're a born teacher: how can you go off to become some kind of glorified social worker?' For me, this was without question the greatest dilemma. I loved teaching and the world of the intellect. What is more I knew I was a good teacher and could look forward to a successful career in education. There were many times when it seemed totally absurd to be leaving something I loved so much. So acute was the dilemma that I hedged my bets. I asked for – and was granted – leave of absence from my school for a year. If things did not work out I could return and resume teaching German and French as if my aberration had never occurred. When I eventually left for Reading University in the autumn of 1967 there was no marked sense of excitement or pleasure. In many ways I was going because it seemed I had to go. For financial reasons (I was once more on a student grant) my wife remained behind in our flat and continued to work in the school. I remember experiencing almost intolerable conflict as I waved goodbye. It seemed that I was leaving behind all that I valued most and that I was doing so because of some inner drive which in my heart I still could not fully trust. This sense of almost being pulled screaming towards the meaning of my life comes back and haunts me still today. When I am exhausted or am caught in an impossibly demanding therapeutic relationship, I can literally scream or shout with resentment and anger. At such times I have little sense of having chosen my life, and come within an ace of rejecting a God whose love seems to have trapped me into a moral compulsion that fills me with loathing.

How did I become a Psychotherapist?

As a student at Cambridge, I had stumbled on the work of Carl Jung as a result of studying the novels of Hermann Hesse for the second part of the Modern Languages Tripos. I was fascinated by Jung's writing and the wide sweep of his conceptual map delighted me. His essentially hopeful view of the human personality came as a refreshing antidote to what I already knew of the Freudian perception of reality and I was particularly enthralled by the Jungian notion of individuation and of the encounter with the Self. It was also a relief to me to discover so eminent a therapist who clearly placed high emphasis on the spiritual dimension in human nature.

One of my most vivid memories of Cambridge is of a glorious summer afternoon in 1961 after I had finished my final examinations and was luxuriating in a period of well-earned idleness. I recall lying on the grassy bank beside the river Cam caught up in the compelling urgency and fascination of Jung's *The Undiscovered Self* and breaking off only to attend evensong at King's College Chapel, sung with the exquisite perfection which can only be attained by a choir of rare distinction. The memory for me is of integration. I can still dimly recall the sense of physical well-being and the delicious heat of the summer sun accompanied by the gentle sound of flowing water. Jung's book spoke of dark forces and the terror of possible annihilation, whilst insisting on the wonder of the human psyche and its potential for transformation. The music of King's spoke of a transcendence and a glory which took the breath away. And, then, at the end of the day there were my friends with whom to drink and talk far into the night. This was heaven.

Reading University Guidance Unit had none of the romantic and powerfully evocative atmosphere of Cambridge in mid-summer and, looking back on it, I believe I began my formal training determined not to be swept into what I suspected could become a psychological ghetto. I remember vowing to myself that I would adopt a critical stance to everything I was taught and that nothing would prevent me from continuing to read novels and poetry or from dabbling in the latest theological issues. In short, I was keen to integrate my training into my life and to avoid being taken over by it. In the event, two significant events occurred in the first months which ensured that no such take-over could happen: my mother died after being in poor health for some time and one of the sixth-form pupils, with whom I had been much involved in the school, committed suicide by hurling himself from the school tower. In the light of such powerful events, it was unlikely that the therapist-in-training would be taken over by new learnings obtained in the lecture room or even in personal supervision sessions. I was too preoccupied incorporating into my life the impact of two such momentous occurrences. I also became aware at this time of the stabilising influence of my theological understandings and of the power of the rituals and offices of the Church to sustain me. I also found myself drawn back repeatedly to Jung's writings whilst I attempted to struggle with dark feelings of despair and impotent rage as my grief came to the surface and demanded attention. For me at this time, Jung was a never-failing repository of hope primarily because he seemed never to evade or deny the negative and yet did not succumb to the dark.

During my first term at Reading, a second Carl edged quietly into my life almost without my being aware that he had slipped in. I shall never know if he would have found such easy access if Christ and Jung had not preceded him into the inner sanctuary of my being. As it was, once I acknowledged his presence, I realised that I had somehow discovered the ideal companion for this phase of my life on which I was now irretrievably embarked. I had, of course, seen Carl Rogers' name on the book lists which had been sent to me before I went to Reading and I had probably read that Bruce Shertzer, my principal trainer from Purdue University in Indiana, was a client-centred practitioner, much influenced by Rogers. It was only gradually, however, that it fully dawned on me that I was being trained as a client-centred therapist and that Carl Rogers was to be the principal source of learning for my new professional identity. By the time I had fully grasped this fact I knew that it was a situation with which I felt wholly content. As I read Rogers' books with increasing enthusiasm I realised that I was not being asked to take on board a whole new perception of reality or a complex theory of human personality. I was not even being required to change my basic way of being with those who sought my help. Instead, I found in Rogers someone who seemed to esteem the validity of my own experience and who gave names to attitudes and activities which I had falteringly attempted to embody for many years. And so it was that Carl Rogers became for me, not the new guru or source of all wisdom for the aspiring therapist, but a gentle companion who spoke of unconditional positive regard, empathy and genuineness and thus gave shape to what, for me, had previously been an almost instinctive and somewhat incoherent response to others in need.

I have spoken above of my early recognition of my capacity to empathise. When I went to Reading I had been a naturally empathic person for as long as I could remember. What was surprising was to discover that this was by no means the case for many of my fellow-trainees. Even more important was the discovery that most people do not expect to be understood and that it is therefore important to let them know when you are actually empathising accurately. I realised that, although I had been understanding others for years, I had not always had the wit to let them know that this was the case: the empathic response had been left incomplete because unexpressed. Rogers' insistence on the quality of unconditional positive regard or non-possessive warmth showed me that, in this respect too, I had always attempted to cultivate just such an attitude towards others. In my grieving, however, I quickly came up against many guilt feelings (especially about the young man who had committed suicide) and realised with the help both of Rogers' writings and of Bruce Shertzer's gentle supervision that I often fell dismally short when it came to offering myself such regard and acceptance. There could hardly have been a more ideal moment for remedying this deficiency and the working-through of my grief was greatly aided by the movement towards self-acceptance which took place in the months immediately after the two deaths.

In Christian terms it would be possible to describe what happened as my growing ability to internalise God's love and forgiveness, whereas previously I had been largely dependent on the sacrament of penance in order to feel acceptable and valuable in my own eyes. It is perhaps a tribute, however, to the basic healthiness of my theology that the movement towards self-acceptance proceeded with commendable speed once Carl Rogers' influence had permeated my thinking and feeling. Since then I have discovered that, for other Christians reared in a more evangelical or judgemental tradition, the encounter with Rogers' work has meant an upheaval of major proportions which not infrequently results either in a rejection of Rogers or of Christianity. It is significant that for me my training as a client-centred practitioner simply deepened and extended my Christian understanding. Carl Jung had shown me that it was wholly reasonable to believe in God and to acknowledge the spiritual dimension in human beings. Carl Rogers showed me what it might mean to take the second great commandment seriously and to attempt to love my neighbour as myself.

Rogers' third core condition for therapeutic movement – genuineness or congruence – also resonated with my previous belief structure and with my own way of being. I had long since valued my uniqueness and had revelled in my own individualism. I was sceptical of experts and had learned to trust my own thoughts and perceptions. Furthermore, I had never seen much point in pretending to be someone I was not. This is not to say that I had always found it easy to resist group pressures or to rise above conventional norms. Often I was as frightened and inhibited as anyone else, but it was clear to me that I did not wish to be so. Therefore Rogers' insistence on the importance of the therapist's own thoughts and feelings, and on his or her willingness when appropriate to express these, was both challenging and confirming of what I truly wished to do and to be for my clients. Once again, Rogers was, in a sense, telling me nothing new. He was giving me the courage and the clarity to develop my own way of being in the knowledge that to do so would be to the benefit of my future clients.

The longer my formal training went on the more clearly I recognised that I was not learning to become a patriarchal figure with wisdom to impart. What is more it was becoming increasingly evident to me that I no longer wished to be such a figure – if indeed, I had ever done so. Weighty theories about personality development and complex maps of the unconscious have their fascination, but they tend to make those who have studied them feel important and erudite. In the behavioural tradition, too, the acquisition of techniques and the development of methodologies for changing overt behaviour can give the therapist a sense of power and competence which, for me, I feel, would not have been healthy. I knew only too well that I was a powerful person and anything which could have added to my sense of power might well have been to the detriment of my growth as a therapist. I was glad to be challenged by the simple but totally demanding task of becoming more empathic, more accepting and more in touch with myself.

Bruce Shertzer offered a compelling model of the client-centred practitioner. He lectured conscientiously and with clarity but it was in his one-to-one relationships and in small groups that he embodied most strikingly the qualities that characterise the client-centred therapist. He listened; he valued those to whom he spoke and made them feel uniquely recognised; he went to infinite pains to make sure he understood; and he did not hesitate to offer his own thoughts and feelings when he believed these would be helpful. In his presence, it was possible to relax into learning and to feel, not pressure, but the space in which to feel and think. In personal development groups, he provided security and absolute attentiveness but never took anything away from trainees by dominating the group or intruding with inappropriate exercises or information. None of this is to deny the value of the more formal opportunities that we were afforded to develop our counselling skills and attitudes through intensive role-play and other experiential workshops. Nor, again, would I wish to undervalue the hours spent in the library and the challenge of writing essays to convey my understanding of therapeutic process and developmental psychology. In the last analysis, however, I know that the deepest learning came from my contact with a therapist who embodied the value system which he sought to impart in the lecture theatre and the seminar room.

My fellow students were also of crucial significance to me. They allowed me to meet them as people and together we shared our strengths and weaknesses. Some of them became important friends during this period and showed me great kindness and understanding, for example, when my mother died. Much of the training took place in small groups and, without this level of openness and responsiveness, it is difficult to imagine what would have happened. As it was, such times were often deeply involving and certainly the hours spent with fellow trainees in pubs and student rooms after the formal training sessions were a rich source of further learning and stimulus. I benefited enormously, I now realise, from being a member of a course where almost all the participants were resident in the same university town and were therefore available to each other almost 24 hours a day.

The sense of openness and responsiveness within the training group as a whole was particularly important when it came to the counselling practicum. We were strongly encouraged to make tape-recordings of our sessions with our clients and these were a primary resource in discussions with our personal supervisors. Of equal importance, however, was the opportunity to present a taped interaction to a whole group of fellow trainees and to receive feedback from them. This discipline was, for me, an invaluable source of learning and its effectiveness would have been greatly reduced if there had not been a willingness to reveal weaknesses and inadequacies on the part of all the members of the training group.

It says much for the flexibility of the course that, in my final term, I was permitted to spend an intensive fortnight at Finchden Manor. For me this provided the ideal opportunity for reflection and for consolidating my learning in an environment where there was no possibility of pretence or self-deception. George Lyward, his staff and the boys of Finchden were my real examiners and it was fitting that the man who had first expressed his confidence in me as a therapist was able at this stage to mark my progress and also gently to tease me if it seemed to him that I was in danger of losing myself in the role. Looking back on the whole training experience, I am aware that, without it, I could not have become a therapist and yet at the same time I knew that the academic study, the formal training sessions, the increasing knowledge of therapeutic process and human development would all have been in vain if it had not been for the quality of the people who were my trainers and fellow students and for the depth of relationship that was offered to me. I suspect, too, that my mother's death, the suicide of my sixth-form pupil and the challenges of the early days of married life, all contributed in a major fashion to my understanding of myself and to my ability to assist those very first 'official' clients who were trusting enough to put themselves in the hands of a somewhat callow apprentice.

When did I become a Psychotherapist?

It is seldom in my professional career that I have referred to myself as a psychotherapist. In the person-centred tradition, the word has about it a certain mystique which is alien to an approach that strives to establish an egalitarian relationship with clients and to eschew the role of the expert. Most of the time, then, I have been content to call myself a counsellor but for me this word implies a professional practitioner with substantial training and experience who enjoys a high level of self-knowledge which he or she brings to therapeutic relationships. When did I become such a person and experience the reality of a confident professional identity? Certainly it was not on the day that I received my diploma from the University of Reading, important as that day was. The movement towards such an identity was more complex and concerned with profounder issues than that of receiving legitimisation from an academic institution.

In the eyes of many of my former colleagues, and certainly as far as my immediate family was concerned, I became a counsellor when I completed my formal training and obtained my first post in a counselling service. For some of the pupils at the school where I had taught, I suspect that I was a therapist long before I embarked on formal training. For me, however, the transition from schoolteacher to counsellor was a lengthy one. The first day I entered my counsellor's consulting room I felt fraudulent and sad. I longed to be back in the classroom with a syllabus to teach and with the stimulus of a responsive and appreciative group. I felt almost trapped by the one-to-one relationship and frightened by the unpredictability of what the client might bring. I felt hopelessly ill-equipped and what a few weeks previously had passed for a sound and creative training experience now seemed in retrospect to be inadequate and superficial. My new colleagues were considerate and helpful, but their very competence added to my sense of ineptitude.

The uncomfortableness with my new professional identity persisted for some weeks during which time I never ceased to be amazed by the way in which clients seemed to be able to trust me and to behave towards me as if I were a *real* therapist. Much of the time, however, I felt as if I were taking part in a dramatic enactment and that soon the curtain would come down and I should be able to return to my familiar environment and resume my teaching of French literature. I believe now that I was grieving for my past identity and that throughout these opening weeks I was mildly depressed. I remember, too, that I was physically ill for a week or so (something that had not happened for years) and that during this illness I seriously wondered if I should resign before I was irrevocably trapped in what appeared to be a somewhat elaborate charade.

Shortly after this illness, two clients appeared who rapidly jerked me out of my transition state. Both were young women and they could not have been more dissimilar in their response to me. The first treated me with cold disdain and as good as challenged me to sort out her problems in half-an-hour. In her presence I felt a rising anger which, after 15 minutes, I could no longer contain. I shouted at her to get out of my room and she left with an arrogant toss of her head while I collapsed on a colleague in the next room, feeling that my counselling career was possibly already at an end. The same afternoon, however, another girl presented herself and revealed within minutes an inner desolation of such intensity that I found myself responding at a level which I had not previously experienced. It was as if my own fear – and ignorance of the young female psyche – evaporated in the presence of her desperation. I was awed, too, by her trust in me and by her preparedness to reveal her total vulnerability. For the first time I experienced what I have come to recognise as an overwhelming surge of loving commitment. What is more, her weakness put me in touch with my own strength. For the first time I felt authentic in my therapeutic role and knew that I could be a faithful companion to my client no matter how dark her world and unpredictable her journey.

These two young women in their different ways forced me to own my new identity. The first revealed to me my inadequacy in the face of her contempt but at the same time showed me that I cared deeply about being a therapist, that I could not bear her scorn. The second compelled me to be real and not to deny the extent of my resources as a person and as a professional. She affirmed me in a way which no amount of praise or encouragement from colleagues or success with less demanding clients could have done. She challenged me to the depth of my being and I found myself not only responding to the challenge but doing so immediately and confidently. In the event, our relationship was to take us into areas of fear and confusion that threatened her sanity and constantly made me question my own competence. But her commitment to me and mine to her never wavered. She showed me that I had the will and the courage to stay with a process come what may and it was this assurance above all others that I needed. When, several months later, she began to smile and to discern a future for herself I knew that my apprenticeship was over. I was a therapist whether I liked it or not and much of the time now I found myself rather liking it.

What sustains me as a Psychotherapist?

I have never attempted to deny to myself or to others the arduous nature of a therapist's work. The intense concentration required in therapeutic relationships, the anxiety generated by close involvement with those who are often highly self-destructive, the relentless pressure of a seemingly endless stream of clients – all these can induce exhaustion and a sense of powerlessness in the face of implacable forces. What is more, there is often the experience of battling against formidable odds because of family or societal pressures which constantly threaten to undermine the client's progress in therapy or seem to reduce the therapeutic relationship to little more than an ineffective palliative administered once or twice a week. It is gruelling and demanding work and the therapist who denies this is mendacious, deluded or incompetent.

There are certain obvious factors that have contributed to my honourable survival for 20 years in the profession. In the first place, I have never had the misfortune to work on my own. Both in educational institutions and in private practice, I have always been a member of a team and have enjoyed the immediate support and stimulus of other therapists working alongside me. Secondly, I have always had easy and ready access to medical and psychiatric resources and this has relieved me of the intolerable burden of coping unsupported with clients who are on the verge of psychosis or seem to have lost the capacity to hold their lives together in the practical world of day-to-day existence. Thirdly, I have a regular and valued supervision relationship where I can talk through those aspects of my work (or of my own life) that are proving particularly difficult or stressful. Fourthly, I have a wife and family who are astonishingly supportive of my curious mode of earning a living and even seem to take some pride and interest in my work.

Clearly, this network of human support forms the context of much of my professional life, but it is not in itself sufficient to explain why I continue to feel, not simply sustained but positively nourished by my work as a therapist. The deeper reasons for this happy state of affairs lie in the nature of the relationships I form with my clients. It is my conviction, as I have argued earlier, that the work of the therapist is not essentially concerned with dispensing wisdom or expertise or even with the deploying of skills. It is more to do with embodying values consistently no matter how great the client's confusion, resistance or even hostility. For me, this means not only that I attempt to demonstrate unambiguously the unique value that I place on an individual life, but also my conviction that in the last analysis it is love with understanding that heals. In a sense, therefore, my work as a therapist, although it is hard, demanding and exhausting, is easy because it gives me the permission and the constant obligation to be the person I truly wish to be. Obviously, I do not always succeed in embodying such values or in being this person, but the very fact that I construe my work in this way means that many of the relationships which I form in the process of being a therapist are a source of the profoundest satisfaction. In the first place, I am enabled to love not in some wishy-washy generalised way, but in a focused manner which is devoid of possessiveness and refuses to be easily side-tracked. What is more, I am challenged to put whatever intellectual abilities I possess at the service of my loving. In short, every therapeutic relationship offers me the possibility of living in as integrated a way as possible. Secondly, I am not infrequently on the receiving end of my client's loving. It is, I believe, one of the therapist's rare privileges to be loved by those who in the past have often experienced their loving as destructive or damaging. I say a privilege because, for such a person to discover that their loving can be creative and positive is often to unleash a flood of energy that can irradiate the therapist and become a source of renewal and refreshment for him or her. There is all the difference in the world between this kind of client loving, which is life-enhancing, and the desperate dependency that is often the mark of the client who has not yet been able to receive the therapist's understanding and acceptance. What is more, the client's discovery that he or she can enter deeply into a relationship without being destructive, not only makes it possible for the therapist to receive love but also provides him or her with the surest evidence of his or her client's development.

One of the chief advantages of working with a predominantly youthful clientèle (as I do in my university setting) is the rapidity with which such development often takes place. I know that I possess qualities of patience and perseverence which enable me to commit myself to clients for years if necessary, but I am equally aware that I would soon be worn down if *all* my clients needed such long-term attention. My brief counselling encounters, lasting perhaps 2 or 3 months, do much to remind me of the remarkable capacity of many human beings to discover their own resources and strengths once they have been offered a modicum of acceptance and understanding. I believe that my long-term clients owe much to these others who continually delight me by their ability to move forward rapidly and confidently and who therefore provide me with constant proof that therapy 'works'.

With those whose journey is more arduous and complex, it is not always so easy to hang on to my faith in the process and it is in these cases that my religious faith becomes of such cardinal importance. With the short-term client, it is comparatively easy to imagine that I have been the chief facilitator of the client's growth and progress. With those who are more damaged, however, the experience is often one of frustration, stuckness and even of powerlessness. It is in such relationships that it becomes so blindingly obvious that I am not a powerful magician who can work miracles by offering acceptance, genuineness and empathy. I am learning increasingly to accept my stuckness and powerlessness to that I can get somewhere near the humility that is necessary if I am to become a channel for a power greater than my own. If I can let go of anxiety and simply relax, I experience what I can only describe as a new resource which becomes available to my client and to me. To non-religious readers this may sound strange, but to those familiar with the disciplines of prayer and worship, it will not be difficult to see the process as akin to that of resting in the presence of God. Such a resting is in no sense a giving up. It is rather a willingness to be open to forces greater than oneself and a readiness to cooperate with them. In Christian terms, it is best expressed as being open to the Holy Spirit or being a willing participant in the operation of grace. Interestingly enough, my experience of opening myself in this way does not seem to be dependent on the spiritual or religious understanding of my client. However, where the client is a fellow Christian and the process can be acknowledged and openly shared, the developments can be all the more surprising and dramatic (Thorne, 1987b) (see Chapter 6).

It will now be clear that for me the practice of psychotherapy is serving my own needs and desires in fundamental ways. It allows me to love and to be loved and encourages me to develop my relationship with God by continually opening myself to His presence. Emotionally and spiritually I am nourished and challenged every day. As I grow older I discover that I yearn for more solitude, although sometimes it feels like a kind of greediness to have more of God and less of His creatures! If I can learn to trust this feeling, then it seems likely that my activities as a therapist may diminish in the years ahead and I can well imagine that by retirement age the day-to-day conduct of my life may be looking very different. Perhaps, too, I will have learned to do without the prestige, the respect and the reasonably generous salary that my work as a therapist has brought me and which have done much to bolster my failing ego when the pressures have seemed too overwhelming.

I cannot conclude this section without referring once more to that part of me which profoundly hates being a therapist at all. There are times when I long to be blissfully unaware, shallow and pleasure seeking. I could easily succumb at such moments to an almost anarchic urge to lose myself in wine, women and self-indulgence. I am heartily sick of the sufferings of others and of the God who tells me to recognise Him in them. It is then that my long-suffering family comes to my rescue. They allow me to rage, usually unjustifiably, at them and not to feel too guilty afterwards and they even listen to my complex anecdotes (often drawn from Army life) which always reduce me, if not them, to uncontrollable mirth and a state of imminent apoplexy. Without such an arena, where I can froth with rage and dissolve in laughter, I do not know what would have become of me.

Implications for Other Therapists

I am doubtful about the usefulness of my experience to other therapists because I am aware of its idiosyncratic nature. Writing about myself in this way has revealed to me that, viewed from the outside, my life may appear to have about it a pattern that would be the delight of many a career planner. My essentially empathic personality, fed by war-time experiences and buttressed by reasonable intelligence, might naturally be expected to find expression first in teaching and then in the therapeutic field. As an only child, too, it is perhaps not surprising that I have sought intimacy beyond the family and have ensured that I always have someone to love and from whom I can, in return, receive affection and esteem. All this in a sense is true, but it does not reach the heart of the matter.

When I first decided to become a teacher (on a summer's day in an Italian cathedral) and when later I decided to seek therapist training, I do not recall anything approaching a 'Eureka' experience. On the contrary, there was a sense of inevitability mingled with something akin to dread. I knew I had little choice if I was to obey the voice within me. In short, my work as a therapist has in a sense been an act of obedience. I suppose this realisation may in itself be of value to others in that it suggests that the overt desire or ambition to be a therapist may be a somewhat treacherous motivation. Certainly, over the years I have found myself being less than enthusiastic about the aspirations of some who have voiced their intention to me of becoming therapists. It has seemed that in some cases there has been a highly romantic and unrealistic view of the therapist's life, whereas in others there has been a scarcely concealed lust for power.

To those who have made it into the profession I would warn against neglect of self. I know how often I have been near the edge of self-sacrificial stupidity and have been pulled back at the eleventh hour by the kindly or stern warnings of colleagues, friends or spouse. I realise furthermore how vital such people are to me in the preservation of my own well-being. Heaven preserve me from the life of solitary private practice where the need to earn money means the rapid disappearance of a social life and the end of friendships and family relationships.

Perhaps the chief insight for me from this autobiographical reminiscence has been the way in which I have somehow incorporated therapy into the overall understanding and conduct of my life. The important people for me in the therapeutic world – Lyward, Shertzer, Rogers – have impressed me primarily as human beings rather than as theoreticians or therapists. Their therapy was an extension of their personalities or an expression of the values which permeated their lives. I have met therapists who seem somehow to have stuck their therapeutic ideas and practice on to a personality which then lives in great discomfort with such an accretion. Strangely enough, such people seem to talk endlessly about therapy and leave me with grave doubts about their effectiveness. I have recorded how, during my period of formal training, I consciously refused to be sucked into a psychological 'Weltanschauung' and stubbornly held on to my literary and theological slants on reality. It is, I believe, dangerous when a psychological understanding of life and a therapeutic approach based on it begin to take the place of religion or of a fervently held philosophical or political credo. The therapist who falls into this trap is in serious trouble when clients fail to behave appropriately or reject what is on offer for he is likely to feel undermined and to have his whole identity threatened. This is even more painful if his identity is in any case a somewhat makeshift affair where therapeutic ideas and practice are an accretion rather than an extension of his personality.

Finally, I doubt if a therapist who is incapable of loving or of allowing himself to be loved can do much good. Therapeutic technicians may perform an effective service for robots or computers but they threaten to finish off human beings who already have little enough sense of belonging to the species. I could not know as I grew up in the dark days of the 1940s that I was receiving an ideal education for someone who was later to accompany those who were struggling with life and death issues and had often run out of hope. The therapist for whom life has not thrown down the gauntlet and compelled love to declare itself may have to follow Jung's guidance and go in search of a deeper reality:

> The man who would learn the human mind will gain almost nothing from experimental psychology. Far better for him to put away his academic gown, to say goodbye to his study, and to wander with human heart through the world.
>
> Jung, 1953, p. 71

References

JUNG, C.G. (1953). *Psychological Reflections* (an anthology of writings, edited by J. Jacobi). London: Routledge & Kegan Paul.

THORNE, B.J. (1987a). A Good Friday encounter: escaping from guilt in the Christian tradition. *Self and Society* 15(1), 4–11.

THORNE, B.J. (1987b). Beyond the core conditions. In: W. Dryden (Ed.), *Key Cases in Psychotherapy*. London: Croom Helm.

Chapter 2
The God who comes: Good Friday 1946

Good Friday 1946 found me playing cricket in a Bristol park which was still full of air-raid shelters and all the bric-à-brac of war. Suddenly there appeared in the street at the side of the park a procession of witness headed by a crucifer, candle bearers and a thurifer swinging a censer. The effect on me was instantaneous. I left my friends, ran all the way home and shut myself in my bedroom and sobbed for what seemed like hours. In the midst of this overwhelming distress, I encountered the living Jesus and, from that day until this, I have had an unshakeable conviction that love is the primary force in the universe no matter how great the evidence may seem to the contrary. Looking back on it, the events of that Good Friday afternoon probably determined the direction of my life because they impinged on me at so many different levels. In the first place, the initial incident was visually stupendous: the contrast between the solemn beauty of the procession and the barrenness of the park still ravaged by war could not have been greater. Secondly, the experience established in a moment an order of values. I suppose I felt mildly guilty that I was playing cricket on Good Friday, but the main feeling was one of quite overwhelming gratitude that I could be so incredibly loved. In that moment I knew that, in the last analysis, all that matters is loving and being loved. I also knew that the love I had experienced brought with it a snse of being fully and profoundly understood. It followed therefore that to love in this way must involve the deepest commitment to understanding. I have since discovered that love devoid of understanding, although it can bring comfort and solace, can never heal. Thirdly, the incident endowed me with an intoxicating sense of my own unique value. At a wholly conscious level I knew that something special had happened to me which I would never be able to deny or eradicate.

From *Behold the Man*, 1991, Darton, Longman & Todd, London, with permission.

I suspect that my 'Good Friday' experience strikes chords for many people. One of the things we know from the recent research into mystical experience is that thousands of us actually have such experiences (some have suggested as many as one in five), but that we seldom talk about them and often, indeed, dismiss them or succeed in banishing them from consciousness. I suppose it is not altogether surprising that we should behave in this way. At a time and in a culture where the so-called scientific method still rules the roost, and objective knowledge is enthroned, it is perhaps too much to expect that we should take such experiences with the utter seriousness that I am convinced they merit. They come as gifts but also as challenges to our concept of reality and it is sad in the extreme when, as a result of conditioning, we dismiss them as unimportant or even crazy.

I was very lucky (if luck can ever be the right word) to have my experience at the age of nine, before those habits of thought had been formed which tend to dismiss subjective knowledge and experience as at best suspect and at worst a positive hindrance to the acquisition of the objective knowledge that alone is believed to have real value. Returning to my experience in the park, there is one aspect of it that merits more detailed exploration.

Undoubtedly the most important and life-transforming outcome was the sense of being loved beyond all the possible limits of my imagining. I know, and have known intermittently ever since, that I am *desired* by Someone or Something who has created me and of whom I am in that sense a part. There are, of course, many times – indeed so many times that it becomes *most* of the time – that such a notion seems patently absurd. In the first place, I experience myself all too frequently as being pretty undesirable. I have some abominable habits and I seem to have been perpetrating the same sins for decades. Secondly, it seems remarkably arrogant to claim that *I* am the desired of God, that God finds *me* infinitely desirable. And yet I know that what I experienced all those years ago is the essential truth about me and, what is more, that if it is true of me it is true of all of us. The corollary of all this is that self-hate, self-contempt, self-denigration and all those other states of mind which tell me that I am no good, that I am unworthy, that I am worthless – all these gloomy self-judgments – are a denial of the truth about myself and separate me from a compassionate and forgiving self-love which is the only possible attitude towards myself in the light of the astounding fact that God finds me desirable.

My experience was given to me on Good Friday. The sobbing in my bedroom took place under a picture postcard (very stylised) of the crucifixion on Calvary and I have tried hard to reconstruct the words of Christ to the 9-year-old me on that day. At the time, of course, the conversation was wordless – it was heart to heart. I can only reconstruct it in the light of the message that still today has not been fully revealed and perhaps never will be in this world. Certainly, I know what it was *not*. Jesus did *not* say to me:

> You know, you are a very naughty boy, more naughty than you can ever know. In fact, if you knew the whole story as I know it, you would realise that you actually helped murder me. But you needn't worry. I care about you so much that I actually chose to let you and all your other friends in the human race murder me so that you could experience how utterly forgiving I am and that I can triumph over your evil. You see, you couldn't really finish me off and however awful you are I really do love you and if you trust me and believe me you'll get a lot better and then you can really be my friend.

No, Jesus did not, I am convinced, talk to me like that. If he had I should have been terrified and I should have wondered how on earth I was ever going to be able to forgive myself enough to merit the friendship of such a superior and strange being. I reckon that what Jesus said was more like this.

> Hello, Brian. It's lovely to have you near me. I'm so glad you're still alive after this dreadful war. I've tried to look after you and I hope you're not feeling guilty about playing cricket because it's a good game. Why I interrupted was to let you know something very important. You know already that life isn't always easy. People do terrible things like dropping bombs and it is very difficult to go on loving them. You get frightened, don't you, and upset and I bet you often feel you're not much good especially when people tell you off or get angry with you. Well, what I wanted to say was that you needn't be scared of people because they do awful things and you certainly need not be scared of dying. People did awful things to me and I died, but I want you to know that it's alright. Whatever you do, don't let people tell you you're no good and go on trying to find out more and more what's going on. Most people don't want to know, it seems, but that's only because they're frightened.

I have come to believe that Jesus spoke to me somewhat like this in 1946, because such a message makes sense of much that has happened since. It explains why, over the years, sometimes it seems, against all the odds, I have managed to keep a shaky hold on the truth that I and, with me, all humanity are infinitely desirable and why, too, I have come to believe that self-awareness and self-knowledge must be pursued, however frightening, and however inimical they are to the part of us that wants a quiet life and resists growth and development. I was delighted to read recently in a book by the Catholic theologian, Sebastian Moore (1985), that he has come to believe that the original, generic sin is precisely this refusal to grow, this resistance to self-awareness. And, of course, such a resistance is closely linked to the feeling that I am no good. If I am no good I do not wish to discover more about myself. It is only when I feel good with conviction that I can go forward to discover more with confidence. Moore points out with telling force that we have now arrived at a situation where all the best counsellors and therapists are coming to understand the root of our evil as a bad self-image, a devaluing of self, whilst Christians tend to say in response, 'Ah, but you are forgetting original sin' – not realising apparently that the counsellors are precisely *pointing* to original sin – namely that attitude of mind which says 'Human beings are hopelessly flawed and cannot therefore change'.

Reference

MOORE, S. (1985). *Let this Mind be in You*. London: Darton, Longman & Todd.

Part II
Theory in Practice

Introduction

This section of the book is by far the longest because it contains some of my most extended attempts to elucidate the theory and practice of the person-centred approach to therapy. Chapter 4 moves the focus from individual work to the facilitation of large groups and recalls for me, not only the exciting summer workshops of the Facilitator Development Institute in Britain, but also the many other large cross-cultural events in which I have been privileged to take part in many different regions of Europe. I am glad to belong to a tradition that has increasingly, in recent years, attempted to apply discoveries first made in the counselling room to the fields of education, cross-cultural communication and peace work. Trusting a group to find its own way forward is for me one of the stiffest challenges to my deeply held belief that, given the right conditions, human beings are capable of behaving lovingly and constructively towards each other and thus of creating a new kind of world.

Chapter 5 is perhaps the contribution of which I am most proud. The elusive 'quality of tenderness' which I attempt to describe there, and which I believe to be mysteriously powerful in the healing of emotional wounds, seems to have touched many readers at the deepest level. Of all the things I have written, this short article has elicited the most letters and the most conversations. It seems as if, in some important way, it permits entry into the realm of the transcendental to those for whom religious and mystical language is alien and outside their world of experience; at the same time for those who *have* a religious allegiance it seems to serve as an enrichment and extension of their understanding. I happen to believe that this short piece may turn out to be my most significant contribution to the development of person-centred theory.

Chapter 3
Person-centred Therapy

Historical Context and Development in Britain

Historical context

Dr Carl Rogers (1902–1987), the American psychologist and founder of what has now become known as person-centred counselling or psychotherapy, always claimed to be grateful that he never had one particular mentor. He was influenced by many significant figures, often holding widely differing viewpoints, but above all he claimed to be the student of his own experience and of that of his clients and colleagues.

Whilst accepting Rogers' undoubtedly honest claim about his primary sources of learning, there is much about his thought and practice which places him within a recognisable tradition. Oatley has described this as:

> the distinguished American tradition exemplified by John Dewey: the tradition of no nonsense, of vigorous self-reliance, of exposing oneself thoughtfully to experience, practical innovation, and of careful concern for others.   (Oatley, 1981, p. 192)

In fact in 1925, while still a student at Teachers College, Columbia, New York, Rogers was directly exposed to Dewey's thought and to progressive education through his attendance at a course led by the famous William Heard Kilpatrick, a student of Dewey and himself a teacher of extraordinary magnetism. Not that Dewey and Kilpatrick formed the mainstream of the ideas to which Rogers was introduced during his professional training and early clinical experience. Indeed, when he took up his first appointment in 1928 as a member of the Child Study Department of the Society for the Prevention of Cruelty to Children in Rochester, New York, he joined an

---

From *Individual Therapy: A Handbook*, 1990, edited by W. Dryden, Open University Press, Milton Keynes, with permission.

institution where the three fields of psychology, psychiatry and social work were combining forces in diagnosing and treating problems. This context appealed to Rogers' essentially pragmatic temperament.

Rogers' biographer, Kirschenbaum (1979), whilst acknowledging the variety of influences to which Rogers was subjected at the outset of his professional career, suggests nevertheless that when Rogers went to Rochester he saw himself essentially as a diagnostician and as an interpretative therapist whose goal, very much in the analytical tradition, was to help a child or a parent gain insight into his or her own behaviour and motivation. Diagnosis and interpretation are far removed from the primary concerns of a contemporary person-centred therapist and, in an important sense, Rogers' progressive disillusionment with both these activities during his time at Rochester mark the beginning of his own unique approach. He tells the story of how, near the end of his time at Rochester, he had been working with a highly intelligent mother whose son was presenting serious behavioural problems. Rogers was convinced that the root of the trouble lay in the mother's early rejection of the boy, but no amount of gentle strategy on his part could bring her to this insight. In the end he gave up and they were about to part when she asked if adults were taken for counselling on their own account. When Rogers assured her that they were, she immediately requested help for herself and launched into an impassioned outpouring of her own despair, her marital difficulties, and her confusion and sense of failure. Real therapy, it seems, began at that moment and was ultimately successful. Rogers commented:

> This incident was one of a number which helped me to experience the fact – only fully realized later – that it is the client who knows what hurts, what direction to go, what problems are crucial, what experiences have been deeply buried. It began to occur to me that unless I had a need to demonstrate my own cleverness and learning, I would do better to rely upon the client for the direction of movement in the process.
>
> (cited in Kirschenbaum, 1979, p. 89)

The essential step from diagnosis and interpretation to listening had been taken and from that point onwards Rogers was launched on his own path.

By 1940, Rogers was a professor of psychology at Ohio State University and his first book, *Counseling and Psychotherapy*, appeared 2 years later. From 1945 to 1957, he was professor of psychology at Chicago and director of the university counselling centre. This was a period of intense activity, not least in the research field. Rogers' pragmatic nature had led to much research being carried out on person-centred therapy. With the publication of *Client-Centered Therapy* in 1951, Rogers became a major force in the world of psychotherapy and established his position as a practitioner, theorist and researcher who warranted respect. In an address to the American Psychological Association in 1973, Rogers maintained that during this Chicago period he was for the first time giving clear expression to an idea whose time had come. The idea was:

> the gradually formed and tested hypothesis that the individual has within himself vast resources for self-understanding, for altering his self concept, his attitudes and his self-directed behavior – and that these resources can be tapped if only a definable climate of facilitative psychological attitudes can be provided. (Rogers, 1974, p 116)

From this 'gradually formed and tested hypothesis', non-directive therapy was born as a protest against the diagnostic, prescriptive point of view prevalent at the time. Emphasis was placed on a relationship between counsellor and client based on acceptance and clarification. This was a period, too, of excitement generated by the use of recorded interviews for research and training purposes and there was a focus on 'non-directive techniques'. Those coming for help were no longer referred to as patients, but as clients, with the inference that they were self-responsible human beings, not objects for treatment. As experience increased and both theory building and research developed, the term 'client-centred therapy' was adopted which put the emphasis on the internal world of the client and focused attention on the attitudes of therapists towards their clients rather than on particular techniques. The term 'person-centred' won Rogers' approval in the decade before his death, because it can be applied to the many fields outside therapy where his ideas are becoming increasingly accepted and valued and because, in the therapy context itself, it underlines the person-to-person nature of the interaction where not only the phenomenological world of the client but also the therapist's state of being are of crucial significance. This 'I–Thou' quality of the therapeutic relationship indicates a certain kinship with the existential philosophy of Kierkegaard and Buber and the stress on personal experience recalls the work of the British philosopher/scientist Michael Polanyi (whom Rogers knew and admired). In recent times, too, Rogers himself reported his own deepening respect for certain aspects of Zen teaching and became fond of quoting sayings of Lao-Tse, especially those that stress the undesirability of imposing on people instead of allowing them the space in which to find themselves.

Development in Britain

Although the influence of Rogers percolated spasmodically into Britain in the post-war years – mainly through the work of the Marriage Guidance Council (now known as 'Relate') and then often in an unacknowledged form – it was not until the mid-1960s that he came to be studied in depth in British universities. Interestingly enough, the reason for this development was the establishment of the first training courses in Britain for school counsellors. These programmes (initially at the Universities of Keele and Reading) were largely dependent in their first years on American Fulbright professors of psychology or counselling, many of whom were steeped in the client-centred tradition and introduced their British students to both the theory and practice of client-centred therapy. It is therefore with the growth of counselling in Britain that the work of Rogers has become more widely known; it is probably true to say that the largest recognisable group of person-centred practitioners currently working in Britain comprises counsellors operating within the educational sector. It is also significant that, when Rogers started working in the 1920s, psychologists in the USA were not permitted to practise psychotherapy so he called his activity 'counselling'. British practitioners of person-centred therapy have tended to use the word 'counsellor' and to eschew the word 'psychotherapist' for perhaps different reasons. They have seen the word 'psychotherapist' as somehow conducive to an aura of mystification and expertise which runs counter to the egalitarian relationship which the person-centred approach seeks to establish between therapist and client. In the last 15 years or so, partly thanks to the growth of the Association for Humanistic Psychology in Britain, there are many signs that the person-centred approach is moving out of the educational arena and making its impact felt more widely. The work of the British Centre of the Facilitator Development Institute (founded in 1974 on the initiative of Rogers' close associate, Dr Charles Devonshire) has introduced person-centred ideas to a wide variety of psychologists, social workers, psychiatrists and others, whilst the establishment in 1980 of the Norwich Centre for personal and professional development gave Britain its first independent therapy and training agency committed to the person-centred approach. The last 5 years have also seen the emergence of two substantial in-depth training courses for those seeking to become person-centred therapists. One is run by the Facilitator Development Institute (Mearns and Thorne, 1988)* and the other is the British programme of the Person-Centered Approach Institute International, which is gradually extending its training opportunities throughout Europe.

Theoretical Assumptions

Image of the person

Person-centred therapists start from the assumption that both they and their clients are trustworthy. This trust resides in the belief that every organism – the human being included – has an underlying and instinctive movement towards the constructive accomplishment of its inherent potential. Rogers (1979) often recalled a boyhood memory of his parents' potato bin in which they stored the winter supply of potatoes. This bin was placed in the basement several feet below a small window and yet, despite the highly unfavourable conditions, the potatoes would nevertheless begin to send out

---

* The Institute was re-named Person-centred Therapy (Britain) in April 1991 insofar as its therapist training is concerned.

spindly shoots groping towards the distant light of the window. Rogers compared these pathetic potatoes in their desperate struggle to develop with clients whose lives have been warped by circumstances and experience, but who continue against all the odds to strive towards growth, towards becoming. This directional, or actualising, tendency in the human being can be trusted and the therapist's task is to help create the best possible conditions for its fulfilment.

The elevated view of human nature which person-centred therapists hold is paralleled by their insistence on individual uniqueness. They believe that no two persons are ever alike and that the human personality is so complex that no diagnostic labelling of persons can ever be fully justified. Indeed, person-centred therapists know that they cannot hope to uncover fully the subjective perceptual world of the client and that clients themselves can do this only with great effort. Furthermore, clients' perceptual worlds will be determined by the experiences they have rejected or assimilated into the self-concept.

Conceptualisation of psychological disturbance and health

The self-concept is of crucial importance in person-centred therapy and needs to be distinguished from the self. Nelson-Jones (1982) has made the helpful distinction of regarding the self as the real, underlying organismic self – that is the essentially trustworthy human organism which is discernible in the physiological processes of the entire body and through the growth process by which potentialities and capacities are brought to realisation – and contrasting this with the self-concept which is a person's conceptual construction of him- or herself (however poorly articulated) and which does not by any means always correspond with the direct and untrammelled experiencing of the organismic self.

The self-concept develops over time and is heavily dependent on the attitudes of those who constitute the individual's significant others. It follows therefore that, where a person is surrounded by those who are quick to condemn or punish (however subtly) the behaviour which emanates from the experiencing of the organismic self, he or she will become rapidly confused. The need for positive regard or approval from others is overwhelming and is present from earliest infancy. If therefore behaviour arising from what is actually experienced by the individual fails to win approval, an immediate conflict is established. A baby, for example, may gain considerable satisfaction or relief from howling full-throatedly but may then quickly learn that such behaviour is condemned or punished by the mother. At this point the need to win the mother's approval is in immediate conflict with the promptings of the organismic self which wishes to howl. In the person-centred tradition, disturbance is conceptualised in terms of the degree of success or failure experienced by the individual in resolving such conflicts.

The badly disturbed person on this criterion will have lost almost complete contact with the experiencing of the organismic self, for the basic need for self-regard can in the most adverse circumstances lead to behaviour that is totally geared to the desperate search for acceptance and approval. The voice of the organismic self in such cases is silenced and a self-concept is developed which bears little relationship to people's deepest promptings from which they are essentially cut off. Not surprisingly, perhaps, such attempts to create a self-concept that denies the nature of the self cannot in the long run be successful. In most cases individuals, whatever face they may present to the world, hold themselves in low esteem and a negative self-concept is usually a further sign of disturbance at some level. In those rarer instances where the self-deception is more extreme, the self-concept may at a conscious level appear largely positive, but it will be quickly evident to others that such self-affirmation has been won at the cost of a deliberate and sustained refusal to allow adverse judgements into awareness whether these threaten from within or from outside sources. Disturbed people can seldom trust their own judgement and, for the person-centred therapist, another sure mark of disturbance is the absence of an internalised locus of evaluation. This somewhat cumbersome term describes the faculty which determines individuals' capacities to trust their own thoughts and feelings when making decisions or choosing courses of action. Disturbed people show little sign of possessing such a faculty: instead they constantly turn to external authorities or find themselves caught in a paralysis of indecison. In summary, then, disturbance may be conceptualised as a greater or lesser degree of alienation form the organismic self prompted by the fundamental need for self-regard. The resulting self-concept, usually negative and always falsely based, is linked to a defective capacity to make decisions which in turn indicates the absence of an internalised locus of evaluation.

If individuals are unfortunate enough to be brought up among a number of significant others who are highly censorious or judgemental, a self-concept can develop which may serve to estrange them almost totally from their organismic experiencing. In such cases the self-concept, often developed after years of oppression of the organismic self, becomes the fiercest enemy of the self and must undergo radical transformation if the actualising tendency is to reassert itself.

The person-centred therapist is constantly working with clients who have all but lost touch with the actualising tendency within themselves and who have been surrounded by others who have no confidence in the innate capacity of human beings to move towards the fulfilment of their potential. Psychologically healthy persons, however, are men and women who have been lucky enough to live in contexts that have been conducive to the development of self-concepts which allow them to be in touch for at least some of the time with their deepest experiences and feelings without having to censure them or distort them. Such people are well placed to achieve a level of psychological freedom which will enable them to move in the direction of becoming more *fully functioning* persons. 'Fully functioning' is a term used by Rogers to denote individuals who are using their talents and abilities, realising their potential and moving towards a more complete knowledge of themselves. They are demonstrating what it means to have attained a high level of psychological health and Rogers has outlined some of the major personality characteristics that they seem to have in common. The first and most striking characteristic is *openness to experience*. Individuals who are open to experience are able to listen to themselves and to others and to experience what is happening without feeling threatened. They demonstrate a high level of awareness especially in the world of the feelings. Secondly, allied to this characteristic, is the *ability to live fully* in each moment of existence. Experience is trusted rather than feared and is therefore the moulding force for the emerging personality rather than being twisted or manipulated to fit some preconceived structure of reality or some rigidly safeguarded self-concept. The third characteristic is the *organismic trusting* which is so clearly lacking in those who have constantly fallen victim to the adverse judgements of others. Such trusting is best displayed in the process of decision-making. Whereas many people defer continually to outside sources of influence when making decisions, fully functioning persons regard their organismic experiences as the most valid sources of information for deciding what to do in any given situation. Rogers put it succinctly when he said 'doing what "feels right" proves to be a ... trustworthy guide to behaviour' (1961, p. 190). Further characteristics of the fully functioning person are concerned with the issues of personal freedom and creativity. For Rogers, a mark of psychological health is the sense of responsibility for determining our own actions and their consequences based on a feeling of freedom and power to choose from the many options that life presents. There is no feeling within the individual of being imprisoned by circumstances, or fate or genetic inheritance, although this is not to suggest that Rogers denies the powerful influences of biological make-up, social forces or past experience. Subjectively, however, people experience themselves as free agents. Finally, the fully functioning person is typically creative in the sense that he or she can adjust to changing conditions and is likely to produce creative ideas or initiate creative projects and actions. Such people are unlikely to be conformists, although they will relate to society in a way that permits them to be fully involved without being imprisoned by convention or tradition.

Acquisition of psychological disturbance

In person-centred terminology the mother's requirement that the baby cease to howl constitutes a *condition of worth*: 'I shall love you if you do not howl.' The concept of conditions of worth bears a striking similarity to the British therapist George Lyward's notion of contractual living. Lyward believed that most of his disturbed adolescent clients had had no chance to contact their real selves because they were too busy attempting – usually in vain – to fulfil contracts, in order to win approval (Burn, 1956). Lyward used to speak of usurped lives and Rogers, in a similar vein, sees many individuals as the victims of countless internalised conditions of worth which have almost totally estranged them from their organismic experiencing. Such people will be preoccupied with a sense of strain at having to come up to the mark or with feelings of worthlessness at having failed to do so. They will be the victims of countless introjected conditions of worth so that they no longer have any sense of their inherent value as unique persons. The proliferation of introjections is an inevitable outcome of the desperate need for positive regard. Introjection is the process whereby the beliefs, judgements, attitudes or values of another person (most often the parent) are taken into the individual and become part of his or her armamentarium for coping with experience, however alien they may have been initially. The child, it seems, will do almost anything to satisfy the need for positive regard even if this means taking on board (introjecting) attitudes and beliefs which run quite counter to its own organismic reaction to experience. Once such attitudes and beliefs have become thoroughly absorbed into the personality, they are said to have become internalised. Thus it is that introjection and internalisation of conditions of worth, imposed by significant others whose approval is desperately desired, often constitute the gloomy road to a deeply negative self-concept as individuals discover that they can never come up to the high demands and expectations which such conditions inevitably imply.

Once this negative self-concept has taken root in an individual, the likelihood is that the separation from the essential organismic self will become increasingly complete. It is as if individuals become cut off from their own inner resources and their own sense of value and are governed by a secondary and treacherous valuing process which is based on the internalisation of other people's judgements and evaluations. Once caught in this trap the person is likely to become increasingly disturbed, for the negative self-concept induces behaviour which reinforces the image of inadequacy and worthlessness. It is a fundamental thesis of the person-centred point of view that behaviour is not only the result of what happens to us from the external world, but also a function of how we feel about ourselves on the inside. In other words, we are likely to behave in accordance with our perception of ourselves. What we do is often an accurate reflection of how we evaluate ourselves and, if this evaluation is low, our behaviour will be correspondingly unacceptable to ourselves and in all probablility to others as well. It is likely, too, that we shall be highly conscious of a sense of inadequacy and, although we may conceal this from others, the awareness that all is not well will usually be with us.

The person-centred therapist recognises, however, that psychological disturbance is not always available to awareness. It is possible for a person to establish a self-concept which, because of the overriding need to win the approval of others, cannot permit highly significant sensory or visceral (a favourite word with Rogers) experience into consciousness. Such people cannot be open to the full range of their organismic experiencing because to be so would threaten the self-concept which must be maintained in order to win continuing favour. An example of such a person might be the man who has established a picture of himself as honourable, virtuous, responsible and loving. Such a man may be progressively divorced from those feelings which would threaten to undermine such a self-concept. He may arrive at a point where he no longer knows, for example, that he is angry or hostile or sexually hungry, for to admit to such feelings would be to throw his whole picture of himself into question. Disturbed people therefore are by no means always aware of their disturbance nor will they necessarily be perceived as disturbed by others who may have a vested interest in maintaining what is in effect a tragic but often rigorous act of self-deception.

Perpetuation of psychological disturbance

It follows from the person-centred view of psychological disturbance that it will be perpetuated if an individual continues to be dependent to a high degree on the judgement of others for a sense of self-worth. Such persons will be at pains to preserve and defend at all costs the self-concept which wins approval and esteem and will be thrown into anxiety and confusion whenever incongruity arises between the self-concept and actual experience. In the example above, the 'virtuous' man would be subject to feelings of threat and confusion if he directly experienced his hostility or sexual hunger, although to do so would, of course, be a first step towards the recovery of contact with the organismic self. He will be likely, however, to avoid the threat and confusion by resorting to one or other of two basic mechanisms of defence – perceptual distortion or denial. In this way he avoids confusion and anxiety and thereby perpetuates his disturbance while mistakenly believing that he is maintaining his integrity. Perceptual distortion takes place whenever an incongruent experience is allowed into awareness, but only in a form that is in harmony with the person's current self-concept. The virtuous man, for instance, might permit himself to experience hostility but would distort this as a justifiable reaction to wickedness in others: for him his hostility would be rationalised into righteous indignation. Denial is a less common defence but is in some was the more impregnable. In this case, individuals preserve their self-concept by completely avoiding any conscious recognition of experiences or feelings which threaten them. The virtuous man would therefore be totally unaware of his constantly angry attitudes in a committee meeting and might perceive himself as simply speaking with truth and sincerity. Distortion and denial can have formidable psychological consequences and can sometimes protect a person for a lifetime from the confusion and anxiety which could herald the recovery of contact with the alienated self.

Change

For people who are trapped by a negative self-concept and by behaviour which tends to demonstrate and even reinforce the validity of such a self-assessment, there is little hope of positive change unless there is movement in the psychological environment which surrounds them. Most commonly, this will be the advent of a new person on the scene or a marked change in attitude of someone who is already closely involved. A child, for example, may be abused and ignored at home but may discover, to her initial bewilderment, that her teachers respect and like her. If she gradually acquires the courage to trust this unexpected acceptance, she may be fortunate enough to gain further reassurance through the discovery that her teachers' respect for her is not dependent on her 'being a good girl'. For the young adult a love relationship can often revolutionise the self-concept. A girl who has come to think of herself as both stupid and ugly will find such a self-concept severely challenged by a young man who both enjoys her conversation and finds her physically desirable. There are, of course, dangers in this situation, for if the man's ardour rapidly cools and he abandons her, the young woman's negative self-concept may be mightily reinforced by this painful episode. Where love runs deep, however, the beloved may be enabled to rediscover contact with the organismic core of her being and to experience her own essential worth. For clients beginning therapy, the most important fact initially is the entry of a new person (the therapist) into their psychological environment. As we shall see it is the quality of this new person and the nature of the relationship which the therapist offers that will ultimately determine whether or not change will ensue.

Practice

Goals of therapy

The person-centred therapist seeks to establish a relationship with a client in which the latter can gradually dare to face the anxiety and confusion that inevitably arise once the self-concept is challenged by the movement into awareness of experiences that do not fit its current configuration. If such a relationship can be achieved, the client can then hope to move beyond the confusion and gradually to experience the freedom to choose a way of being which approximates more closely to his or her deepest feelings and values. The therapist will therefore focus not on problems and solutions but on communion or on what has been described as a person-in-person relationship

(Boy and Pine, 1982, p. 129). Person-centred therapists do not hesitate therefore to invest themselves freely and fully in the relationship with their clients. They believe that they will gain entrance into the world of the client through an emotional commitment in which they are willing to involve themselves as people and to reveal themselves, if appropriate, with their own strengths and weaknesses. For the person-centred therapist, a primary goal is to see, feel and experience the world as the client sees, feels and experiences it and this is not possible if the therapist stands aloof and maintains a psychological distance in the interests of a quasi-scientific objectivity.

The theoretical end-point of person-centred therapy must be the fully functioning person who is the embodiment of psychological health and whose primary characteristics were outlined above. It would be fairly safe to assert that no client has achieved such an end-point and that no therapist has been in a position to model such perfection. However, there is now abundant evidence, not only from the USA but also, for example, from the extensive research activities of Reinhard Tausch and his colleagues at Hamburg University (Tausch, 1975) that clients undergoing person-centred therapy frequently demonstrate similar changes. From my own experience, I can also readily confirm the perception of client movement that Rogers and other person-centred practitioners have repeatedly noted. A listing of these perceptions will show that, for many clients, the achievement of any one of the developments recorded could well constitute a 'goal' of therapy and might for the time being at least constitute a valid and satisfactory reason for terminating therapy. Clients in person-centred therapy are often perceived to move, then, in the following directions:

1. Away from the façades and the constant preoccupation with keeping up appearances.
2. Away from 'oughts' and an internalised sense of duty springing from externally imposed obligations.
3. Away from living up to the expectations of others.
4. Towards valuing honesty and 'realness' in oneself and others.
5. Towards valuing the capacity to direct one's own life.
6. Towards accepting and valuing one's self and one's feelings whether they are positive or negative.
7. Towards valuing the experience of the moment and the process of growth rather than continually striving for objectives.
8. Towards a greater respect for and the understanding of others.
9. Towards a cherishing of close relationships and a longing for more intimacy.
10. Towards a valuing of all forms of experience and a willingness to risk being open to all inner and outer experiences however uncongenial or unexpected.

(Frick, 1971, p. 179)

Selection criteria

Person-centred therapy has proved its effectiveness with clients of many kinds presenting a wide range of difficulties and concerns. Its usefulness even with psychotics was established many years ago when Rogers and his associates participated in an elaborate investiagation of the effect of psychotherapy on schizophrenics. Rogers himself, however, offered the opinion that psychotherapy of any kind, including person-centred therapy, is probably of the greatest help to the people who are closest to a reasonable adjustment to life. It is my own belief that the limitations of person-centred therapy reside not in the approach itself, but in the limitations of particular therapists and in their ability or lack of it to offer their clients the necessary conditions for change and development. Having said this I freely admit that in my own experience there are certain kinds of clients who are unlikely to be much helped by the approach. Such people are usually somewhat rigid and authoritarian in their attitude to life. They look for certainties, for secure structures and often for experts to direct them in how they should be and what they should do. Their craving for such direction often makes it difficult for them to relate to the person-centred therapist in such a way that they can begin to get in touch with their own inner resources. Overly intellectual or logically rational people may also find it difficult to engage in the kind of relationship encouraged by person-centred therapy, where often the greatest changes result from a preparedness to face painful and confusing feelings which cannot initially be clearly articulated. Clients falling into these categories often turn out to be poorly motivated in any case and, not infrequently, they have been referred in desperation by an overworked medical practitioner, priest or social worker. Inarticulacy is in itself no barrier to effective therapeutic work, for inarticulate people are often brimming over with unexpressed feeling which begins to pour out once a relationship of trust has been established.

Clients who perhaps have most to gain from person-centred therapy are those who are strongly motivated to face painful feelings and who are deeply committed to change. They are prepared to take emotional risks a. d they want to trust even if they are fearful of intimacy. In my own work I often ask myself three questions as I consider working with a prospective client:

1. Is the client really desirous of change?
2. Is the client prepared to share responsibility for our work together?
3. Is the client willing to get in touch with his or her feelings, however difficult that may be?

Reassuring answers to these three questions are usually reliable indicators that person-centred therapy is likely to be beneficial.

The person-centred approach has made significant contributions to small and large group work and the person-centred therapy group (with two therapists or 'facilitators') is a common modality. Clients who give evidence of at least some degree of self-acceptance, and whose self-concept is not entirely negative, may well be encouraged (but never obliged) to join a group from the outset. More commonly, however, membership of a counselling group will occur at the point when a client in individual therapy is beginning to experience a measure of self-affirmation and is keen to take further risks in relating. At such a stage, membership of a group may replace individual therapy or may be undertaken concurrently. In all cases it is the client who will decide whether to seek group membership and whether or not this should replace or complement individual therapy.

The person-centred therapist will be at pains to ensure that a client whose self-concept is very low is not plunged into a group setting prematurely. Such an experience could have the disastrous outcome of reinforcing the client's sense of worthlessness. In such cases individual therapy is almost invariably indicated.

Person-centred therapists can work successfully with couples and with family groups but in these contexts much will depend on the therapist's ability to create the environment in which the couple or the family members can interact with each other without fear. In order for this to be possible, it is likely that the therapist will undertake extensive preparatory work with each individual in a one-to-one relationship. Ultimately, the principal criterion for embarking on couple or family therapy (apart, of course, from the willingness of all members to participate) is the therapist's confidence in his or her own ability to relate authentically to each member. Such confidence is unlikely to be achieved in the absence of in-depth preliminary meetings with each person involved. Indeed, in couple therapy it is common for the therapist to agree to work for a negotiated period with each partner separately before all three come together in order to tackle the relationship directly. With a family, the process is clearly more complex and the preparatory work even more time-consuming. Perhaps this is the main reason why person-centred family therapy remains comparatively rare. In a sense it is therapists who select themselves for such work and not the clients who are selected.

Qualities of effective therapists

It has often been suggested that, of all the various 'schools' of psychotherapy, the person-centred approach makes the heaviest demands upon the therapist. Whether this is so or not I have no way of knowing. What I do know is that, unless person-centred therapists can relate in such a way that their clients perceive them as trustworthy and dependable *as people*, therapy cannot take place. Person-centred therapists can have no recourse to diagnostic labelling nor can they find security in a complex and detailed theory of personality which will allow them to foster 'insight' in their clients through interpretation, however gently offered. In brief, they cannot win their clients' confidence by demonstrating their psychological expertise, for to do so would be to place yet another obstacle in the way of clients' movement towards their own innate resources. To be a trustwothy person is not something which can be simulated for very long and, in a very real sense, person-centred therapists can only be as trustworthy for another as they are for themselves. Therapists' attitudes to themselves thus become of cardinal importance. If I am to be acceptant of another's feelings and experiences, and to be open to the possible expression of material long since blocked off from awareness, I must feel a deep level of acceptance for myself. If I cannot trust myself to acknowledge and accept my own feelings, without adverse judgement or self-recrimination, it is unlikely that I shall appear sufficiently trustworthy to a client who may have much deeper cause to feel ashamed or worthless. If, too, I am in constant fear that I shall be overwhelmed by an upsurging of unacceptable data into my own awareness, then I am unlikely to convey to my client that I am genuinely open to the full exploration of his own doubts and fears.

The ability of the therapist to be genuine, accepting and empathic (fundamental attitudes in person-centred therapy which will be explored more fully later) is not developed overnight. It is unlikely, too, that such an ability will be present in people who are not continually seeking to broaden their own life experience. No therapist can confidently invite his client to travel further than he has journeyed himself but, for the person-centred therapist, the quality, depth and continuity of his own experiencing becomes the very cornerstone of the competence which he brings to his professional activity. Unless I have a sense of my own continuing development as a person, I shall lose faith in the process of becoming and shall be tempted to relate to my clients in a way which may well reinforce them in a past self-concept. What is more, I shall myself become stuck in a past image of myself and will no longer be in contact with that part of my organism that challenges me to go on growing as a person, even if my body is beginning to show every sign of wearing out. It follows, too, that an excessive reliance on particular skills for relating or communicating can present a subtle trap because such skills may lead to a professional behavioural pattern, which is itself resistant to change because it becomes set or stylised.

Therapeutic style

Person-centred therapists differ widely in therapeutic style. They share in common, however, a desire to create a climate of facilitative psychological attitudes in which clients can begin to get in touch with their own wisdom and their capacity for self-understanding and for altering their self-concept and self-defeating behaviours. For person-centred therapists, their ability to establish this climate is crucial to the whole therapeutic enterprise, because if they fail to do so there is no hope of forming the kind of relationship with their clients which will bring about the desired therapeutic movement. It will become apparent, however, that the way in which they attempt to create and convey the necessary climate will depend very much on the nature of their own personality.

The first element in the creation of the climate has to do with what has variously been called the therapist's *genuineness*, realness, authenticity or congruence. In essence, this realness depends on therapists' capacities for being properly in touch with the complexity of feelings, thoughts and attitudes which will be flowing through them as they seek to track their clients' thoughts and feelings. The more they can do this, the more they will be perceived by their clients as people of real flesh and blood who are willing to be seen and known, and not as clinical professionals intent on concealing themselves behind a metaphorical white coat. However, the issue of the therapists' genuineness is more complex than it might initially appear. Although clients need to experience their therapists' essential humanity and to feel their emotional involvement, they certainly do not need to have all the therapist's feelings and thoughts thrust down their throats. Therapists therefore must not only attempt to remain firmly in touch with the flow of their own experience, but must also have the discrimination to know how and when to communicate what they are experiencing. It is here that, to the objective observer, person-centred therapists might well appear to differ widely in style. It my own attempts to be congruent, for example, I find that verbally I often communicate little. I am aware, however, that my bodily posture does convey a deep willingness to be involved with my client and that my eyes are highly expressive of a wide range of feeling – often to the point of tears. It would seem therefore that in my own case there is frequently little need for me to communicate my feelings verbally: I am transparent enough already and I know from experience that my clients are sensitive to this transparency. Another therapist might well behave in a manner far removed from mine but with the same concern to be genuine. Therapists are just as much unique human beings as their clients and the way in which they make their humanity available by following the flow of their own experiencing and communicating it when appropriate will be an expression of their own uniqueness. Whatever the precise form of their behaviour, however, person-centred therapists will be exercising their skill in order to communicate to their clients an attitude expressive of their desire to be deeply and fully involved in the relationship without pretence and without the protection of professional impersonality.

For many clients entering therapy, the second attitude of importance in creating a facilitative climate for change – *total acceptance* – may seem to be the most critical. The conditions of worth, which have in so many cases warped and undermined the self-concept of the client so that it bears little relation to the actualising organism, are the outcome of the judgemental and conditional attitudes of those close to the client which have often been reinforced by societal or cultural norms. In contrast, the therapist seeks to offer the client an unconditional acceptance, a positive regard or caring, a non-possessive love. This acceptance is not of the person as she might become, a respect for her as yet unfulfilled potential, but a total and unconditional acceptance of the client as she seems to herself *in the present*. Such an attitude on the part of the therapist cannot be simulated and cannot be offered by someone who remains largely frightened or threatened by feelings in himself. Nor again can such acceptance be offered by someone who is disturbed when confronted by a person who possesses values, attitudes and feelings different from his own. Genuine acceptance is totally unaffected by differences of background or belief system between client and therapist, for it is in no way dependent on moral, ethical or social criteria. As with genuineness, however, the attitude of acceptance requires great skill on the part of the therapist, if it is to be communicated at the depth that will enable clients to feel safe to be whatever they are currently experiencing. After what may well be a lifetime of highly conditional acceptance, clients will not recognise unconditionality easily. When they do, they will tend to regard it as a miracle that will demand continual checking out before it can be fully trusted. The way in which a therapist conveys unconditional acceptance will again be dependent to a large extent on the nature of his or her personality. For my own part, I have found increasingly that the non-verbal aspects of my responsiveness are powerfully effective. A smile can often convey more acceptance than a statement which, however sensitive, may still run the risk of seeming patronising. I have discovered, too, that the gentle pressing of the hand or the light touch on the knee will enable clients to realise that all is well and that there will be no judgement, however confused or negative they are or however silent and hostile.

The third facilitative attitude is that of *empathic understanding*. Rogers (1975) himself wrote extensively about empathy and suggested that of the three 'core conditions' (as genuineness, acceptance and empathy are often known), empathy is the most trainable. The crucial importance of empathic understanding springs from the person-centred therapist's overriding concern with the client's subjective perceptual world. Only through as full an understanding as possible of the way in which clients view themselves and the world can the therapist hope to encourage the subtle changes in self-concept which make for growth. Such understanding involves, on the therapist's part, a willingness to enter the private perceptual world of the client and to become thoroughly conversant with it. This demands a high degree of sensitivity to the moment-to-moment experiencing of the client so that the therapist is recognised as a reliable companion even when contradictory feelings follow on each other in rapid succession. In a certain sense, therapists must lay themselves aside for the time being with all their prejudices and values if they are to enter into the perceptual world of the other. Such an undertaking would be foolhardy if the therapist feels insecure in the presence of a particular client, for there would be the danger of getting lost in a perhaps frightening or confusing world. The task of empathic understanding can be accomplished only by people who are secure enough in their own identity to move into another's world without the fear of being overwhelmed by it. Once there, therapists have to move around with extreme delicacy and with an utter absence of judgement. They will probably sense meanings of which the client is scarcely aware and might even become dimly aware of feelings of which there is no consciousness on the part of the client at all. Such moments call for extreme caution, for there is the danger that the therapist could express understanding at too deep a level and frighten the client away from therapy altogether. Rogers, on a recording made for *Psychology Today* in the 1970s, described such a blunder as 'blitz therapy' and contrasted this with an empathic response which is constructive because it conveys an understanding of what is currently going on in the client and of meanings that are just below the level of awareness, but does not slip over into unconscious motivations which frighten the client.

If the communication of genuineness and acceptance presents difficulties, the communication of empathic understanding is even more challenging. In this domain there can, I believe, be less reliance on non-verbal signals. Often a client's inner world is complex and confusing as well as a source of pain and guilt. Sometimes clients have little understanding of their own feelings. Therapists need therefore to marshal the full range of their emotional and cognitive abilities if they are to convey their understanding thoroughly. However, if they do not succeed there is ample evidence to suggest that their very attempt to do so, however bumbling and incomplete, will be experienced by the client as supportive and validating. What is always essential is the therapist's willingness to check out the accuracy of his understanding. I find that my own struggles at communicating empathic understanding are littered with such questions as 'Am I getting it right?', 'Is that what you mean?'. When I do get a complex feeling right, the effect is often electrifying and the sense of wonder and thankfulness in the client can be one of the most moving experiences in therapy. There can be little doubt that the rarity of empathic understanding of this kind is what endows it with such power and makes it the most reliable force for creative change in the whole of the therapeutic process.

It was Rogers' contention – and he held firm to it for over 40 years – that if the therapist proves able to offer a facilitative climate where genuineness, acceptance and empathy are all present, then therapeutic movement will almost invariably occur. In such a climate, clients will gradually get in touch with their own resources for self-understanding and will prove capable of changing their self-concept and taking over the direction of their life. Therapists need only to be faithful companions, following the lead which their clients provide and staying with them for as long as it is necessary. Nothing in my own experience leads me to dispute Rogers' contention that the core conditions are both necessary and sufficient for theraputic movement, although I have argued that, when a fourth quality is present, which I have defined as tenderness, then something qualitatively different may occur (Thorne, 1985) (see Chapter 5). This fourth quality is characterised chiefly by an ability on the part of the therapist to move between the worlds of the physical, the emotional, the cognitive and the mystical without strain and by a willingness to accept and celebrate the desire to love and to be loved if and when it appears in the therapeutic relationship. I cite my own thinking as evidence for the fact that person-centred theory and practice is in no sense a closed system and is constantly being refined and developed by person-centred practitioners.

Major therapeutic strategies and techniques

There are no strategies or techniques which are integral to the person-centred approach. Person-centred therapy is essentially based on the experiencing and communication of attitudes and these attitudes cannot be packaged up in techniques. At an earlier point in the history of the approach, there was an understandable emphasis on the ebb and flow of the therapeutic interview and much was gained from the microscopic study of client–therapist exchanges. To Rogers' horror, however, the tendency to focus on the therapist's responses had the effect of so debasing the approach that it became known as a technique. Even nowadays, it is possible to meet people who believe that person-centred therapy is simply the technique of reflecting the client's feelings or, worse still, that it is primarily a matter of repeating the last words spoken by the client. I hope I have shown that nothing could be further from the truth. The attitudes required of the therapist demand the highest level of self-knowledge and self-acceptance and the translation of them into communicable form requires of each therapist the most delicate skill, which for the most part must spring from his or her unique personality and cannot be learned through pale imitations of Carl Rogers or anyone else.

In a recent work (Mearns and Thorne, 1988), a colleague and I have drawn attention to the fact that the most productive outcomes seem to result from therapeutic relationships which move through three distinct phases. The first stage is characterised by the establishing of *trust* on the part of the client. This may happen very rapidly or it can take months. The second stage sees the development of *intimacy* during which the client is enabled to reveal some of the deepest levels of his experiencing. The third stage is characterised by an increasing *mutuality* between therapist and client. When such a stage is reached, it is likely that therapists will be increasingly self-disclosing and will be challenged to risk more of themselves in the relationship. When it occurs, this three-stage process is so deeply rewarding for the therapist that a cynical critic might view it as the outcome of an unconscious strategising on the therapist's part. So insidious is this accusation that I am now deeply concerned to monitor my own behaviour with the utmost vigilance in order to ensure that I am *not* embarked on a manipulatory plot which is aimed at achieving a mutuality that may be deeply satisfying for me but quite irrelevant to the client's needs.

The change process in therapy

When person-centred therapy goes well, clients will move from a position where their self-concept, typically poor at the entry into therapy and finding expression in behaviour which is reinforcing of the negative evaluation of self, will shift to a position where it more closely approaches the essential worth of the organismic self. As the self-concept moves towards a more positive view so, too, clients' behaviour begins to reflect the improvement and to enhance further their perception of themselves. The therapist's ability to create a relationship in which the three facilitative attitudes are consistently present will, to a large extent, determine the extent to which clients are able to move towards a more positive perception of themselves, and to the point where they are able to be in greater contact with the promptings of the organismic self.

If therapy has been successful, clients will also have learned how to be their own therapist. It seems that when people experience the genuineness of another and a real attentive caring and valuing by that other person, they begin to adopt the same attitude towards themselves. In short, a person who is cared for begins to feel at a deep level that perhaps she is after all *worth* caring for. In a similar way, the experience of being on the receiving end of the concentrated listening and the empathic understanding, which characterises the therapist's response, tends to develop a listening attitude in the client towards herself. It is as if she gradually becomes less afraid to get in touch with what is going on inside her and dares to listen attentively to her own feelings. With this growing attentiveness, there comes increased self-understanding and a tentative grasp of some of her most central personal meanings. Many clients have told me that, after person-centred therapy, they never lose this ability to treat themselves with respect and to take the risk of listening to what they are experiencing. If they do lose it temporarily or find themselves becoming hopelessly confused, they will not hesitate to return to therapy to engage once more in the process which is in many ways an education for living.

In Rogers and Dymond (1954), one of Rogers' chapters explores in detail a client's successful process through therapy. The case of Mrs Oak has become a rich source of learning for person-centred therapists ever since and, towards the end of the chapter, Rogers attempts a summary of the therapeutic process which Mrs Oak has experienced with such obvious benefits to herself. What is described there seems to me to be so characteristic of the person-centred experience of therapy that I make no apology for providing a further summary of some of Rogers' findings.

The process begins with the therapist providing an atmosphere of warm caring and acceptance which, over the first few sessions, is gradually experienced by the client, Mrs Oak, as genuinely *safe*. With this realisation, the client finds that she changes the emphasis of her sessions from dealing with reality problems to experiencing herself. The effect of this change of emphasis is that she begins to experience her feelings in the immediate present without inhibition. She can be angry, hurt, childish, joyful, self-deprecating, self-appreciative and, as she allows this to occur, she discovers many feelings bubbling through into awareness of which she was not previously conscious. With new feelings, there come new thoughts and the admission of all this fresh material to awareness leads to a *breakdown of the previously held self-concept*. There then follows a period of disorganisation and confusion, although there remains a feeling that the path is the right one and that reorganisation will ultimately take place. What is being learned during this process is that it pays to recognise an experience for what it is rather than denying it or distorting it. In this way the client becomes more open to experience and begins to realise that it is healthy to accept feelings whether they be positive or negative, for this permits a movement towards greater completeness. At this stage the client increasingly comes to realise that *she can begin to define herself and does not have to accept the definition and judgements of others*. There is, too, a more conscious appreciation of the nature of the relationship with the therapist and the value of a love which is not possessive and makes no demands. At about this stage, the client finds that she can make relationships outside of therapy which enable others to be self-experiencing and self-directing and she becomes progressively aware that at the core of her being she is not destructive but genuinely desires the well-being of others. Self-responsibility continues to increase to the point where the client feels able to make her own choices – although this is not always pleasant – and to trust herself in a world which, although it may often seem to be disintegrating, yet offers many opportunities for creative activity and relating (Rogers, 1954).

Limitations of the approach

After 20 years as a person-centred therapist I am drawn to the conclusion, as I stated earlier, that the limitations of the approach are a reflection of the personal limitations of the therapist. As these will clearly vary from individual to individual and are unlikely to be constant over time, I am sceptical about the usefulness of exploring the limitations of the approach in any generalised fashion. Nonetheless I am intrigued by the question with respect to two particular issues. I believe that person-centred therapy may be in danger of selling itself short because of its traditional emphasis on the 'here and now' and because of what is seen as its heavy reliance on verbal interaction. Both these tendencies are likely to be reinforced when the therapist's congruence remains at a relatively superficial level.

In my own practice, I have discovered that the more I am able to be fully present to myself in the therapeutic relationship, the more likely it is that I shall come to trust the promptings of a deeper and more intuitive level within myself. Cautiously, and with constant safeguards against self-deception, I have come to value this intuitive part of my being and to discover its efficacy in the therapeutic relationship. (For a further discussion of this issue see my chapter in *Key Cases in Psychotherapy*: Thorne, 1987.) What is more, when I have risked articulating a thought or feeling which emanates from this deeper level, I have done so in the full knowledge that it may appear unconnected to what is currently happening in the relationship or even bizarre to my client. More often than not, however, the client's response has been immediate and sometimes dramatic. It is as if the quality of the relationship that has been established, thanks to the powerful offering of the core conditions, goes a long way towards ensuring that my own intuitive promptings are deeply and immediately significant for the client. Often, too, the significance lies in the triggering of past experience for the client – not in the sense simply of looking at memories of past events but in releasing a veritable flow of feeling whose origin lies in past experience which is then vividly re-lived. Commonly, also, the therapist's intuitive response seems to touch a part of the client's being which cannot find immediate expression in words. I am astonished how often, at such moments, the client reaches out for physical reassurance or plunges into deep but overflowing silence or even requests materials for writing or sketching (see also Chapter 6).

The person-centred approach is frequently applauded for its usefulness in promoting beneficial changes in self-concept and criticised at the same time for its failure to change behaviour. There may well be some truth in this judgement but I do not believe that this limitation is inherent to the approach. I am increasingly convinced that it is in the area of therapist congruence that the greatest advances can and should be made. In my own case, this has meant a developing trust in my intuitive responses and the discovery that, for my client, this has often resulted in a profound re-living of past experience and an engagement with me on a non-verbal level which has proved remarkably productive. These outcomes, not commonly associated with the person-centred approach as it has been traditionally practised, are, of course, powerfully conducive to behavioural change both within and beyond the therapeutic relationship. This having been said, I suspect that clients who are in the grips of behaviour disorders, such as phobias or obsessive compulsive neuroses, are unlikely to be much helped by person-centred therapy unless, that is, they conceptualise their difficulties as being an outcome of their way of being in the world. If, as is often the case, they view their disorder as a disability to be cured, then they are more likely to be rewarded by a visit to the nearest behavioural therapist.

Case Example

The client

Louise, a married postgraduate student in her mid-20s, presented herself for the first time at the university counselling service in the early autumn. She had been persuaded to come by her GP. She seemed taut and uncertain and began smoking within minutes of the start of the interview. She announced in a somewhat staccato fashion that she had a long history of tension and anxiety and was determined to tackle this directly. Recent asthma attacks had further strengthened her motivation to do something about her 'screwed-up' state. As if to reassure me that not everything was negative, she added the astonishing information that she had cured herself of a stammer and was an absolute expert at evolving strategies for coping. In fact, she was constantly preoccupied with the detailed working out of such schemes and strategies.

All this came out in an enormous rush with Louise scarcely seeming to draw breath; also she did not look at me much during her monologue. When she stopped, it was to convey to me that she was sceptical about the likely value of counselling and to ask me what I thought about continuing with her.

The therapy

I was astonished by the strength of feeling within myself during these opening minutes. I was aware of a deep compassion for Louise and of sheer admiration at the way in which she was apparently holding her life together despite the great cost she was paying in tension and anxiety. I was also conscious of the difficulty of making contact with her. She seemed almost incarcerated in her anxiety and therefore insulated from me. I responded to her scepticism about the value of therapy by describing my own approach with particular reference to the core conditions and by suggesting that she might like to consider an 'experimental' period of, say, four sessions at the end of which she could decide whether she would like to continue. The proposal seemed to reassure her and for the first time she relaxed a little. She then began to talk about her earlier years and especially about the difficult relationship with her parents.

When she left I felt puzzled. I had no idea of how she had experienced the session nor did I feel that I had made much contact. I was sure, however, that I liked her and only hoped that she had sensed something of my respect for and acceptance of her. When she came a fortnight later for the first of three weekly sessions, I made what could have been a costly mistake. For some reason I needed to prove to this highly intelligent woman that I, too, was intellectually alert. I made prodigious efforts to empathise with her thought processes and constantly interjected 'understanding' responses. Almost every time I miscued disastrously. It seemed as if her frame of reference was so removed from my own that the more I tried to come alongside her the more elusive she became. Somewhat crestfallen, I gave up, stopped trying to be empathic and contented myself with listening and simply being present to her. As in the first session, she began to relax at this and talked at length about her annual depressive bouts, sometimes lasting weeks and involving almost total withdrawal, which invariably began in the month of February. She spoke of the effect of these bouts on her marriage and of her concern for her husband, even though she was not at all sure that she actually loved him.

In the third session, Louise began to look me in the eye for the first time. There was a new liveliness about her which did not seem fuelled by her anxiety. She told me that she was rather proud of the way in which she had coped with much of her adult life, especially with motherhood and its demands. She smiled at this and actually exuded the confidence which she was expressing. A few minutes later, however, she took me quite by surprise by plunging into the most painful recollections of her childhood and adolescence. There was no way, it seemed, in which she could win her parents' approval. Two stories exemplified her predicament. Her parents apparently admired those who had the courage to own up to their misdemeanours. Louise therefore concluded that she should deliberately commit an offence so that she could own up to it and thus win her parents' love. She stole biscuits and then openly admitted the theft. The plan, of course, backfired and she was punished for her criminal behaviour. On another occasion she achieved outstanding results in her 'O' level examinations only to be told by her father that it was typical of her to excel in the wrong subjects.

After this third session I found myself profoundly moved at the process. I was aware of the fact that not only was Louise already prepared to experience deep feelings, both positive and negative, in my presence, but also that she was doing so on only the flimsiest evidence of my capacity to receive and understand her. She seemed to be letting me or allowing me to experience diectly that she was both strong and weak, coping and confused, self-affirming and yet craving for approval. What is more I began dimly to perceive that it was these apparent contradictions which made life intolerable for her. It was as if she experienced herself as many conflicting elements and could consequently find no firm identity on which to build.

During the weeks which followed (she was in no doubt after the fourth session that she wished to continue), Louise experienced breathless attacks in my presence and short periods of agitation when she would shake or chain-smoke. She even ran out on one occasion because the fear of suffocation was so overwhelming. Gradually, however, it became clear that her life outside the counselling room was becoming increasingly satisfactory to her. She was making friendships at a deeper level than ever before. She had overcome her awe of her academic supervisor and, as Christmas approached, she coped effectively with a visit from her parents. It was only in the seventh session that she referred directly to me and our relationship. In the most delicate way possible, she indicated how much she had felt able to have confidence in me almost from the outset ('something about how you listen and how you sit') and that this permitted her to feel free to be whatever she happened to be and to 'leave things behind' with me in a way which was not possible even with her friends. Because I was clearly not out to pass judgement, she felt able to experiment freely with the situation and to take risks which would not have been possible in the 'real' world.

By the time February arrived (the month of the cyclical depression), Louise seemed in fine fettle. She declared that she seldom now engineered particular responses from others and that she no longer saw herself as a permanently anxious person. However, she was still aware of tension within herself and wondered if this might be to do with blocked energy. This was the prelude to a period of intense self-exploration during which she discovered new resources in herself and became deeply involved in student politics and radical activism. Perhaps more importantly, she began to face her feelings about her marriage and to acknowledge her dissatisfaction with many aspects of it. One day she appeared in different clothes and announced that she now felt happy about the person she was discovering herself to be and that other people seemed to like her too.

By the beginning of May, it seemed that Louise was approaching the end of therapy. She admitted that she came now to her weekly sessions mainly because she enjoyed them rather than because she needed them. Completely taken in by this apparent breakthrough into psychological health, I asked Louise if she would be interested in working with me on a new video project in which I had been asked to participate with a long-term client. She readily agreed and the fact that the project would require us to spend many hours together as we travelled to another university some distance away seemed to make the proposal all the more attractive to her. Five days later (and a week before the video was due to be made), I was telephoned in alarm by one of Louise's close friends who reported that Louise had cut her wrist and was hopelessly drunk. The following day Louise herself arrived unexpectedly and asked to be seen as an emergency. She was totally incoherent, unable to focus and clearly very frightened. Although her behaviour was bizarre in the extreme, I found myself able to contain my own anxiety, to hold her silently for some minutes and to let her go at the end of the session, although she literally staggered from the building and remained slumped against the wall outside for a further half-hour before moving off. The agitation of others in a neighbouring building was such that I went out to her during this period and asked if she could manage. 'I shall be all right', she said although she was crying. An hour or so later she sent a message from the university's health centre to assure me that she was not in danger.

It is clear in retrospect that for Louise this was her final test of my acceptance of her and of my trust in her own inner resources. I am not suggesting that she consciously planned the whole episode and it is evident that she experienced great fear as she allowed herself to move into chaos. Suffice to say that 4 days later, we travelled together to make the video film and actually spent almost 8 hours in each other's company, during which we established a depth of mutuality which had not been possible previously. (Readers who are interested in seeing the video can purchase it or hire it from the Audio Visual Services Department, University of Leicester.)

Therapy continued for another 10 months during which time Louise fell deeply in love, faced the complexities of her marriage and found a new direction for her life. To all intents and purposes hers is a success story. For me, however, the experience of working with her reinforced in a moving and dramatic way the truth that the client knows best even if this means, as in Louise's case, the rejection of coping behaviours and the descent into chaos. What is more, my relationship with her showed me that, as a therapist, I can be taken completely by surprise and make apparently profound errors of judgement without losing the privilege of being a faithful companion who goes on trying to be accepting, empathic and open to the flow of my own experiencing within a relationship.

References

BOY, A.V. and PINE, G.J. (1982). *Client-centered Counseling: A Renewal.* Boston, MA: Allyn & Bacon.

BURN, M. (1956). *Mr Lyward's Answer* London: Hamish Hamilton.

FRICK, W.B. (1971). *Humanistic Psychology: Interviews with Maslow, Murphy and Rogers.* Columbus, OH: Charles E. Merrill.

KIRSCHENBAUM, H. (1979). *On Becoming Carl Rogers.* New York: Delacorte Press.

MEARNS, D. and THORNE, B.J. (1988). *Person-centred Counselling in Action.* Beverly Hills, CA: Sage.

NELSON-JONES, R. . (1982). *The Theory and Practice of Counselling Psychology.* London: Holt, Rinehart & Winston.

OATLEY, K. (1981). The self with others: the person and the interpersonal context in the approaches of C.R. Rogers and R.D. Laing. In F. Fransella (Ed.), *Personality.* London: Methuen.

ROGERS, C.R. (1954). The case of Mrs Oak: a research analysis. In C.R. Rogers and R.F. Dymond (Eds), *Psychology and Personality Change*, Chicago. IL: University of Chicago Press.

ROGERS, C.R. (1961). *On Becoming a Person*, Boston: Houghton Mifflin.

ROGERS, C.R. (1964). Towards a modern approach to values: the valuing process in the mature person. *Journal of Abnormal and Social Psychology* 68 (4), 160–167.

ROGERS, C.R. (1974). In retrospect: forty-six years. *American Psychologist* 2, 115–123.

ROGERS, C.R. (1975). Empathic: an unappreciated way of being. *The Counseling Psychologist* 2, 2–10.

ROGERS, C.R. (1979). The foundations of the person-centered approach. Unpublished manuscript.

ROGERS, C.R. and DYMOND, R.F. (Eds) (1954). *Psychology and Personality Change.* Chicago, IL: University of Chicago Press.

TAUSCH, R. (1975). Ergebnisse und Prozesse der klienten-zentrierten Gesprächspsychotherapie bei 550 Klienten und 115 Psychotherapeuten. Eine Zusammenfassung des Hamburger Forschungsprojektes. *Zeitschrift für Praktische Psychologie* 13, 293–307.

THORNE, B.J. (1985). *The Quality of Tenderness.* Norwich: Norwich Centre Occasional Publications.

THORNE, B.J. (1987). Beyond the core conditions. In W. Dryden (Ed.), *Key Cases in Psychotherapy.* Beckenham: Croom Helm.

Chapter 4
The Person-centred Approach to Large Groups

From Non-directive Therapy to Person-centred Learning Communities

From 1938 until 1950, the late Carl Rogers was discovering what it might mean to relate to another person in a way that was truly helpful and effective. He dedicated himself to the experience and the understanding of the one-to-one therapeutic relationship and emerged from this period with the conviction, tested repeatedly in experience, that what mattered was the facilitative climate that the counsellor or therapist could create for his client who could then be trusted to develop in life-enhancing ways. Since that time, Rogers frequently reiterated this belief that constructive personality growth and change can only occur when the client is both aware of and experiences a special psychological climate in the relationship. Furthermore, this climate does not spring from the therapist's knowledge or his or her intellectual training or from techniques learned in some particular school of thought. The conditions which characterise the creative therapeutic relationship are feelings and attitudes that must be experienced by the therapist and recognised by the client if they are to prove effective. These feelings and attitudes which Rogers deemed essential for creative personality growth are now well known. The therapist, he believed, must be genuine in the relationship, that is to say, properly in touch with his own feelings and thoughts and capable of expressing them when appropriate, he must be unconditionally accepting of his client and he must show a sensitive empathic understanding of the client's feelings and personal meanings. When these 'core conditions' are present in a therapeutic relationship then, Rogers discovered, creative movement will take place. This is a position from which he never deviated, although the

From *Group Therapy in Britain*, 1988, edited by M. Aveline and W. Dryden, Open University Press, with permission.

theory has been both refined and elaborated over the years in the light of experience and research both by Rogers himself and by other person-centred (a fairly recent label) practitioners.

Carl Rogers encountered individual human beings in his consulting room and gradually discovered that his work as a clinician had profound implications for human relationships in general. Although he professed to be astonished at the way in which the person-centred approach has now permeated so many areas of human activity, it is clear that almost from the outset Rogers believed that if he could discover even one essential truth about the relationship between two people he would inevitably have something important to say in a whole range of other human arenas. Significantly, Rogers was also the kind of man who was highly motivated to exercise influence and, in the latter part of his life, he showed an astonishing determination, both through his involvement in countless workshops and seminars throughout the world and through his voluminous writings, to bring the insights first culled from individual psychotherapy to bear upon a whole range of human situations.

The movement out of the consulting room was publicly registered with the appearance in 1961 of *On Becoming a Person*, where Rogers clearly demonstrates the application of his work as a therapist to human relationships in general. This book had an instant appeal to people outside the professional circles of psychology and mental health and it continues to have a profound impact on many contemporary readers who find articulated in its pages thoughts and feelings of which they have been dimly aware, but which they have never been able clearly to formulate. It was during the 1960s, following the publication of *On Becoming a Person*, that the focus of Rogers' professional activity shifted from the one-to-one relationship to the small group. The era of the so-called 'encounter group' had arrived. As early as the late 1940s, Rogers had used the group setting as a primary context for the training of counsellors, but the encounter group had different objectives and attracted a far wider spectrum of participants. Essentially it offered the opportunity to a participant both for self-exploration and for providing sensitive support to other members of the group (usually of about 8–15 persons) who also wished to develop their self-understanding and their capacities for relating more creatively to others. The role of the group leader (usually known as 'the facilitator') is to engage in the process in such a way that an atmosphere or climate is established in which members can gradually exhibit towards each other the qualities of genuineness, acceptance and empathic understanding which characterise the effective therapeutic relationship. The facilitator eschews the role of the expert or the consultant and, if he does his work effectively, his behaviour and involvement may well become indistinguishable from that of other group members.

During the 1960s, the encounter group movement swept the USA and many strange and bizarre events were reported in both the professional and popular press. Rogers and his colleagues were horrified at many of the developments, and especially at the emergence of manipulatory and gimmicky 'techniques' which were perpetrated by untrained and unskilled group leaders who seemed launched on irresponsible and potentially dangerous power trips. With the proliferation of groups and with the ubiquitous use of the word 'encounter', it was difficult to preserve both the integrity and the credibility of the person-centred model but, during this period, Rogers and his associates nevertheless discovered that their experience in individual therapy was confirmed and further enhanced by what happened in small groups when they were facilitated by experienced person-centred practitioners. The belief in the innate wisdom and resourcefulness of the individual, once he or she is offered a relationship in which acceptance, genuineness and empathy are present, was mirrored by a growing trust in the capacity of a small group to discover its own wisdom and resourcefulness for meeting the needs of its members, given the presence of the same qualities in the overall 'climate' of the group's interactions. In the same way that an individual could be trusted to find the way forward to a more creative way of being, so too could the small group be relied upon to evolve a more satisfying approach to its group life – provided always that the 'core conditions' were established and cultivated.

It was in the context of the so-called La Jolla Programme, established in the latter half of the 1960s by associates of Rogers in order to provide learning opportunities for the development of facilitative skills, that for the first time the staff experimented with the notion of the community meeting at which all the participants in a training programme (some 100 or so people) could meet frequently together. Even if total institutions could not be transformed overnight, it seemed appropriate to discover whether or not a temporary community of some size could create for itself a climate where the core conditions were powerfully present. Rogers himself commented on this experiment in hopeful terms in his book *Encounter Groups* which appeared in 1970:

> Last year the staff [of the La Jolla Programme] experimented with the concept of the community meeting – frequent and intensive meetings for the entire community of participants, a development which it was felt would have particular application to their back-home settings. This proved definitely successful. (Rogers, 1970, p. 153)

The large group experience was launched and, in the years following, commanded an increasing amount of Rogers' time and energy. By the mid-1970s, the man who had begun his career as the non-directive counsellor in a one-to-one relationship was increasingly to be found sitting patiently in the midst of large groups of people, often of different nationalities and cultures. What is more he displayed the same kind of faith in the potential of such a heterogeneous community as he had formerly shown in an individual client.

Background to the Large Group Approach

Although with hindsight it seems that the gradual movement from the one-to-one relationship to the large group was simply a logical and inevitable progression, this would I believe, be to underrate the strong and initially unostentatious thread running through Rogers' work which has justifiably been labelled political. For Rogers, the individual human being is innately good and creative and can be relied upon to move in a positive direction as long as the right conditions for growth are provided. The enemy, clearly, is 'society', which has somehow managed to produce pressures and constraints and to invent organisations and institutions which, far from encouraging the growth of human beings, actually stunt and cripple them. The source of such mismanagement was never fully explored by Rogers, but clearly he would have little sympathy with such notions as 'original sin' or the 'glorious flaw' which might seem to indicate that men and women are *not* innately good and forward-moving. Instead he tended to focus on *the abuse of power* and saw this as the primary cause for much human misery. Human beings, when they are afraid or feel threatened, resort to defensive or aggressive postures in order to preserve their own shaky security. Such measures tend to increase the aura of fear, and certainly do nothing to develop increased understanding within and between people. Differences are automatically seen as divisive and dangerous and are, therefore, not open to exploration and negotiation. Instead they are more likely to result in power struggles and conflicts where one side or faction attempts to dominate the other. The political animal in Rogers strove consistently to attack this process whereby differences lead inexorably to mistrust and hostility. It was his goal, which he pursued with great single-mindedness, to create large group learning situations where individuals have the chance to experience a totally different outcome.

Developments in Britain

In the spring of 1974, Dave Mearns, a young psychologist from Glasgow, had recently returned from a year's study with Rogers as a Visiting Fellow at the Center for Studies of the Person in La Jolla. At the same time Charles (Chuck) Devonshire, a close associate of Rogers and founder of the Center for Cross-Cultural Communication, was in the early stages of what could appropriately be called a 'mission to Europe'. It was thanks to the initiative of these two men that, in the following year, a Facilitator Development Institute (FDI) was established in Britain (whose four co-directors were Mearns, Devonshire, Elke Lambers, a Dutch person-centred therapist, and myself) which had as its aim the creation of residential summer workshops on the person-centred approach to groups. The first such workshop took place in Glasgow in August 1975 and similar workshops have occurred every summer since then in various parts of the country. In each case, a primary task has been to create a learning community where individuals can experience the large group as an environment conducive to personal and professional development. Over the years, some 500 people have participated in the workshops (including many from countries other than Britain) and there seems to be no lack of people still coming forward to take part in what is a unique and intensive opportunity to learn about the person-centred approach and its many different aspects. The recently established Person-Centred Network has drawn on the experience of FDI (Britain) in the conduct of its large group activities, and both the Group Relations Training Association and the Association for Humanistic Psychology have explored the large group through 'person-centred' eyes. However, there is in Britain no other organisation as yet regularly offering the kind of experience afforded by the FDI summer workshops.*

The Aims of the Large Group Experience

The fundamental aim of the FDI Workshop (and of similar person-centred large group experiences) is to provide an environment where the maximum learning can take place for every participant. Emphasis is placed in the advertising brochure on the interrelatedness of personal and professional development and the workshop is presented as an opportunity for participants, who are drawn principally but not exclusively from the helping professions, to find strength and support for both their personal and professional lives through the exploration of new ways of working and being together. It is made clear that the staff members do not see it as their responsibility to plan the workshop beyond its initial stages and that what happens during the week will be the outcome of a community design, created to meet the initial and emerging needs and interests of all participants, including the staff. At the same time, the staff members indicate in the publicity material that they have particular interests and experience which they will be willing to share with participants. The person-centred philosophy of trust in the individual's capacity for development and for taking responsibility for his or her own learning is spelt out as clearly as possible. In short, the expressed aim of the workshop is to enable individual participants, given the over-arching philosophy of the person-centred approach and the different experience and competencies of the staff members, to discover and explore their own needs and to create both an environment and a structure where those needs can be met. In the event, the kind of programme which evolves usually includes a number of large group or community meetings,

---

* These workshops are still continuing (in 1991) under the FDI banner.

smaller encounter groups and a number of options or workshops around specific themes. In no way, however, is the week pre-planned by the staff nor do they seek to push the participants in a particular direction. The invitation to share in a community design is an authentic one and, on occasions, has resulted in unusual and unexpected structures which could not possibly have been foreseen.

The person-centred approach is concerned with the development of attitudes and the large group experience clearly provides a powerful context for attitude change and formation. The attitudes in question are those which have been shown to be *facilitative* of positive changes in clients and others, and one way of looking at the FDI large group experience is to focus on the essential meaning of the Institute's own name. What does it actually entail to be in the business of developing *facilitators*? How can people be 'trained' to develop an unconditional regard for each other? How can they be encouraged to be more honest and authentic so that their outward behaviour and utterances are in correspondence with their inner thoughts and feelings? How can they be enabled to understand another individual from that person's own frame of reference and then communicate their understanding with clarity and sensitivity? In short, how can a large group become an effective context for individuals to learn how to be more accepting, congruent and empathic?

A common and conventional educational approach is to focus mainly on the cognitive component in learning. In this model, students are likely to read books, listen to lectures and write about their growing knowledge in essays and examinations. Such a model is unlikely to be effective in the development of attitudes, because it tackles only one component (the cognitive) in attitude formation and pays little attention to the affective (feelings) and behavioural components. Attitudes are only likely to be affected if people prove totally involved as thinking, feeling and behaving persons. The implications for the large group experience are well summarised by Dave Mearns and Elke Lambers in an article contributed to *Self and Society* in 1976:

> ...our philosophy...in our workshops is to emphasise experiential learning involving the thinking, feeling and behaviour of the participant. We try to create an environment in which the participants will be fully involved as persons not as 'students' or 'trainees'. A vitally important aspect of this environment is that participants are encouraged *to take responsibility for themselves* and for what happens during the programme. There is considerable *freedom* for them to design a programme which they consider worthwhile. The individual participant is encouraged to express his wishes and to endeavour to have them met in the context of the wishes of others.
>
> (Mearns and Lambers, 1976, p. 11)

From the outset, participants in the FDI Workshops have been encouraged to take part in on-going participative research into the process and effectiveness of the events. In the early years John McLeod,* at that time a doctoral research student in Edinburgh University, acted as researcher to FDI and his doctoral thesis presented in 1977 draws extensively on his involvement with the summer workshops. He continued to perform an important research function for the Institute for many years subsequently and discusses his research methodology in a chapter co-authored with Dave Mearns which appears in a later symposium on the person-centred approach published in the USA (Mearns and McLeod, 1984). McLeod believes that research which attempts to explore complex and often shifting subjective experience can only be undertaken by a researcher who is himself known and trusted by the subjects of the research. He was, therefore, fully participant in the workshops and openly discussed his research objectives with the workshop members. He invited them to keep journals throughout the events and to share these or parts of them with him subsequently. In this way those participants (and they were many) who agreed to cooperate in the research were enabled to have a close and confidential relationship with the researcher and witnessed his own struggles to make sense of his experience. Both the journal material and the letters and other information which were passed to the researcher were, therefore, offered within the context of a trusted relationship and to someone who was himself fully participant in the process that he was seeking to elucidate.

McLeod's doctoral thesis explores in some depth the FDI Workshops of 1975 and 1976 and, among other things, he examines the expectations of participants prior to their involvement in the workshop experience. It is evident that, for most of them, there was indeed the expectation of learning which would embrace both the personal and the professional. It is also clear that many hoped for opportunities to work at a feeling level and to experiment with their interpersonal behaviour. Although there were wide differences when participants attempted to elaborate their expectations, there was a common hope that close relationships would be possible and that there would be an involvement of the total person. Such expectations were, in fact, justifiable and McLeod comments:

> Finally, members' expectations – of forming 'intimate' relationships, undergoing personal learning and change, talking about personal problems and so on – were generally fulfilled. As one participant wrote: 'If people come they will work to get what they came for'. (McLeod, 1977, p. 269)

---

* Dr McLeod now trains counsellors at Keele University.

Preparing for the Large Group: The Role of Staff as Convenors

In much that has been written about the large group experience, both by Rogers himself and by his close associate John Wood, considerable emphasis is placed on the significance of the preparatory stages before the group itself actually assembles (i.e. Rogers, 1977; Wood, 1984). What may seem, for example, like mere administrative issues, turn out to have important implications and the dynamics within the staff group are shown to have particular relevance to the large group's subsequent evolution. The British experience confirms these findings.

An FDI Workshop begins, in an important sense, with the composition and publication of the advertising brochure. The staff struggle with its compilation so that nothing appears that is not fully acceptable to everyone. This usually means much hard work and several re-draftings before the brochure is fully and accurately expressive, not only of the workshop's aims but also of the personal interests and preoccupations of each staff member. Even at this early stage, the staff group is modelling the kind of cooperative and responsive way of being together which encourages the expression of personal differences in the interests of arriving at a satisfactory group decision.

Financial issues are also of great significance at this point. Staff members' desire or need to ensure at least a reasonable financial return for their work and commitment has to be balanced against the fact that many likely participants will have limited financial resources, especially if they are students or working outside the conventional structures. A number of strategies have been adopted over the years to ease this dilemma, including differential payments for those who are self-financing and those supported by agencies or organisations, an invitation to wealthy participants to pay more than the workshop fee, the establishing of a bursary or scholarship fund, the acceptance of payment by instalments, and so on. Scholarships are awarded to anyone who asks for them and each individual is asked to determine the size of his or her own scholarship up to a maximum of 50% of the participation fee. Although the FDI staff have never adopted the method devised by Rogers and his colleagues of allowing all participants to determine their own fee (having been given basic data about accommodation and tutorial costs), I believe that it is true to say that no applicant for an FDI Workshop place has had to withdraw because of financial difficulties. Certainly many students and several unemployed people have taken part.

Once the brochure has been published and distributed (usually some 8–10 months before the event), a period of correspondence begins which intensifies as the workshop draws nearer. Every attempt is made to personalise this process. Those who register or enquire about the workshop receive individualised replies and great care is taken to ensure that a warm and responsive attitude is conveyed by the tone and content of letters or telephone calls. Only at the last stage, when joining instructions and information are sent out to the participants, do we resort to a 'packaged' communication and even then a scribbled note or post-script will often add a personal touch. These may seem to be trivial points, but there is no doubt that for some participants such attentive behaviour conveys an attitude of respect and caring which does much both to reinforce the tone of the brochure and to provide evidence of its genuineness.

The importance of the staff meeting immediately prior to large group workshops cannot be overestimated. At least a whole day needs to be allotted for this purpose and, in the case of particularly large workshops where the staff may number as many as 20 people, 3–4 days is not excessive. The FDI team has been small (usually no more than six) and the members well known to each other. Nevertheless, the profound significance of the pre-workshop staff meeting has been proved on every occasion. It is not simply an opportunity for attending to last-minute administrative details, although clearly this often has to be done. Much more important is the quality of the relating which the staff members can achieve in this comparatively short time. They attempt to create an environment in which it is possible to listen to each other, to express important feelings and to share hopes and fears about the forthcoming workshop. Frequently the meeting gives rise to interpersonal issues which have to be addressed or to the discovery that a particular theme seems to be a shared preoccupation, even if there is little agreement on its precise nature let alone its resolution. What is aimed at is a preparedness to live in depth with each other and a willingness to be honest, open and supportive even when confrontation has to be risked. In brief, the major task of the staff group during this preliminary time together is to be themselves. Rogers and his associates have described the process in the following terms:

> ... we spend time together before the workshop convenes, so that insofar as we are capable:
> We can be fully open to each other, and later to the whole group;
> We can explore new and unknown areas of our various life styles;
> We are truly acceptant of our own differences;
> We are open to the new learnings we will receive from our fresh
>   inward feelings, from the group and from each other, all stimulated by the group experience (Villas-Boas Bowen et al., 1978).

Beginnings

By the time the first participants appear the staff group, if all has gone well, are feeling relaxed with each other and open to experience. They are 'tuned up' for what is to follow. The reception of people as they arrive now engages

Person-centred Approach to Large Groups 59

their whole attention. It is very easy at this stage for the staff to take on a kind of proprietary air as if they are the real 'owners' of the workshop and the other participants merely temporary tenants. Every effort is therefore made to convey the message that the workshop 'belongs' to everyone and is not something being 'put on' by the staff group. Early arrivals, for example, may be quickly incorporated into the reception team and may find themselves escorting other participants to their rooms or conveying information about facilities. Other participants may take charge of the Polaroid cameras and assume the task of persuading workshop members to have their photographs taken in order to aid identification in the early stages of the workshop. When these photographs are subsequently displayed the staff members' pictures will not be placed apart but will be mixed up with all the others. These details of behaviour are not part of an elaborate plot on the part of the staff to deny or reject their roles, nor do they stem from a laid-down set of procedures which the staff feel obliged to follow. It is in no sense 'policy' to suggest that early arrivals help with the organisation, but it tends to happen because of the *attitude* adopted by the staff towards participants. Indeed, much of what goes on in these early stages is the outcome of the staff's desire to communicate that they wish to be attentive and responsible *to* participants but have no desire to be responsible *for* them or to arrange their lives during the workshop.

When the community assembles for the first time, usually within an hour or so of the end of the registration period, the tension is high. Over the years, the FDI summer workshop group has ranged in size from 25 to over 80 but even when the *numbers* have been relatively small, the group at the outset will appear enormous to many of the participants. For some, the sense of being overwhelmed and of the sheer impossibility of relating to what appears an amorphous mass will be predominant. Their initial reaction will be one of fear and even of an urgent desire to escape. A staff member will usually be the first to speak and who this will be will probably have been decided by the staff group prior to the meeting. Nobody, however, will know what the particular facilitator is going to say and it is unlikely that even he or she will know until the words have been uttered. The chances are, however, that what is said will be a mixture of feeling and expectation:

> I feel very nervous but at the same time excited now that we're all together. I've no idea what we're in for but I hope we shall be able to make something good of this week together. I'm Dave, by the way, in case there are some of you who haven't identified me yet.

Such a statement is saying many things. It gives high priority to feelings, it is hopeful, it refutes any notion of staff prescience or omnipotence, it points to the corporate responsibility of the group and it indicates a desire to be known as a person. It is likely to be followed by silence but in some way it will have sown the seeds for what is to follow. The likelihood is that, in a first meeting of this kind, the ensuing process will actually seem haphazard and fragmented. Several people may speak, expectations and fears may be voiced, there may even be some tentative self-disclosure but there will be little sense of coherence or continuity. The task of the staff members will be to remain attentive to everyone in the room and to attempt, as far as is possible, to hear fully what is said and to acknowledge it, especially in cases where an individual's contribution seems in danger of disappearing into the black hole of silence which a large group can so easily create. It is unlikely to be helpful if the staff find themselves adopting a high profile in these early stages, but at the same time they must feel free to express strong feelings if and when they experience them. In short, they will be attempting to be real and they will be doing all they can to show that they value the contributions of others, especially when these appear confused or negative or seem destined to sink without trace. Perhaps, more than anything else, they will be attempting to listen and to maintain this listening attitude in a group where the fears and expectations of the majority make this an acutely difficult activity. They will be listening, however, not only to the contributions of others, but also to the changing and probably chaotic flow of experience taking place within themselves. It is exhausting and demanding work.

Development of the Large Group

In a large group which reaches a creative state, a number of stages in its development are generally discernible. Clearly, not every group does achieve such a state and there are many occasions when large groups seem to attain few capacities beyond those of a crowd or collective. The creative state (if it is reached) is characterised chiefly by the ability of the members to be both autonomous and cooperative. Initially, it is of overriding importance that participants experience their own validity and significance. If they feel that they are mere cogs in a machine or pawns in some elaborate and incomprehensible game, they will not be able to attach value to the community as a whole. Instead, they will see it as threatening, a kind of prison where they are without identity. Much of what occurs in the early stages of a workshop can therefore be seen as attempts by individuals to discover if they can be autonomous without being rejected or ostracised by the community. Such attempts will take various forms, but commonly some participants will become angry at what they see as a lack of effectiveness on the part of the staff, others will give expression to feelings of confusion or frustration and others again may register their disapproval by absenting themselves from group meetings or leaving in the middle of sessions. During this period, it is important that the staff members seek to respect and to understand the feelings and behaviour of those participants who test out their autonomy in this way without, however, denying feelings of hurt or irritation which, as staff members, they themselves may be experiencing. The residential setting provides many additional contexts in which the feelings of individuals can be acknowledged and explored, and staff members will often find themselves drawn into or seeking exchanges at meals or in the bar.

Most often the need of individuals to feel valued and significant as people results in an early request for the large group to split up into smaller groups. This development serves to focus on the comparative fragility of the large group, and there are usually those who oppose the movement into smaller units because they fear that the community will not survive such fragmentation. Such people are expressing a care and concern for the total community and act as a counterbalance to those whose main need at this early stage is to find a place where they can feel a sense of security. It is these 'community carers' who usually ensure that, if the large group does break up into smaller units, a time is established at which the whole community can come together again to review its position.

It is not always easy for the large group to decide *how* to divide itself into smaller units and often there is a period of pain and struggle as various permutations are suggested and rejected. The role of the staff members can again become the focus of attention and much discussion will often centre around whether or not each smaller group shall have a staff member as its facilitator. Frequently, a number of small groups will be formed, some of which will have staff members while others opt to be 'leaderless'.

Whether the large group splits into small groups or whether, as in exceptional cases, it remains as a total community, the next stage of development is critical if a creative state is ultimately to be achieved. I have come to think of this part of the process as the search for mutuality or the quest for intimacy. Within the context of a small group, especially if it is ably facilitated, most participants in the workshop will quickly discover a sense of belonging and of acceptance. This in itself, however, is insufficient if the total community is to make significant advances. Participants need to know not only that they are acceptable, but also that they can contribute significantly to the well-being of others. In short, they must experience themselves as givers as well as receivers. This achievement of mutuality or intimacy can happen in a variety of ways. Often it will take place within the small group as group members establish strong bonds and experience their interdependency. Sometimes, though, it will happen on the periphery of the workshop, in the bar or walking in the grounds. As always, the example of the staff members is powerfully influential at this stage. If they are self-sufficient and appear to be omnicompetent, they are unlikely to encourage the quest for mutuality. If, however, they show themselves to be vulnerable as well as resourceful, willing to relate in depth rather than remaining aloof or distant, then the move towards mutuality within the community is likely to be hastened.

It is my belief that, once the majority of participants in the workshop have experienced at least the beginnings of mutuality, there is a strong likelihood that the large group itself will undergo a transformation. People will begin to listen to each other with greatly increased attentiveness, and individuals will be bold enough to express their needs or to offer their ideas without being undermined if these are not immediately taken up. The large group will begin to have confidence in its capacity to make decisions and will be willing to experiment with a variety of structures, both formal and informal. This confidence springs, I believe, from an increasing willingness on the part of the workshop members to be changed by experience. Having found a modicum of security and having discovered that they are important to at least one other person, the participants are eager to take risks and to trust that the large group will provide an environment for growth. There is often a much greater degree of self-disclosure and the increased attentiveness leads to intimate exchanges and sometimes to considerable physical contact. Gradually, the large group seems to shrink in size and is no longer threatening to its members. Instead they begin to perceive that this previously unwieldy community has its own patterns and that they have a contribution to make to its own life. At one and the same time, there is a realisation of corporate identity and of individual uniqueness. When the large group attains, however momentarily, this supremely creative state, the ancient problem of the one and the many melts away.

Not all groups, of course, attain such a creative state or do so only fleetingly. For some participants, the anger and frustration with the workshop staff may persist for many days and, when this happens, there is little chance of forward movement until the feelings have been fully expressed and acknowledged. There are times when the staff may have to work hard at enabling this anger to emerge or when they may feel it necessary to explain that their reluctance or refusal to impose a plan of action on the workshop springs from a deep respect for the needs and resources of the group as a whole, and not from indifference or some underlying urge to manipulate through inaction. Particular difficulties can arise when the workshop membership contains a number of participants who have been 'sent' by their organisations or institutions. Such people have come under authority rather than through personal motivation and are therefore ill-prepared for the struggle to achieve personal autonomy. They are resentful of the authority which has placed them in a situation where there is apparently no authority and, as a result, can rapidly become not only angry but highly confused. Such individuals are often helped by the preparedness of staff members or other participants to spend lengthy periods of time with them outside group meetings in order to discover whether or not they can identify goals and objectives for themselves, which they can pursue during the workshop without reference to the stated or assumed objectives of the employing organisation that originally sent them. Such one-to-one explorations often involve deep ethical issues about the moral rightness of a member of the helping professions seeking to satisfy his or her own needs and longings while the employer is footing the bill.

The atmosphere of intimacy and closeness which is increasingly generated as the community develops is itself a stumbling block for some participants. Often, the desire for intimacy is accompanied by a fear that to take the risks involved in opening up to others will mean a confrontation with deeply buried feelings which will then prove intolerable. Here again, when there are several such people in a workshop, the facilitators may have to be highly sensitive to their needs and fears and must be willingly available to respond to them in private session if need be. Often, of course, such persons are greatly assisted if they are fortunate enough to belong to a caring small group which is patiently responsive to their fears and anxieties. In most instances the final realisation that nobody is going to *coerce* them to be more intimate or self-revealing than they wish proves to be the key to alleviating their fear. What is more, this realisation often engenders the very openness which had previously seemed so threatening.

In many ways, an FDI Workshop is a space apart, for some a kind of 'magic island', and for most at the very least a place where different conditions prevail to those under which they normally live. The problem of re-entry is therefore a major one for almost all participants and the return home is sometimes far from easy. McLeod's (1977) research reveals the agony for some participants of attempting to share with spouses or intimate friends and colleagues the learnings and experiences of the workshop. Often it is difficult to find appropriate language and, especially when the week has been powerfully creative, participants are shocked at the inability or unwillingness of their intimates to share their enthusiasm or understand and accept the changes which they have undergone. Some provision is made for responding to these re-entry problems by convening a follow-up to each workshop which takes place some 2–6 months after the original event. In most cases the organisation of these follow-ups has been undertaken by workshop participants themselves who have usually arranged the appropriate venues. On average, about 50% of the participants attend and most of the staff members. The follow-up event has usually taken the form of an intensive weekend, some of which is spent in the whole group and some in small groups. During the workshop itself, it is common for the issue of re-entry to be raised during the closing days, and groups have often been convened specifically to explore the kind of difficulties which participants are expecting or might encounter. In addition, net-working is encouraged and staff members make it clear that they are happy to respond to letters or even to arrange meetings with individuals, if participants encounter grave difficulties on re-entry. For some years, an informal *Newsletter* also circulated among former workshop members. Research on person-centred encounter groups, undertaken by Rogers himself, has indicated that a fair number of participants report a temporary change in behaviour which rapidly disappears (Rogers, 1970, p. 126). The aim of the FDI follow-up and of the net-working between individuals is to create opportunities for participants to capitalise on and reinforce learnings, whether these be in the personal or professional domains or, as is likely, in both.

Modes of Group Learning

There is little doubt that large group experiences, such as that offered by the FDI Workshops, have about them a strong element of unpredictability. It is safe to assume that many factors contribute to this, not least the effects of setting, sunshine, the holiday spirit, romantic love and the composition of the group membership. Nevertheless, there are certain forms of group learning which commonly recur and deserve special comment.

Issues of power

Most large groups are notorious for their tendency to render individuals powerless. In a person-centred workshop, however, the large group can become the arena in which an individual feels *empowered* and this comes about through the conscious valuing of differences. First the staff members, then others demonstrate by their behaviour that validating and empowering others is the facilitator's chief art. The person who feels him- or herself respected and valued is then willing to put his or her skills and resources at the disposal of the community. People who are empowered are unlikely later to abuse their power. Many organisations and institutions would be transformed if they could capitalise on this simple truth.

Dealing with crisis

It is seldom that a workshop takes place without a crisis of some kind, and frequently this will occur within the large group setting. Crises can take such forms as an apparently irreconcilable conflict between participants or bizarre behaviour which smells of psychosis. It is very common, too, for a member of the community to 'break down' and for there to be prolonged tearful episodes during a large group meeting. In most instances, the large group shows itself to be a remarkably healing environment when such incidents occur. The concentrated attention and concern of a large number of people creates a network of safety and the deep respect which is usually shown for the member's distress gradually turns the crisis into an opportunity for change and development. In everyday life, the response to crisis is so often one of panic and of 'doing something'. The large group behaves differently. It contains the crisis and gives space and attention to the person or persons involved. It is in no hurry and is concerned not with solutions but with staying alongside until the crisis is defused. What is more, when the large group session ends, individuals are not left alone unless they wish to be. The community continues to care through those who elect to stay closely in contact with the person or persons who have undergone the crisis. Sometimes it may be staff members who provide this continuing support but, as a workshop proceeds, it is much more likely to be other participants. One of my own most powerful memories is of collapsing in the large group myself and of the way in which the group accepted my vulnerability and my inability to cope. I did not feel a less effective facilitator as a result.

Decision-making and planning

In the initial stages of a workshop the large group seems particularly inept at making decisions and formulating plans. The brochure's promise of a 'community design', created to meet the needs of all participants, seems far removed from the capabilities of an ill-organised and apprehensive crowd of bewildered people. Decisions are made on impulse, plans are drawn up by power groups or by forceful individuals. Gradually, however, as the quality of listening improves and as members feel valued and resourceful, the process of decision-making and planning changes completely. Proposals are made or suggestions offered and these in turn are discussed, modified or perhaps opposed. Indeed, particular attention is given to individuals who have strong negative feelings, and this encourages those who may normally sit on their misgivings to speak up and register their disquiet. The decisions and plans which emerge from this often long and complex process are often beautifully crafted and take note of the desires and feelings of all members of the community, some of whom may well, of course, have undergone radical shifts of attitude during the process itself. This kind of decision-making goes beyond the normal structures of democracy and it is seldom that the large group resorts to head-counting or to calling for a vote. Occasionally, when the group members have achieved an exceptional degree of sensitivity and openness to each other, there develops what John Wood has called a 'participatory intuition', which leads the whole community to adopt a course of action which is not consciously decided upon in the large group meeting but which evolves in each individual as a result of the group's previous interaction. Wood recounts how one day every member in the community woke up knowing that it was a holiday and that there would be no planned activities that day. Nobody had apparently made the decision and yet everybody knew (Wood, 1984, p. 307).

Transformation through awareness

Many of the participants at an FDI Workshop and at similar person-centred events are members of the helping professions and, for them, the workshop, whatever else it may be, can be a powerful training experience. Undoubtedly, depending on the structure and the content of the programme which evolves, such people will learn much of relevance to their professional activity. At the very least, they will gain insight into the facilitation of small and large groups but they may learn much, too, about the person-centred approach to education and psychology and to institutional life. They will certainly undergo an intensive training in empathy development! None of these gains, however, can explain the radical shift in perception which has been reported by several participants and which seems to spring primarily from experience in the large group itself. It is difficult to avoid religious terminology in attempting to explain this shift. It seems that the heightened awareness which develops in the context of the intensive residential community leads to a fresh interpretation of reality for many participants. It is as if the large group both confirms and illuminates the uniqueness of individuals, while at the same time establishing beyond any shadow of doubt their interconnectedness. Such a perception reveals a pattern behind the surface of things and therefore gives to individuals a sense of meaning and of belonging to an orderly creation which is both mysterious and supportive. When this transformation through heightened awareness comes about, in a large group consisting of people from many different nations and cultures, there is the added excitement of glimpsing the essential unity of humanity which is currently obscured by warring power blocs and international strife.

Effective Leadership in the Large Group

Most of this chapter tells of large groups that attain a high degree of creativity. It has been stressed that the leaders or facilitators of such groups need to be persons who are capable of embodying to a high degree the facilitative attitudes that are the cornerstone of the person-centred approach. The facilitator who cannot be congruent, even when this means revealing his or her own vulnerability and inadequacy, should not embark upon this kind of work, nor should persons who are not deeply accepting of their fellow human beings. What is more, the level and intensity of empathic listening and communicating which is required of the large group facilitator, especially in the early stages of the group's existence, is unlikely to be attained by someone who is not deeply involved in therapeutic work in the normal course of his or her professional life. The large group facilitator, in short, needs to be wise, experienced, self-aware and deeply self-accepting.

Having portrayed such a paragon, it is important as a counterbalance to stress what is perhaps the most crucial attitude of all, namely humility. The facilitator needs to be totally free of the temptation to play the role of expert or teacher or, even worse, of psychological technician armed with a bag of manipulative 'techniques'. On the contrary, he or she enters the large group experience as a learner who is prepared to be with the group as a whole person. I have written here of 'successful' large groups, but their success has depended to a high degree on the willingness of the facilitators for the group to fail. Chuck Devonshire, himself the personification of the inspiring learner, has summed up the whole matter:

> When the facilitator allows a group to struggle freely with its own success or failure and joins in that struggle him or herself, it becomes increasingly clear that growth for persons depends upon their free interaction and not upon the super ability, skill or techniques of the 'expert' (Devonshire and Kremer, 1980, p. 16).

It will be clear that the task of the large group facilitator demands a somewhat formidable array of personal and professional qualities and, in the long run, the presence or absence of such qualities will determine the facilitator's effectiveness. There are, however, skills to be learned, not the least of these being the ability to distinguish between those times when it is appropriate for the facilitator to be self-effacing and those when an intervention is called for. Such skills are in no sense techniques. They evolve from the facilitator's growing capacity to remain congruent even in the most chaotic interactions and to be able to deploy that congruence in the interests, if need be, of one individual in a group of 100 – all this, however, without losing sight of the needs of the group as a whole even if such needs have to be left for the moment in the care of others. Large group facilitators need, therefore, to be experienced counsellors or therapists who are also practised in the facilitation of the small encounter group. Additionally, it is highly desirable that they have taken part as an ordinary participant in at least one residential large group experience before attempting to undertake a staff role. FDI has made it possible for a number of people to experience the role of co-facilitator as a form of additional apprenticeship for this work. A co-facilitator is a member of the staff team who is nonetheless using the workshop both to monitor closely the behaviour of other staff members and to receive help and feedback from them. Steps are also taken to ensure that co-facilitators do not find themselves overloaded with responsibilities during a workshop so that they are unable to reflect on their experience or lose touch with their own needs and limitations.

The Large Group as a Training Experience

Mention has already been made of the obvious benefits which are likely to be derived by members of the helping professions through participation in large group experiences such as those offered by the FDI residential workshops. However, in addition to the knowledge gained of the person-centred approach in its many different facets, there are perhaps other and deeper issues at stake. Essentially, participants in a large group experience of this kind come as people rather than as professionals. And yet they often arrive weighed down by the burdens of their professional activity and by the ravages which their work may have wrought in their personal lives. Often they feel drained, tired and uncared for either by their professional superiors or by their spouses and families. For many such people, the workshop becomes an oasis where they can take stock of their lives and reveal their own wounds and need for emotional nourishment. In this sense, the workshop is often a powerful form of therapy for the helpers. It can also serve as a necessary warning for those who are, sometimes unwittingly, moving towards exhaustion and burn-out. Such a warning can often make a profound impact on the individuals involved. It tells them, before it is too late, that they, too, are persons of value and deserve just as much care and attention as they are wont to lavish on their clients.

Much suffering in the helping professions is caused by insensitive bureaucracy and authoritarian hierarchical structures. Such situations frequently demand assertive behaviour from the potential victims, but there is little in the training of the helping professions which encourages such a response to the abuse of power by those in positions of authority. The FDI Workshop, with its insistence on cooperative planning and on the unique importance of each individual, presents a model which is non-hierarchical and non-authoritarian. For many, it is an empowering experience which gives them the confidence and the energy on their return to do battle with insensitive authority and the courage not to be intimidated by apparently intractable structures. An indication of this kind of personal development is often provided during the workshop by the participant, who for the first time in his or her life speaks with conviction to a group of over 50 people and finds that they listen and are even prepared to change their plans as a result.

In brief, organisations which encourage their members to participate in large group experiences of the kind described here should not be surprised if their employees return with a greatly heightened awareness of their own needs and a quiet determination to have those needs acknowledged and met. In many instances this may well entail a questioning of perhaps time-honoured administrative procedures and a refusal to accept structures which pay scant regard to individual needs and differences.

Therapy or a Therapeutic Experience?

It will be clear that the large group experience is, for most of the participants, a highly therapeutic event from which they derive benefit both personally and professionally. It should not, however, be seen as therapy. In the brochure of the FDI summer workshops, it is clearly stated that those undergoing counselling or therapy should discuss participation with their therapist before applying (see Appendix). The reasons for this are many. In the first place, such an experience is by its nature unpredictable: distressed and highly vulnerable people may find its demands too great and its evolution frustrating or even damaging. Furthermore, if their needs for help and safety are disproportionate, they are likely to hinder the kind of risk-taking in other participants who wish to extend the boundaries of their own self-awareness. Secondly, the presence of a number of manifest 'clients' can make it virtually impossible for those participants who are members of the helping professions to lay aside their professional roles and anxieties and to derive from the group the kind of nourishment and learning which comes from confronting themselves and others as people without role expectations. Thirdly, it would be irresponsible of the staff members even to appear to be offering individual or group therapy when they are likely to be outnumbered by about 12 to 1 by the participants and where there can be no possibility of interviewing applicants prior to the group.

Clearly, from time to time, the large group experience throws up for participants conflicts and personal issues which require subsequent therapy. In such cases staff members do their utmost to ensure that the individuals in question are put in touch with therapists in their own locality and make a point of maintaining contact over the following months. Indeed, it seems likely that a small number of participants attend such events in order to precipitate a crisis which will then ensure that they are forced to seek the therapeutic help which they require. In this sense, therefore, the large group experience can be seen as a stepping stone to therapy for those who, whether consciously or unconsciously, have previously lacked either the courage or the insight to acknowledge the depth of their own needs.

Societal and Cross-cultural Implications

From the outset, the FDI summer workshops have attracted participants from countries other than Britain. They have also brought together members of many different helping professions and people of widely differing religious, philosophical and political viewpoints. Since 1978, when a large cross-cultural workshop was organised in Spain (shortly after Franco's death), the Center for Cross-Cultural Communication (founded by former FDI co-director Chuck Devonshire) has sponsored similar workshops annually in many different countries of the world, including Hungary. These events, too, have been facilitated in the person-centred tradition described in this chapter and have added immeasurably to an understanding of the processes involved (Devonshire and Kremer, 1980). Most importantly, they have shown repeatedly that large groups of almost unimaginable heterogeneity are capable, given the appropriate conditions, of finding ways of working constructively together which affirm individual experiences and respect human differences. In the FDI Workshops, there have sometimes been as many as 10 different nations represented, but this pales into insignificance when contrasted with the 20 or more represented each year in the specifically cross-cultural events.

Our own country is currently more divided than it has been for many years. A period of economic recession has led to a mass of unemployed people and an increasing gap between north and south. The inner cities are often a tinder box where inter-racial feeling runs high. In the world at large, too, the divisions between nations and cultures are as wide as they have ever been and the nuclear threat does not diminish. The appalling scourge of HIV (the virus which can cause AIDS) has now focused attention on the urgent need to discover forms of relating intimately which, in the face of so grotesque a plague, do not further endanger our species.

In such a context, the need to discover ways of enabling individuals to transcend their differences of culture, education and upbringing becomes all the more critical. The temptation may well be to resort to authoritarian modes of control so that differences are not transcended but rather suppressed or stifled. Certainly, the fear of the large group increases as conflicts become more overt and the challenge to authority grows. It is my belief, however, that the large group experiences which I have attempted to describe have within them the seeds of an approach to the pressing problems of our time which preserves a faith in the human spirit which is neither naïve nor foolishly optimistic. What is more, if therapists profess to minister to the individual, but fall silent on the needs of the world, I for one cannot help feeling that there is a dereliction of responsibility somewhere.

Appendix: Extracts from a Current FDI Brochure

Facilitator Development Institute   Summer Workshop 1986

The Workshop

The workshop has a primary training function for those who are working with individuals or groups, and it also provides a context for personal growth and development. Because of its international nature it serves to foster cross-cultural as well as interpersonal communication. It is designed to provide an intensive learning experience in which the participants can discover their own and others' power and resources, find strength and support for their personal and professional lives and explore new ways of working with individuals and groups.

The basic philosophy of FDI is person-centred in the tradition of Dr Carl Rogers. This approach is one in which there is trust in the individual's responsibility and capacity for development.

Only the initial steps of the workshop will be planned by the staff. The overall format will be a community design, created to meet the initial and many as 10 different nations represented, but this pales into insignificance when contrasted with the 20 or more represented each year in the specifically cross-cultural events.

Our own country is currently more divided than it has been for many years. A period of economic recession has led to a mass of unemployed people and an increasing gap between north and south. The inner cities are often a tinder box where inter-racial feeling runs high. In the world at large, too, the divisions between nations and cultures are as wide as they have ever been and the nuclear threat does not diminish. The appalling scourge of HIV (the virus which can cause AIDS) has now focused attention on the urgent need to discover forms of relating intimately which, in the face of so grotesque a plague, do not further endanger our species.

In such a context, the need to discover ways of enabling individuals to transcend their differences of culture, education and upbringing becomes all the more critical. The temptation may well be to resort to authoritarian modes of control so that differences are not transcended but rather suppressed or stifled. Certainly, the fear of the large group increases as conflicts become more overt and the challenge to authority grows. It is my belief, however, that the large group experiences which I have attempted to describe have within them the seeds of an approach to the pressing problems of our time which preserves a faith in the human spirit which is neither naïve nor foolishly optimistic. What is more, if therapists profess to minister to the individual, but fall silent on the needs of the world, I for one cannot help feeling that there is a dereliction of responsibility somewhere.

Appendix: Extracts from a Current FDI Brochure

Facilitator Development Institute   Summer Workshop 1986

The Workshop

The workshop has a primary training function for those who are working with individuals or groups, and it also provides a context for personal growth and development. Because of its international nature it serves to foster cross-cultural as well as interpersonal communication. It is designed to provide an intensive learning experience in which the participants can discover their own and others' power and resources, find strength and support for their personal and professional lives and explore new ways of working with individuals and groups.

The basic philosophy of FDI is person-centred in the tradition of Dr Carl Rogers. This approach is one in which there is trust in the individual's responsibility and capacity for development.

Only the initial steps of the workshop will be planned by the staff. The overall format will be a community design, created to meet the initial and the first place, such an experience is by its nature unpredictable: distressed and highly vulnerable people may find its demands too great and its evolution frustrating or even damaging. Furthermore, if their needs for help and safety are disproportionate, they are likely to hinder the kind of risk-taking in other participants who wish to extend the boundaries of their own self-awareness. Secondly, the presence of a number of manifest 'clients' can make it virtually impossible for those participants who are members of the helping professions to lay aside their professional roles and anxieties and to derive from the group the kind of nourishment and learning which comes from confronting themselves and others as people without role expectations. Thirdly, it would be irresponsible of the staff members even to appear to be offering individual or group therapy when they are likely to be outnumbered by about 12 to 1 by the participants and where there can be no possibility of interviewing applicants prior to the group.

Clearly, from time to time, the large group experience throws up for participants conflicts and personal issues which require subsequent therapy. In such cases staff members do their utmost to ensure that the individuals in question are put in touch with therapists in their own locality and make a point of maintaining contact over the following months. Indeed, it seems likely that a small number of participants attend such events in order to precipitate a crisis which will then ensure that they are forced to seek the therapeutic help which they require. In this sense, therefore, the large group experience can be seen as a stepping stone to therapy for those who, whether consciously or unconsciously, have previously lacked either the courage or the insight to acknowledge the depth of their own needs.

Societal and Cross-cultural Implications

From the outset, the FDI summer workshops have attracted participants from countries other than Britain. They have also brought together members of many different helping professions and people of widely differing religious, philosophical and political viewpoints. Since 1978, when a large cross-cultural workshop was organised in Spain (shortly after Franco's death), the Center for Cross-Cultural Communication (founded by former FDI co-director Chuck Devonshire) has sponsored similar workshops annually in many different countries of the world, including Hungary. These events, too, have been facilitated in the person-centred tradition described in this chapter and have added immeasurably to an understanding of the processes involved (Devonshire and Kremer, 1980). Most importantly, they have shown repeatedly that large groups of almost unimaginable heterogeneity are capable, given the appropriate conditions, of finding ways of working constructively together which affirm individual experiences and respect human differences. In the FDI Workshops, there have sometimes been as emerging needs of all participants, including the staff. Each person shares the power to influence the course of the workshop. Group experiences, now spanning many years and many countries, lead us to trust that self-direction and collaborative decision-making in a climate where feelings and intellect are equally respected, contribute to constructive personal and social change. The workshop offers the possibility of experience in small groups and large community meetings. In addition, areas of exploration may develop around the interests of staff and participants, for example:

- Experience and theory of group facilitation
- Empathy development
- Person-centred approaches to psychotherapy
- Person-centred approaches in education
- Person-centred approaches in organisation and training
- Voice work and creativity

PARTICIPANTS

The Workshop has particular relevance for those working in education, counselling, research, social work, psychology, psychiatry, community work, management, the churches, the health professions, trade unions and the armed services. Those taking part in the workshop are not, however, in any way restricted to these professions. Since the primary language of the workshop will be English, a working knowledge of that language is highly desirable. For this workshop an upper limit of 50 participants is envisaged.

TEAMS

Organisations and institutions are encouraged to send teams of participants to the workshop. This can be particularly valuable where the aim is team-building or where organisational innovation is being considered.

RESEARCH

Individual reflection and evaluation of the workshop experience has been characteristic of FDI in the past, primarily through journal keeping. The staff very much hope that this feature will be continued and that a new method of research may evolve during the summer workshop. It is the staff's experience and belief that participation in this way can contribute significantly to the individual's own understanding of the workshop experience. Members of the workshop are invited to keep their own private journals. Participants are under no obligation to contribute to any new research programme.

CONDITION FOR PARTICIPATION

An FDI educational workshop is not a substitute for psychotherapy or counselling. Participants are in all ways taking part because of their own free will, and are fully responsible for themselves during the workshop. Those currently undergoing psychotherapy or counselling are required to discuss participation in the workshop with their therapist or counsellor.

Information about FDI Summer Workshops and about FDI Counsellor and Psychotherapy Training* may be obtained from:
  The Administrator,
  Norwich Centre for Personal and Professional Development,
  7 Earlham Road,
  Norwich   NR2 3RA.

References

DEVONSHIRE, C.M. and KREMER, J.W. (1980). *Toward a Person-centred Resolution of Intercultural Conflicts.* Dortmund: Pädagogische Arbeitsstelle.

MCLEOD, J.A. (1977). *A study, using personal accounts and participant observation, of two 'growth' movements as social–psychological phenomena, with a discussion of the possibility of a Humanistic Science of Persons.* Unpublished thesis, Edinburgh University.

MEARNS, D. and LAMBERS, E. (1976). Facilitator Development Institute. *Self and Society* 4 (12), 9–12.

MEARNS, D. and MCLEOD, J. (1984). A person-centered approach to research. In R.F. Levant and J.M. Shlien (Eds), *Client-centered Therapy and The Person-centered Approach.* New York: Praeger.

ROGERS, C.R. (1970). *Carl Rogers on Encounter Groups.* New York: Harper & Row.

ROGERS, C.R. (1977). *On Personal Power.* New York: Delacorte Press.

VILLAS-BOAS BOWEN, M., JUSTYN, J., KASS, J., MILLER, M., ROGERS, C.R., ROGERS, N. and WOOD, J.K. (1978). Evolving aspects of person-centred workshop. *Self and Society* 6 (2), 43–49.

WOOD, J.K. (1984). Communities for learning: a person-centered approach. In R.F. Levant and J.M. Shlien (Eds) *Client-centered Therapy and the Person-centered Approach.* New York: Praeger.

---

* From 1991, the counsellor training section of FDI has been re-named Person-centred Therapy (Britain).

Chapter 5
The Quality of Tenderness

Those of you who are familiar with my preoccupations in recent years will know that I have long since been concerned with the problem of guilt and the way in which its pervasiveness destroys individuals and contaminates so many of our relationships. Last summer I was invited to give a paper at the annual general meeting of the Norwich Diocesan Board for Social Responsibility and I want to quote something I said then as one of the starting points of my reflections this evening. In attempting to unravel the knots which result from guilt feelings I had arrived in my paper at the point where the indissoluble link between body and soul in the genesis of guilt was all too clear. This led me to comment as follows:

> In these cases where guilt has exerted a strangle-hold for many years and perhaps since birth or before, the therapist needs to be at home in both the worlds of the soul and of the body. (Thorne, 1985)

My second starting point is a meeting in Paris which I attended in January of this year. The object of the meeting, which brought together about 40 people – mainly young people – from many different nations, was to explore the task of how to set up temporary communities in which it would be possible for people to communicate in depth across language and cultural barriers. The meeting was difficult and challenging. There were many moments of frustration: at times we seemed very stuck. On the last afternoon a 16-year-old English girl went to the blackboard and began to write there the results of her recent researches into the dictionary. Her efforts had focused on one word – the word *tender*. As she wrote I felt an instant attentiveness within myself. I knew that she was providing a key. This paper is some attempt to understand both the nature of the key and of the door which it promises to unlock.

A lecture delivered at the Norwich Centre on December 13 1982 and repeated at the University of East Anglia on March 18 1983, published 1985 by Norwich Centre Publications – reproduced with permission.

Many in this audience are well acquainted with the work of Dr Carl Rogers. Indeed, the influence of Rogers on the development both of the UEA Counselling Service and of the Norwich Centre in the city is immense. His belief in the self-actualising tendency of human beings and his understanding of the nature of the therapeutic relationship are cardinal factors in the approach which we have embraced here during the last decade.* Perhaps Rogers' greatest contribution to therapeutic knowledge has been the thorough and painstaking way in which he has researched the elements which make for growth in a counselling relationship. We are perhaps now so familiar with the concepts of unconditional acceptance, genuineness and empathy that we no longer realise the full significance of the staggering claim which Rogers makes for these qualities, when he states that if the counsellor can offer them to his client then therapeutic movement will occur – not might or can but will occur.

One of the questions which perhaps lies behind this paper this evening is whether or not I still believe this claim. In fact, I am confident that I do. After 15 years or more working as a person-centred counsellor in the Rogers' tradition I am convinced that, if I can really accept my client, if I can seek to understand his or her inner world and to communicate this understanding to him or her and if I can be authentically myself in the relationship, then positive movement will occur. Sometimes that movement will seem slow, almost imperceptible, at others it will seem so swift that it is almost breathtaking. But that it happens I have no doubt. When it does not happen I can be fairly sure that I have not offered those conditions adequately or that, if I have, my client's exposure to them has been so short-lived that no benefit has accrued.

In the face of such an affirmation of Rogers' beliefs you might well ask why I am devoting this evening to the exploration of a fourth quality. Is it that despite my affirmation I am, after all, dissatisfied with the therapeutic trinity? Must I somehow complete the square in some such manner as that adopted by the Catholic Church, if we are to believe Carl Jung, when the doctrine of the Assumption elevated the Virgin Mary to a seat beside the Holy Trinity? The answer is something like 'yes and no'. Let me be more specific. I do not doubt the efficacy of acceptance, genuineness and empathy in providing a growth-promoting climate nor do I wish to maintain that tenderness has to be added to them in order to make them more effective. What I wish to propose is that, if tenderness is present, something qualitatively different may occur. What I mean by tenderness and what, further, I mean by something qualitatively different are the two questions to which I shall now address myself.

---

* The Student Counselling Service at the University of East Anglia was founded in 1974, the Norwich Centre in 1980.

The word 'tender' is so multifaceted that to comprehend its total significance is, I suspect, impossible. Indeed, it is partly for that reason that I find myself so fascinated by it. Let me, at least, though, give some glimpses of its complex nature. It is, to start with, both an active and a passive attitude. Compare, for example, 'He is feeling very tender and bruised after the conflict with his boss' and 'She was tender and gracious towards those she loved'. Then, again, it is a word which can be literal and physical or supremely metaphorical and abstract. 'My feet are very tender after the route march. He has a very tender spot on his right arm', contrasted with 'The first tender shoots of an emerging confidence appeared in his reply. When you speak to me of my mother you touch me on my most tender spot'; and then there is the usage which seems to embrace the physical and the abstract, the literal and the metaphorical: 'His tender eyes gazed into hers. So tender was her heart that it came as no surprise when she became delirious at the news of the disaster.' If we track this remarkable word further many more avenues open up. Here is a word which means both vulnerable and warmly affectionate, easily crushed and merciful, not tough and sympathetic. It seems to incorporate both weakness and gentle strength, great fragility and great constancy. But there is more. It is a word which has about it the breath of youth: 'He knew this at a very tender age.' It is a word which expresses sensitivity to moral or spiritual feelings: 'He is a person of tender conscience', and it can also indicate protectiveness towards emotions: 'She is very tender of her suffering.' It even has a nautical sense insofar as a tender vessel is one which can be easily keeled over by the wind (the opposite incidentally is a stiff vessel!).

I am sure you will not be unaware that in the last three minutes we have journeyed through vast territories! It is almost as if this one word opens up the whole panorama of human experience. What is more, it seems effortlessly to bridge the worlds of the material and carnal, of the feelings and emotions, of the moral and spiritual, of suffering and of healing, of youth and age, of active and passive. It is, if you like, a supremely holistic word. This being the case, I have wondered to myself why it is that on those occasions in recent weeks when I have found myself telling people the title of this paper, I have sometimes experienced a slight embarrassment inside me, almost a hint of shame, a trace of disquiet as if I were mentioning something slightly indecent. And then I realised that such feelings were present only in my conversations with men. What was ever so slightly indecent was the fact of two men talking about tenderness.

This reflection made me think again of the Holy Trinity, Carl Jung and the Blessed Virgin Mary. Could it be that there was something faintly male dominant about the therapeutic trinity of acceptance, genuineness and empathy, and that my attempt to introduce tenderness into the picture was an infiltration of the feminine into the sanctuary – and not only the feminine but also the carnal and fleshly? Remember, incidentally, that the doctrine of the Assumption of the Blessed Virgin Mary proclaims that she was raised *bodily* into heaven. As I meditated on this possibility, I was instinctively drawn to my experience of Carl Rogers himself and to considering those things I know about him and his life. I remember the strict protestant upbringing, the young man who intended to be a pastor and then his refusal to be trapped in what seemed a narrow doctrinal strait jacket. I remembered, too, his inhibition until late in life about physical contact and how he valued the encounter group experiences which had enabled him to feel more free in his body and in his physical relating. I remember, too, his wonderful, lifelong marriage with Helen, but also the difficulties of the last years before she died. And I am aware of how, since her death, he has felt an openness to women which has been a source of new discovery and fulfilment. Could it be, in short, that the man who himself discovered and embodied the therapeutic trinity is himself further on in his journey thanks to those very qualities which he has so consistently offered to others and to himself? Could it be that he, too, as he approaches death knows and enjoys the world of tenderness where male and female flow together without inhibition and without shame? I hope so.

I cannot dodge the task any longer. I must now attempt to define what I mean by tenderness, to draw together the hints and half-thoughts with which I have laboured so far. What does it mean for a person to possess the quality of tenderness in all its fullness? In the first place it is a quality which irradiates the total person – it is evident in voice, the eyes, the hands, the thoughts, the feelings, the beliefs, the moral stance, the attitude to things animate and inanimate, seen and unseen. Secondly, it communicates through its responsive vulnerability that suffering and healing are interwoven. Thirdly, it demonstrates a preparedness and an ability to move between the worlds of the physical, the emotional, the cognitive and the mystical without strain. Fourthly, it is without shame because it is experienced as the joyful embracing of the desire to love and is therefore a law unto itself. Fifthly, it is a quality which transcends the male and female but is nevertheless nourished by the attraction of the one for the other in the quest for wholeness.

It will be evident that so breath-taking a quality is rare. What is more no one person can hope to embody it more than fleetingly and intermittently, for to be irradiated by it is to achieve a level of humanness which belongs to the future and not to now. It is precisely for that reason, however, that those of us who have chosen to dedicate our lives to counselling and to the education of the person have the awesome responsibility of developing this quality in ourselves and others now. If we can do this in our generation, then we can have hope that there will indeed be a future and that it will be a time in which something qualitatively different can happen between human beings.

I have now arrived at the *second* question to which I wish to address myself this evening. What do I mean when I claim that where tenderness is present between two people then something qualitatively different can occur? I want

The Quality of Tenderness

to begin by answering that question as concisely as I can. Only then will I attempt the far more daunting task of illuminating what may well seem a fairly hermetic statement. *When tenderness is present in a relationship I believe that there is the possibility of finding wholeness and of recognising the liberating paradox.*

The unpacking of this statement will not be easy. I will begin by attempting to describe the nature of the fleeting moments when I believe the quality I am calling tenderness is present in my *own* interactions as a counsellor. This is an attempt to grasp in words a state of being which eludes definition and, I know at the outset, that I can do no more than grope after the inexpressible. Inwardly, I feel a sense of heightened awareness and this can happen even if I am near exhaustion at the end of a gruelling day. I feel in touch with myself to the extent that it is not an effort to think or to know what I am feeling. It is as if energy is flowing through me and I am simply allowing it free passage. I feel a physical vibrancy and this often has a sexual component and a stirring in the genitals. I feel powerful and yet at the same time almost irrelevant. My client seems more accurately in focus: he or she stands out in sharp relief from the surrounding decor. When he or she speaks, the words belong uniquely to him or her. Physical movements are a further confirmation of uniqueness. It seems as if for a space, however brief, two human beings are fully alive because they have given themselves and each other permission to risk being fully alive. At such a moment I have no hesitation in saying that my client and I are caught up in a stream of love. Within this stream there comes an effortless or intuitive understanding and what is astonishing is how complex this understanding can be. It sometimes seems that I receive my client whole and thereafter possess a knowledge of him or her which does not depend on biographical data. This understanding is intensely personal and invariably it affects the self-perception of the client and can lead to marked changes in attitude and behaviour. For me as a counsellor, it is accompanied by a sense of joy which, when I have checked it out, has always been shared by the client. The difficulty lies in trusting such experiences, for there seems to be in all of us *a deep and almost pathological distrust* of something which brings such joy and such clarity. It is as if *joy and knowledge are forbidden fruits* and the experience of them must therefore be evidence of dubious motives and unhealthy desires or of insanity. Or to put the matter into slightly different terminology 'If I am full of understanding and of the joy of desiring then it can only be that I have fallen into the hands of Satan'. If, however, both the client and I are able to trust the moment, that is to trust the working of tenderness, then a number of things can happen and I have come to recognise a whole range of possibilities. Tears, for example, may flow without warning and without apparent cause or there may be a sudden release of laughter. There may be an overwhelming desire for physical contact which can result in holding hands or in a close embrace. There may be an urgent need to talk about death or God or the soul. There may be a desire to walk around or lie down. In one instance, a client expressed the desire to be naked and removed clothing without hesitation or shame. Always there is a sense of well-being, of it being good to be alive and this in spite of the fact that problems or difficulties which confront the client remain apparently unchanged and as intractable as ever. Life is good and life is impossible, long live life.

Perhaps by now my original statement is beginning to have more meaning. 'When tenderness is present there is the possibility of finding wholeness and of recognising the liberating paradox.' It appears increasingly to me that, when I can be tender or when I experience tenderness in another, neither I nor they can any longer be satisfied with a fragmented existence. We no longer wish to be mere facets of ourselves, and as a result we find the courage to cross the bridge into new areas which had previously been hidden or feared. What is more, the other person is perceived not as a threat to our own wholeness, but as a beloved companion who is on the same journey. We are truly members one of another. As for the liberating paradox, this is, I believe, the most important door of all to which tenderness provides the key. So often we remain trapped by a paradox because we experience it as a contradiction. The resulting paralysis can hold us captive for years, sometimes for life. I love my mother but I hate her – therefore I can neither rebel nor conform. I am strong but I am weak – therefore I can bring myself neither to lead nor to follow. To be trapped by paradox is, in the end, to capitulate to meaninglessness. In the agony of either–or, we reject all meaning and settle for the paralysis of the stuck life or, if there comes a moment of unendurable pain, we opt for death. And all the time the liberating paradox is standing there in the shadows like a candle waiting to be lit. In the moments of tenderness, I have experienced both my weakness and my strength and known them to be not contradictory but complementary, not paralysing but releasing. Often, too, I have known clients who, sensing the paradox at the very source of tenderness itself, have dared to own their love–hate and have discovered that by doing so they are able to quit the emotional prison in which they were paralysed and impotent. The world of the 'both and' is infinitely wider and more invigorating than the cramped conditions prevailing in the world of 'either–or'. We men need constant reminding of this truth. So often with our highly developed objective reasoning we strain for the tidy and logical answer. 'It must be chalk or cheese', we cry in frustration and cannot understand the sadness and bewilderment in our wives or lovers or, more tragically still, in the blocked off recesses of our own hearts for they know and we know, if we did but know it, that it is both chalk *and* cheese.

For me, it is a matter of great regret that I waited until the imminent arrival of our third child before deciding to be present at a birth. The birth of this child proved to be the means whereby I learned more fully what it is to dwell in the paradox and why it is that women have a greater chance of being at home there. As a child is born into the world we must be aware, however dimly, of pain and joy, tears and laughter, toil and relaxation, bloody mess and peach-like purity, power and weakness, anxiety and peace. Perhaps most poignantly of all for me, there was an awareness of violent expulsion and gracious welcoming and the realisation that I had a part to play in the latter. My hunch is that, with some of my clients, it is in a moment of tenderness that I am able to extend to them that welcome to the world which they never received at birth. It is as if they have been waiting all their lives for the completion of the liberating paradox.

In the final part of this lecture, I want to spell out more the significance of tenderness as I have described it to issues of sexuality and spirituality, and to suggest also an important link with the quest for peace in our time. I shall conclude with a few observations about how those of us in the counselling movement might hope to become more tender in the work we undertake with clients.

It is, I am sure, highly significant that Carl Jung has come repeatedly to mind as I have worked on this lecture. I defer to him again as I recall that he frequently stated his belief that those who came to him with sexual problems generally had spiritual problems and vice versa. I use as my starting point, then, the hypothesis that, for us humans, sexuality and spirituality are intimately entwined. You will recall, too, that I began this evening by talking about guilt and it is here I believe that the entwining of the sexual with the spiritual becomes most obvious. So often the person in spiritual anguish is burdened with guilt and so often, too, the person with sexual problems is similarly burdened. Guilt requires a context of shame for shame is the soil in which unhealthy desire or lust grows, but tenderness, you will remember, does not know shame but only the joyful embracing of the desire to love.

I am enormously indebted to Dom Sebastian Moore, a monk of Downside Abbey, who in a recent book entitled *The Inner Loneliness* (1982) throws for me a penetrating shaft of light on to the whole issue of shame. He argues that the original generic sin from which all sins flow and which is therefore the cause of all shame and all guilt is a radical distrust of our Creator. If we attempt to put that idea into secular terms we arrive at a statement something like this: 'The basic trouble with human beings is that they cannot trust that they are so constituted that they need not be anxious about their sexuality, their survival or their death.' By shifting the focus of the original sin from disobedience to distrust, Moore makes possible an immensely rewarding chain of thought. His exegesis of the Genesis story of the Fall is riveting in itself. 'She ate of the fruit and gave some to her husband and he ate. And immediately their eyes were opened, and they saw that they were naked. So they sewed for themselves loincloths out of figleaves.' Moore says of this passage: 'The immediate effect of losing touch with God is the awkwardness of the sexes with each other ... and this awkwardness, this non-alignment is the root of all our sexual disorders' (Moore, 1982). In other words, this awkwardness comes from distrust in God, distrust that He knew what He was about when He created men and women and gave them the freedom to be naked with each other. Once the distrust is there, the shame immediately follows and the necessity to cover up the genitalia. Distrust leads to shame which generates in its turn a distrust of the body so that it must be covered up. And then the scene is set for lust and the anxious preoccupation with mastering desires. Once we are out of friendship with our bodies, we can no longer trust our desires and so the endless process is set in motion. We distrust God, we distrust our bodies, we distrust our desires, we seek to control, we fail, we feel guilty, we seek to placate God the judge, we may succeed temporarily but soon we are back again, distrusting, guilty, seeking vainly to control.

When tenderness as I have attempted to describe it is present between two people, I believe that this endless process can be interrupted. For a moment, shame gives way to wholeness and the liberating paradox and at this moment God is trustworthy, the body is trustworthy, desires are trustworthy, sexuality is not a problem, survival is not a problem, death is not to be dreaded. For a moment, perhaps a fraction of a second, we are transformed and are utterly free of shame. We are restored to full friendship with God or, in secular terms, we know that we are born to be lovers and to be loved. That which I have described as qualitatively different has happened and we are never quite the same again, however much we forget, deny or deride the experience.

The relevance of all this to the urgent quest for peace in our time can be explored in many ways. I wish to confine myself to one line of thought only. The nightmarish possibility of a nuclear holocaust is now daily before us. In prophetic films and books we are confronted by bodies hideously disfigured, bodies in their millions ravaged and dismembered, suppurating and contaminated. But in the moment of tenderness the body is infinitely precious. To destroy it would be unthinkable or to see it wasted away without food would be to condone sacrilege. Need more be said? The more tenderness is released into the world the more impossible it becomes to tolerate war or to tolerate starvation. Mother Teresa of Calcutta relates a story about her sisters:

> 'During the mass', I said, 'you saw the priest touch the body of Christ with great tenderness. When you touch the poor today you will be touching the body of Christ. Give them that same tenderness.' When they returned several hours later, the new sister came up to me, her face shining with joy. 'I have been touching the body of Christ for three hours' she said. I asked her what she had done. 'Just as we arrived, the sister brought in a man covered with maggots. He had been picked up from a drain. I have been taking care of him. I have been touching Christ, I knew it was him' she said.
> (Mother Teresa, 1977)

I began this paper with the observation that the therapist needs to be at home in both the worlds of the soul and of the body if he is to stand much chance against the pervasive power of guilt. I hope I have demonstrated why

I believe that the cultivation of tenderness will enable him or her to move towards that 'at homeness' and thus to make it possible for his or her clients to enjoy a qualitatively different experience to that engendered simply by acceptance, genuineness and empathy. The experience of wholeness and of the liberating paradox, be it ever so fleeting, is indeed the very self-actualisation for which most of the time we can but dimly struggle. And yet such moments are indelible and eternal no matter how much we repress them or deny them.

How then, finally, can those of us who are counsellors hope to become more tender, more capable of being with our clients in such a way that we and they are transformed, however fleetingly, into what we are capable of becoming? The short answer must be that we take our bodies and our souls seriously, and not only our minds and feelings, and do not for a moment forget that we are all four. To do this will involve a form of self-love which extends to a trusting of our desires so that we can take risks and not be for ever worrying about losing control. To this end, I have some specific suggestions for activities that do not perhaps appear on every counsellor training programme: they include prayer and meditation, the study of one's own psychosomatic disorders, attendance at childbirth, deliberate attempts to understand and remedy the awkwardness between the sexes (and that probably means losing the fear of nakedness), assaulting the heavy cultural endorsement of male sexual identity over female, overturning the obsession with genital sex and liberating the many other varieties of human warmth, the study of sacramental religion and, for Christians, the cultivation of a deep devotion to the Eucharist. In short, I am proposing a programme which takes as one of its starting points the belief that people dislike or abuse sex and physicality because they don't know God let alone realise that He or She dwells within them.

Tenderness becomes a possibility at the moment when two human persons meet and are able to give way to the liberating urge to trust without anxiety. There is then no longer a need to control because desire fills the whole personality, body, mind and soul, and such desire is the food of the will which can then obey with joy. The more we counsellors can manifest such tenderness, the more we shall hasten the evolution of the human species – and if that sounds hopelessly fanciful let us not forget that to live without anxiety about sex, survival or death is to dwell with God or, pace Carl Rogers, to acknowledge that our own personal power thus conceived can move mountains.

References

THORNE, B. (1985). Guilt, conscience and the helping professions. In: *Resources Handbook*, vol. 1. Leicester: Diocesan Board of Social Responsibility.

MOORE, S. (1982). *The Inner Loneliness*. London: Darton, Longman and Todd.

TERESA, MOTHER (1977). The poor in our midst. In *New Covenant*, Ann Arbor, Michigan.

Part III
Values and Meaning

Introduction

It is often suggested that person-centred therapists are value-free creatures who have no strong views on anything. They are caricatured as nodding empathisers who are prepared to accept everyone and everything in the interests of a non-conflictual life. In this section of the book, I expose the fallacy of this fantasy. I believe there to be a strong ethical and moral stance inherent in person-centred therapy. There is, too, an understanding of the nature of human beings which often brings the person-centred practitioner into fierce conflict with other views of reality. Chapters 7 and 9 explore these issues in theoretical terms while drawing on material from therapeutic relationships and, in the latter case, from the life of Carl Rogers himself. Chapter 8 seeks to tease out ethical issues as they present themselves in the course of the therapeutic process itself and illuminates the agonising dilemma for the therapist when his or her client is clearly choosing to opt for death rather than life. The final chapter in this section is overtly political. It reveals the escalation of stress in Britain's higher education institutions after 10 years of Thatcher government and shows how the person-centred counsellor is increasingly the guardian of a value system which stands in sharp conflict with the prevailing political climate.

Chapter 6
In Search of Value and Meaning

The word counsellor is open to such misunderstanding that I feel it necessary at the outset to quote from the literature of my own professional association so that the word can be more adequately understood in its educational context:

> Clients consult a counsellor because they are in difficulties and hope that by discussing their concerns with the counsellor they will gain fresh insights and move towards a more creative response to their problems. The professionally trained counsellor is seldom an advice giver... Instead he will try to assist a person to see his own situation more clearly and then provide the opportunity for looking at ways of behaving differently or of arriving at decisions... The client himself is the primary judge of what is or what is not an appropriate concern to take to a counsellor. Counsellors should be prepared and equipped to respond to a wide range of personal, emotional, social and educational difficulties ... All counsellors observe a code of professional confidentiality and information is not divulged to others unless the client gives specific permission for this to occur. Often a single interview with a counsellor may be enough to point the way forward. On the other hand, where someone is experiencing more serious difficulties it is possible for him, if he so wishes, to maintain contact with a counsellor for longer periods of time, in which case counselling may continue over many sessions.
>
> (Association for Student Counselling, 1977)

This, then, is the nature of the work in which I have been engaged for a decade and during that time I have met with increasing frequency the intelligent man or woman who can find no value or purpose in living. For me such an encounter constitutes a challenge and a threat, for each time it happens I am faced again by the task of re-examining the purpose of my own life and the nature of my own beliefs. In short, it calls for the kind of faith which risks its own extinction by offering intimate companionship to pointlessness and absurdity.

From *Theology* **LXXXII**, no. 685, 1979, with permission.

Many years ago now a student I knew uttered words which I have never forgotten: 'I feel I am adrift on a limitless ocean of relativity.' He was not a person who was overtly struggling – on the contrary he was sociable and articulate, he had friends of both sexes and he was an above-average student in academic performance – in short he possessed many of the distinctive features of the successful young man.

More recently Penelope, a young woman of 23, entered my office and collapsed on the floor after indicating that she had taken a mild overdose – a mixture of her mother's and her grandmother's sleeping tablets. It was only later that I discovered that, by putting herself to sleep in this way, she had successfully avoided a consultation with her GP with whom she was to have discussed contraception at the insistent request of her boyfriend who wished her to go on the Pill.

An American therapist, Clark Moustakas, in his recent book *Creative Life* (1977) tells of Don, an adolescent who during the course of therapy changed from an inhibited, restricted individual to an outgoing, socially effective person. His parents and teachers regarded the change as a blessing, but Moustakas himself became alarmed when Don began to boast about his conquests and achievements over peers to whom he had once felt distinctly inferior. He was troubled even further when Don told him gleefully of the strategies by which his mother was twisting money out of an insurance company with the help of lawyers and accountants who were only too happy to connive at covert dishonesty. When therapy ended – abruptly and prematurely in Moustakas's eyes – it was deemed highly successful by Don's parents in that the problems which had brought the boy to the clinic were now resolved. Moustakas himself was conscious of letting loose on the world a young man who had learned to be assertive and autonomous, but who remained totally divorced from any knowledge of the moral core of his being.

These three people were confronting or failing to confront the task that constitutes the individual's stiffest challenge in his search for identity – the task of establishing value and meaning or, as I should prefer to define it, of being rooted in the knowledge of what is good and just and true. Moustakas puts it well: 'Being free to be is the right of every human being. Freedom is necessary to maintain one's humanity; the denial of freedom is equivalent to giving up an essential human characteristic. Freedom within the framework of ethical and moral value means not simply the will to choose but choice growing out of a knowledge of the good and a willingness to choose the good' (Moustakas, 1977).

It is important to say more about this sense of moral and ethical value for it is not the same as a *value system*. The latter refers to beliefs, hopes, expectations, expressed preferences which can offer direction to a person and influence his or her decisions and choices. Such a system may indeed be grounded in the sense of moral and ethical value, but it need not be. Hitler had a value system. The sense of value to which I refer is the dimension of the self which unites and integrates. Without it there can be no wholeness. With it there is a commitment to life and to the enrichment of life in its highest forms. With it, too, there is meaning. It is the highest sense of identity and it is the most crucial of all in the development of the individual and in the evolution of a civilisation. Furthermore, I believe it to be much neglected in our society. Neither in education nor in counselling do I see it as a primary concern, let alone the central force. And so it is that much that happens in education and in counselling is destitute of enduring value and that even freedom, knowledge and autonomy are sometimes bereft of meaning. Shortly before he died, the humanistic psychologist Abraham Maslow gave an interview to Professor Willard Frick and at one point, with great emotion, he cast an ominous shadow over the theory of human needs which he had himself so painstakingly evolved.

> I'd always assumed ... that if you cleared away the rubbish and the neurosis and the garbage and so on, then the person would blossom out, that he'd find his own way. I find especially with young people that it just ain't so sometimes. You get people who are in the ... beautiful ... need-gratifying situation and yet get kind of a value pathology. That is, it's possible to be loved and respected, etc., and, even so, to feel cynical and materialistic, and to feel there's nothing worth working for ... Especially in younger rather than older people you can see this. It's sort of a loss of nerve, and I think we're at this point where the traditional culture has broken down altogether, and for many people they just feel, 'My God, there's nothing'.
>
> (Frick, 1971)

In the face of such an existential vacuum – and how immediately recognisable it is to any counsellor working in higher education – it becomes clear that we cannot be content with education which focuses primarily on knowledge, skill and professional competence, nor can we place trust in a therapeutic process which is concerned primarily with change towards self-confidence, social effectiveness and realness in expression. Maslow himself had indicated the answer to his own dismay when a decade before he had insisted that education and therapy reach into the moral realm and enable the individual to encounter the inner experience of value from which comes the will and the strength to become more honest, good, just and beautiful.

It is perhaps hardly surprising that teachers are slow to engage in a battle for moral truth and that counsellors shy away from encountering their clients in the area of moral and ethical value. The spectre of meaninglessness haunts this battlefield and the fear of drowning in the limitless ocean of relativity is never far distant. But what, after all, is the point of teaching anything or counselling anyone if there is no moral value and thus no meaning to life? What kind of counselling success is it if my client feels loved and autonomous and utterly futile? What kind of satisfaction is it for a teacher when his student gets a first-class degree but sees no point either in his success or in his life ahead? What more natural then than that counsellors and teachers alike should remain indifferent to the moral realm in order to cherish a false sense of accomplishment? If I do not seek to enter the world of my client's futility or of my student's pointlessness, I can congratulate myself on my effective performance – see how independent he is after my counselling, or what a brilliant examination script he has produced after my teaching!

The ocean of relativity was partly induced by my student's university education. The development of a critical, enquiring mind has often been acknowledged as the primary aim of higher education and such an aim has a long and honourable history. Students are required to examine their basic assumptions and to reject them if they do not stand the test of rigorous intellectual scrutiny. There is no doubt that, through such a process, many individuals are delivered from ignorance and prejudice and from false and lazy thinking. However, the very same individuals can be confronted simultaneously by a world where everything seems to depend on a point of view and where there are no longer any certainties. Such apparent relativity can often be the herald of meaninglessness. In a society where values are secure and traditions strong such uncertainty – and even the loss of meaning itself – can often be contained, at least long enough for the individual to re-orient him- or herself and rediscover some firm reference points. But at a time when traditions and values are themselves crumbling, the individual is horrifyingly vulnerable. The individual cannot rely on a prevailing stability within his culture to see him through his personal crisis. He has only his personal resources to call upon.

Cardinal Newman saw a university as a place for the exercise of the *whole* intellect and for him a truly great intellect was 'one which takes a connected view of old and new, past and present, far and near and which has insight into the influence of all these, one on another' (Newman, 1852). Owen Chadwick has recently suggested, however, that there is a fatal flaw even in Newman's vision, and if Chadwick is right it is all the more surprising when one remembers Newman's religious convictions (Chadwick, 1976). Newman, according to Chadwick, believed that mental development could take place independently of or at least without direct reference to ethical development and that a university should be primarily concerned with the former. I do not believe that in a post-Christian era this can any longer be advocated without condoning the irresponsibility which springs from failing to make the essential connection between thinking, feeling and caring. We now know only too well that mental development *can* indeed proceed without ethical growth and we see the results all around us and in the history of the twentieth century. The time has come to affirm what logical thought reveals to us without any possibility of contradiction – that mental development *must not* proceed independently of ethical development if we are to have any chance of halting our present gallop towards self-extermination. In short, I am suggesting that, unless a university commits itself to the creation of an environment where emotional and ethical development command parity of esteem with mental development, it will not nourish the logical thought processes which can alone come to grips with the appalling problems of the contemporary world.

Commitment is a word that strikes terror in the hearts of many. It means taking a stand and affirming values. There are times at the end of a day when I feel engulfed by a wave of despair that we cannot affirm two simple values which, if we embraced them, might transform education overnight. The first would be an affirmation that mankind is of infinite worth and the second that the world is worth saving.

These two values are certainly not reflected in the society on which educational institutions uncomfortably depend. Competitive materialism remains the motivating force there, however much politicians may wrap it up in fine-sounding words – although of late they have ceased even to do that. Unashamedly now, we are exhorted to exercise self-denial but only so that we may have more goodies later. We must sacrifice one motor car this year so that we may have three in 5 years' time. What kind of democracy can it be where men are prepared to down tools and take up industrial arms not because they lack money but because their differentials have been eroded? In the face of such a secular ethic, the universities seem at present to stand powerless. They must either collude with it or somehow pretend it has nothing to do with them – the academic washing of hands which betrays the irresponsibility of educators who are no longer inspired by what William Arrowsmith described as 'a care and concern for the future of man, a Platonic love of the species not for what it is but what it might be' (Arrowsmith, 1967).

The situation of Penelope, the second student, was different but no less common. Caught in a network of conflicting values and judgements, she could dimly hear her own voice but not act upon it. She consequently felt ashamed and impotent and finally desperate. Her actions demonstrated her almost complete inability to stay in touch with her own sense of value. In conflict about her relationship with her boyfriend, she went home to a house inhabited by a depressive mother and an ailing grandmother – a home she knew she should not visit in a vulnerable state. Once there she was swept into an addiction culture and stole tablets (of which she heartily disapproved) and used them to avoid a consultation about contraceptive measures which she did not wish to take. Only after this grisly process of self-betrayal was she able, in the counselling relationship, to affirm her own sense of value and to hear her own voice stating plainly that she did not wish to have intercourse without commitment, that she wanted to take responsibility for her own convictions and that she scorned pills as a means of deadening psychological pain or relieving tension. With support she was then able to live out this sense of value and confront her boyfriend with her deep feelings about the physical side of their relationship. Most strikingly, Penelope's experience illustrates that when a person's own essential nature is encouraged and supported his or her sense of value assumes its rightful authority. Penelope was initially unable to act upon the messages emanating from her own sense of value and therefore her sense of shame was intense and her despair predictable. She experienced what I have come to recognize as *appropriate guilt* – i.e. a guilt which springs from having failed to be true to the deepest regions in oneself. Such guilt bears no comparison with the inappropriate guilt experienced by so many which springs from having failed to live up to someone else's judgement or expectations. For the counsellor, nothing is more crucial than his or her ability to help a person distinguish between these two forms of guilt, for the one points directly to the personal sense of moral and ethical value, whereas the other blocks the individual's path to such a sense and lumbers him instead with a burden which he often finds himself both unable to carry and unable to reject. Appropriate guilt calls for forgiveness and an affirmation of the nature which has been betrayed. Inappropriate guilt calls for the identification of the usurping judge and a refusal to accept his authority. Both states cause great distress and demand all the love and understanding a counsellor can muster if the context is to be created in which the necessary work – so different in the two cases – can be done.

The case of Don is the most perturbing of the three, for it reveals the power of a culture to obstruct a person's path to the deepest sense of moral and ethical value because it has lost the map of the world where such journeys have meaning. The search for truth, beauty, love, justice and wisdom makes no sense in a culture where the expertise of lawyers and accountants is exploited to develop fraudulent strategies to beat insurance companies at their own game, and where such behaviour is seen as both typical and normal. Materialism, if it is all-pervasive, affords no signposts for the journey to ethical and moral value and no nourishment for the would-be traveller. Furthermore, it creates a moral desert in which the conscience is stillborn.

Conscience is not a word which leaps from the pages of secular counselling literature and, when it does, it is often presented as the harbinger of guilt, the rod with which a person continues to beat his already bruised back, the weapon of self-punishment. As such it is seen as the enemy of growth or interpreted as the result of conditioning processes associated with religion or the outmoded moral code of a previous generation. But true conscience or conscience that is healthy does not collude with this world of inappropriate guilt nor does it feed the fires of self-rejection. On the contrary, it is the only capacity left to human beings with which they can continue to find the unique meaning of their own life in the face of crumbling values and waning traditions.

It is to his enormous credit that the Austrian psychotherapist Viktor Frankl has rehabilitated the conscience and in so doing has redefined it in such a way that words such as good and bad take on fresh significance. Looking to the future, Frankl sees that morality 'will no longer define what is good and what is bad in terms of what one should do and what one must not do. What is good will be defined as that which fosters the meaning fulfilment of a being. And what is bad will be defined as that which hinders this meaning fulfilment'. In line with this definition, Frankl sees the conscience as the 'means to discover meanings, to "sniff them out" as it were'. 'True conscience', says Frankl, 'has nothing to do with the fearful expectation of punishment. As long as a man is still motivated by either the fear of punishment or the hope of reward – or, for that matter, by the wish to appease the super-ego – conscience has not yet had its say' (Frankl, 1977).

Let me summarise and then look at the implications for educators:

1. An ultimate moral sense is present in the deepest region of the self and it is this sense that establishes meaning and value. Unless it is encountered, the life of the individual hovers ceaselessly on the brink of meaninglessness.
2. In an age when values and traditions are in the melting pot, the individual receives little help from his environment as he seeks to confront the ultimate questions of his own meaning and value. Indeed, he may for a while be separated altogether from these questions by an all-embracing materialism.
3. It is tempting for counsellors and teachers to avoid confronting their clients and students in the moral and ethical realm, for to do so may be to call into question the very validity of what is being offered as therapy or education.
4. By focusing on the undoubted evils of inappropriate guilt and self-punishing shame, counsellors may fail to identify the healthy but equally painful guilt and shame which come from a failure to accept the responsibility of fulfilling the meaning of a personal and unique life.
5. It is the conscience which – however much it is prone to err – can alone serve the individual in her search for the unique meaning of her life. To neglect conscience or to repress it is to surrender the one human capacity that can give direction to the person lost in the ocean of relativity or the fog of meaninglessness.

The message in all this for the counsellor and the teacher is no easy one. Nobody can give meaning to someone else and the counsellor who tries to offer meaning to his or her client or the teacher who attempts to teach moral and ethical principles are both equally doomed to failure. The moral sense cannot be taught or imposed: it can only be discovered. The educator's task, therefore, is to create a context in which such discovery can take place and no task could be more formidable. It involves a willingness to move beyond views of counselling and education which concern themselves with knowledge, skill, social effectiveness, personal autonomy, beyond even the revered concepts of self-acceptance and self-fulfilment. The counsellor and the teacher faced by such a task have no alternative but to demonstrate their own personal commitment to the search for truth and meaning. It is with their whole being that they will reveal the attentiveness and the obedience of their own consciences in the midst of the countless situations with which life confronts them. They will show that they are not afraid to enter the moral struggle and that they do so not as professionals doing a job but as human beings who refuse to be bound by rules, routines and the endless absurdities of bureaucratic and procedural red tape. They will show their willingness to risk even the deepest uncertainty in response to the internal directive which, to quote Clark Moustakas again, 'keeps alive the mind and heart and soul of all humanity' (Moustakas, 1977).

In my own life I have come to the stark realisation that, when I lose contact with that internal directive, I risk inoculating others with despair – and that sounds cause enough for appropriate guilt and true shame in the breast of any counsellor. But I know, too, that when I am bold enough to affirm and embrace the meaning of my own life, with all the self-doubt and agony of spirit which that sometimes entails, I extend to others an invitation to do the same. There is no other way.

References

ARROWSMITH, W. (1967). The future of teaching. In: C.B.T. Lee (Ed.), *Improving College Teaching*. Washington DC: American Council on Education.

ASSOCIATION FOR STUDENT COUNSELLING (1977). *The Role of the Counsellor in Higher and Further Education*: Policy document.

CHADWICK, O. (1976). *Poet of the university's timeless ideal.* London: Times Higher Education Supplement (9 July).

FRANKL, V.E. (1977). *The Unconscious God*. London: Hodder & Stoughton.

FRICK, W. (1971). *Humanistic Psychology: Interviews with Maslow, Murphy and Rogers*. Columbus, OH: Charles E. Merrill.

MOUSTAKAS, C. (1977). *Creative Life*. New York: Van Nostrand Reinhold Co.

NEWMAN, J.H. (1852). *The Scope and Nature of University Education*.

Chapter 7
Ethical Confrontation in Counselling

In 1979, I contributed an article to the journal *Theology* in which I attempted to tease out some of the complex issues surrounding the themes of guilt and conscience (Thorne, 1979) (see Chapter 7). The article was prompted by my experience as a counsellor working in the person-centred tradition of Carl Rogers and by my struggle to make sense of the Christian contribution to these issues. Not long ago, I was counselling a student who was shortly to leave the University of East Anglia and, during the session, I almost came to believe that she was consciously presenting me with a textbook illustration of my own theories. I should like to say something about that counselling session: it will serve as a useful summary of my previously expounded ideas and will also form a springboard for the further reflections I now wish to make.

The client in question (I shall call her Margaret) was exploring the many difficulties which would confront her at the end of the term when she would cease to be a member of the university. Chief among these difficulties was her fear of returning to live once more with her family. Her parents, whom she loved, were worthy people much given to good works and with a strong sense of their own values and what constitutes a worthwhile life. Margaret experienced them as powerful and influential and she found it painfully difficult to question their view of reality and their firmly held, if often unspoken, convictions about life and how it should be lived. As a result she found that, after a couple of days in the parental home, she felt stifled and oppressed. What is more she began to feel guilty and confused. It became clear during our counselling session that Margaret had to avoid living at home after graduation if she was to have any chance of hanging on to her own identity and developing as the person she wanted to be. As this realisation

From *Ethical Issues in Caring*, 1988, edited by G. Fairbairn and S. Fairbairn, Gower, London, with permission.

became increasingly focused, Margaret came out with the following statement: 'If I don't try and live away from home I shall be going against my conscience.' At this point I let out an inward cheer of delight for here was a client who was using the word 'conscience' to denote the faculty that enables a person to keep in touch with the meaning and significance of his or her life and to discover what course of action is in accord with that meaning. It is my contention that this is indeed the true conscience and that failure to listen to it will evoke an *appropriate* form of guilt – namely that profound dissatisfaction at having failed to live and act in accordance with the meaning and potential of one's own unique life and identity. Such guilt is useful and even desirable insofar as it can aid a person in the search for wholeness and fulfilment. It is the guilt which springs from attentiveness to the true conscience which, in Cardinal Newman's marvellous words, speaks as 'the voice of God in the nature and heart of man'.

You will remember though, that when Margaret was at home she quickly became guilty and confused. The guilt she experienced in that setting has nothing to do with the *appropriate* guilt I have described. Rather it was the feeling of being somehow unworthy and delinquent in the eyes of her parents whose values and view of reality she found herself defenceless to resist, having presumably been conditioned by them for most of her life. Her confusion was the result of the rapid slipping away of her own sense of identity once she was plunged back into the parental home. In a disturbing and frightening way she quickly lost herself and began confusedly to assume again the personality her parents would have wished her to have. The guilt she then experienced was the *inappropriate* guilt which ensnares us when we have failed to live up to someone else's view of how we should live and act. This guilt tells us nothing about the meaning and potential of our own unique existence: on the contrary it conceals such meaning from us and condemns us to an alienated existence in which we attempt to live out a destiny which is not ours and in all probability brings in its wake sickness both of soul and body and often of mind as well. Furthermore, the internal voice which provokes this inappropriate guilt is *not*, I would submit, the voice of conscience at all. It is rather the internalised prompting of an external authority, whether this be parents, boss, church, government or the writings of Karl Marx or the Hebrew prophets. This is not to suggest that the true conscience and the internalised prompting of an external authority cannot speak the same message simultaneously. Of course they can and such unison does occur. Unfortunately, however, it is my experience that all too often they do *not* speak the same message or even the same language. What is more, the internalised external authority is frequently so strident in its dogmatic demands that the true conscience cannot be heard at all except perhaps as a faint whisper when inappropriate guilt relaxes its feverish grip for a fleeting moment.

For those of us in the helping professions I believe that one of our most formidable and yet essential tasks is to create an environment where such fleeting moments can occur and then to assist our clients to be attentive to this faint whisper which is the attempt of the true conscience to make itself heard. Such a task demands infinite patience and delicacy. It also demands that we are not ourselves living out alienated lives, mere puppets jerking frenetically on the strings of an external authority in a vain attempt to keep our own inappropriate guilt at bay. How sad it is to come across those helpers – sometimes in prestigious professional positions – who care for others not because that is the meaning of their lives, but because not to do so would release such a flood of inappropriate guilt that life for them would scarcely be tolerable. They are not only painfully out of touch with the core of their own being, but they are a danger to those they feel compelled to help. Full of inappropriate guilt themselves, they are likely to exacerbate a similar guilt in their clients.

I wish to explore further the task of creating an environment in which the true conscience can make itself heard. I have said that such a task demands infinite patience and delicacy, and so it does for it involves most importantly the offering of a deeply felt acceptance whose unconditionality communicates itself to the very heart of the person in need. There must be an utter absence of judgement and a deep faith in the other person's capacity and desire to move towards the good. Such an environment is not created overnight: often it needs months or even years of consistent and unconditional acceptance before the first whisper of the true conscience can make itself heard. Such waiting is a great test for the helper and it will sometimes drive him to the limits of his patience. In this respect it is important to remember that many of those who are most alienated from themselves and are in the deepest distress have lived for many years in an environment where they feel judged and found wanting every minute of the day. It is not therefore surprising that it sometimes takes an unconscionable time for unconditional acceptance to be recognised for what it is, let alone for it to be experienced as a real and liberating response from one human being to another. Mother Julian of Norwich would have it that the helper shares in the parenthood of God as he or she offers unconditional acceptance to the client, and that is saying something very big indeed.

If the truth be known, most of us *expect* to be adversely judged by others and we spend a great deal of time and effort trying to win favourable judgement. Even the delinquent is following the same pattern for he seeks to win the favourable judgement of his peer group by ensuring that he earns the condemnation of those authorities he hates or despises. For most of us it is, I believe, a rare experience to feel unconditionally accepted. When it happens to me I notice that an almost predictable process occurs. At first I feel hesitant and disbelieving – I can hardly credit my good fortune. I test it out probably by trying to shock or provoke a little. When the moment arrives that confirms me in my hope I sense a great relaxation which permeates every fibre of my being. I often feel sleepy and sometimes there is a faint urge to curl up in the other person's arms. I rest awhile and then there comes flooding in a wave of new energy. I feel creative and excited. I can think and feel with clarity and intensity. I do not have to worry if I appear powerful or weak, virtuous or scandalous. I am alive and on the move towards the meaning of my life. My true conscience speaks to me and I might even find the courage to obey its promptings. If I do I shall almost certainly have whiffs of inappropriate guilt or even a cloud of it and shall have to struggle to remind myself that I do not accept the jurisdiction of the court into which I have allowed myself misguidedly to wander. On the worst occasions, obeying my true conscience seems to involve a determined effort on my part not to heed a furious judge with a red face who suddenly jumps into my path and would have me locked up.

One of the saddest discoveries I have made during my 15 years as a professional counsellor is that for many of my clients this furious judge comes masquerading as God himself. The sequence of events in such cases goes something like this. The distressed person comes full of pain, guilt and deeply self-rejecting. If I am lucky a relationship gradually develops in which I attempt to offer those conditions for therapeutic change which Carl Rogers elucidated long ago – unconditional acceptance, empathic understanding and my own genuineness. The feelings of guilt become increasingly susceptible to exploration as the client gradually relaxes and becomes less self-rejecting. In most cases the guilt can be traced back to the failure to live out parental wishes or to come up to the expectations of significant others. There is then a period of agonising confusion as the client seeks to struggle free of the powerful, but inappropriate, guilt feelings without as yet being able to hear the voice of true conscience and without therefore having any sense of direction. Constantly, there is the urge to return to the known prison of guilt and self-rejection: the familiar cell seems preferable to the unknown and frightening world of freedom. The day comes at last when the first whisperings of true conscience are heard. The client experiences the first ineffable feelings of self-love and senses that he or she yearns for the good and the true. It is a precious moment which is sometimes almost overwhelming in its intensity.

At this point I rejoice with my client that he has found himself, recognised his own value and is now in a position to offer himself to life. But then comes the most agonising part of the whole process. The next time the client arrives he is full of despair, confusion and anger. He looks at me as if I have taken on satanic characteristics. He has met the red-faced furious judge whom he identifies as God and at a stroke I am cast in the role of Lucifer to whom he has all but lost his soul. The words of the furious judge come through loud and clear:

> Have you forgotten all you have ever learned? Have you not heard of the sin of egotism? How dare you spend so much time dwelling on your own absurd feelings. Have you forgotten that you are a worm and no man? Have you forgotten that without

me you are nothing – I could extinguish you with a flick of my fingers. How dare you inflate your self-importance. Cross out the I and take up your cross. Be concerned for others, abhor this appalling me-worship. You are on the point of falling into the clutches of a guru of the me-generation which has forgotten all about sacrifice, constraint and renunciation. One step further and you are lost.

What is perhaps astonishing is that clients who have no religious allegiance are almost as likely to meet this furious judge as the practising Christian who is plunged back at this stage into a whole system of Christian education and training which is based essentially on anxiety and fear and a lack of confidence in human nature. It would seem that the condemnatory God of the neurotic Church is rampant still in the unconscious realm of secular man.

It is not easy to endure the experience of being perceived as satanic and there are times, I confess, when it seems easier to give up the struggle and to leave the client in a far more glorious prison than the one she inhabited before calling upon my help. Perhaps, after all, it is a perverse therapeutic triumph to have enabled a client to reach the top-notch prison where God is the governor – much better than the grimy provincial gaol staffed by parents, schoolteachers or the faceless purveyors of society's norms.

It will be clear from my preoccupation with conscience, guilt and judgement that I perceive many of my clients as caught in the grips of the most furious ethical conflicts where oughts and wants struggle desperately for some kind of inner harmony. And yet, prior to the moment when I am suddenly cast in the role of Lucifer, the bringer of false light, it is unlikely that I shall have experienced any desire to confront my client in the ethical arena. On the contrary, as I have stressed, it is highly probable that I shall have bent over backwards to refrain from such confrontation. It is only too evident to me that many of those who seek counselling help have had numerous judges in their lives already without my being added to the list. Indeed, both Freud and Rogers, despite very different concepts of human nature, identify moralism as the root of much psychic disorder. Furthermore, it is possible to encapsulate much of what I have already said by stating the belief (which I certainly hold) that the healing of neuroses is dependent upon the creation of a non-moralistic relationship in which a person can experience that his worth as a human being is without conditions.

Up to the Lucifer moment too, although my patience and my faith may have been sorely taxed, nothing has happened to disturb profoundly my optimistic view that, given the right conditions, a person will develop in self-enhancing ways and in a manner which will advance the common good. Nothing too has made me doubt to any serious degree my belief that my client has the right and the capacity for self-direction and does not stand in need of my guidance whether this be overt or covert. Moral non-intervention has been a logical outcome of my positive view of mankind and of my understanding of the therapeutic process.

Now, however, as I experience my client's rejection of me and of the process to which I have attached such value. I find myself shaken to the foundations. I seem to be witnessing the most shocking act of self-betrayal on my client's part. He has found himself, only to be overcome with such fear and dismay that he is now striving to lose himself again as quickly as possible. What am I do do? If I value my client's freedom so highly must I not allow him to be free to reject me and the healing process itself? Does not my own value system require me to extend to my client the liberty to choose the prison of his neurosis rather than the freedom of unconditional self-regard? If I turn to Carl Rogers I receive what seems a plain enough answer. Rogers speaks of the therapeutic process and its outcomes in these words:

> But is the therapist willing to give the client the full freedom as to outcomes? Is he genuinely willing for the client to organise and direct his life? Is he willing for him to choose goals that are social or anti-social, moral or immoral? If not, it seems doubtful that therapy will be a profound experience for the client. Even more difficult, is he willing for the client to choose regression rather than growth or maturity? to choose neuroticism rather than mental health? to choose to reject help rather than accept it? to choose death rather than life? (Rogers, 1951)

The implication of all this is evident. According to Rogers the counsellor should indeed honour his or her client's freedom to choose death and destruction if that is how he or she so decides. Not to do so would be a kind of denial of the rationale of the therapeutic process. It is but a short step from this position to a stance which sees ethical confrontation or moral intervention as inevitably in conflict with the therapeutic efficacy of unconditional acceptance. Using different language Freud arrives at much the same conclusion. The analyst too is forbidden to play the part of mentor. The patient must be free to select what he or she will and the therapist's 'conscience is not burdened whatever the outcome' (Freud, 1949).

I must confess to an increasing uneasiness with both Rogers and Freud on this issue, an uneasiness which now threatens to bubble over into rebellion. I am utterly certain that my own right to exist does not depend upon my client choosing goodness and wholeness, but that is a very different matter to adopting a posture of silence or neutrality at the very moment when my client faces the choice of life and good or death and evil. I can no longer rest comfortably with the notion that therapeutic necessity demands that I display a kind of ethical emptiness in the face of my client's fear of freedom. Indeed, I am rapidly approaching a contrary point of view and yet, as I do so, I like to feel that I am not deviating essentially from the person-centred approach which characterises all that I undertake as a counsellor. Nor am I sure, incidentally, that I am deviating from the model that Rogers *actually* offers as I have witnessed in his own moment-to-moment relating with another person.

It will be remembered that unconditional acceptance is not the only condition for therapeutic growth that Rogers cites. Genuineness or congruence on the counsellor's part is of equal importance and it is on genuineness that I stake my right to give expression, when the moment demands it (and that moment is not always easy to identify), to those truths and values which I cherish. So great can be my own anguish when I experience the kind of self-betrayal in a client which I have described above that I feel increasingly compelled to give expression to that anguish and to the values which underpin it. As I do so I sense in myself nothing of the judgemental attitude towards the other which is the curse of moralism. Instead, I experience a deep regard for my client which would make it unthinkably insulting on my part not to share as graciously and lovingly as I can those truths which give meaning to my own life and actions. My client may of course continue to reject me and reject his or her own apparent journey towards health but at least he or she will be rejecting me as a person with my feelings and values and not simply me as a counsellor wedded to a belief (often justified) in the therapeutic efficacy of moral non-intervention.

My deep desire to be genuine in my relationship with my client does not impede my acceptance of him when the ethical witness which I proclaim points to what John Hoffmann (1979), in a book bearing the same title as this chapter, has called 'an empowering acceptance at the heart of life', by which he means a source of being which validates by the very unconditionality of its acceptance all that is created. At the same time, if I speak with an authority that is not truly moral, I am refusing to acknowledge that for every person ethical development is a fundamental part of growth towards wholeness. This seems to me of tremendous importance. Mental health is the outcome not simply of basking in the unconditional acceptance of a person-centred therapist or being in the unreal environment of a permanent encounter group where nothing has any lasting ethical significance. Mental health is the outcome of relating what happens in therapy to the real world where moral decisions have to be made and where prejudice, injustice, oppression and degrading inequalities are rampant. Faced with such a world, a person who neglects his or her ethical development can never hope for personal healing and a counsellor who allows that to happen in a client is ignoring an essential dimension of his or her therapeutic work.

The task, as I see it then, is to embody as far as I am able an utterly gracious authority. I strive to adopt a response which accepts unconditionally the other person, which avoids all overtones of moralism and yet points unerringly to a non-moralistic morality whose attractiveness is irresistible. That for me is the nearest I can get (and again I am indebted to the insights of John Hoffmann) to describing a gracious authority which is truly moral. If I can embrace such an authority I shall not lapse into a posture which offers cheap grace – 'I'll forgive you whatever you do' – nor shall I run the risk of colluding with immorality by adhering to a form of therapeutic authority which forbids me to express my own deepest sense of life's meaning. I have come to conclude therefore that there will be critical times in my counselling encounters when, if I am to be fully genuine and if I am to care about the ethical growth of my client, I must seek to give expression to an authority which at one and the same time attracts my client towards the greatest effort for moral development while granting him or her the absolute right to be apart from such development. I do not for one moment deny the difficulty or complexity of such a task. Not only must I feel the deepest possible respect for and acceptance of my client's freedom and autonomy, but I must experience also the deepest desire to be fully present in the relationship, and that includes my ethical self with all its passion and yearning. To embrace all these feelings and values within a unified response to another person is demanding enough, but to give expression to them without lapsing into moralism on the one hand or empty permissiveness on the other is perhaps the stiffest challenge that any counsellor can face.

What is more I become increasingly persuaded that it is precisely this capacity in the counsellor which needs to be demonstrated at those vital times when, metaphorically, death threatens to take away the life of the psychologically newborn person. I have heard it said by wise midwives that it is not the moment of birth itself which demands the greatest skill and attentiveness, despite its enormous excitement, but what happens during the first hour of life. I suspect that, in the case of some clients, the counsellor, like the midwife, needs to be particularly alert to the fears which follow immediately upon the client's profound experience of unconditional acceptance and self-love. If these fears are such that the client moves rapidly away from life and heads back towards neurosis and destruction, then I submit it is not enough for the counsellor to remain passively acceptant of this flight from health. His or her response must convey that being alive and healthy is right and desirable *and that* the client who is fleeing in fear from life and health is totally acceptable. Not one or the other but both at the same time.

I have chosen to focus on the client who by his or her words and behaviour denies the validity of the therapeutic process and runs in angry terror from his or her incipient feelings of self-regard. I have done so because such behaviour causes me the deepest kind of personal anguish and constitutes the most savage assault on my own value system and ethical convictions. For others, it may be a quite different form of client behaviour or expression that brings about a similar shaking of the foundations. It may be, for example, that a client is expressing every intention of committing a deed which morally the counsellor finds utterly repugnant. For person-centred counsellors, however, the dilemma is the same in every case. How can they simultaneously convey their continuing acceptance and confront their clients with the moral issue which lies at the heart of his or her struggle? I have suggested that there is much in the person-centred tradition (and in the analytical for that matter) which implies that unconditional acceptance and moral confrontation are incompatible activities. That is a view to which I can no longer subscribe. On the contrary, I have come to believe that it is the very holding of these two in healthy tension which constitutes the counsellor's greatest challenge and can prove to be his or her most potent force for healing at those crucial times when the client hovers between health and neurosis. Such a conviction brings with it the somewhat daunting reflection that I shall have no chance whatever of offering to my client such a life-giving force unless I have succeeded in extending to myself the same healing attitude of love and challenging confrontation. To quote John Hoffmann once more, I need to experience again and again that 'empowering acceptance at the heart of life' if I am to acknowledge my yearning for a perfection which is beyond all moralism and if I am then to strive towards it however feebly and intermittently.

References

FREUD, S. (1949). *The Ego and the Id*. London: Hogarth.
HOFFMANN, J. (1979). *Ethical Confrontation in Counselling*, p. 107. Chicago: University of Chicago Press.
ROGERS, C.R. (1951). *Client-centered Therapy*. Boston: Houghton Mifflin.
THORNE, B. (1979). In search of value and meaning. *Theology*, **82**, 685.

Chapter 8
Carl Rogers and the Doctrine of Original Sin:
Carl Rogers, Christianity and the person-centred approach

I have been a person-centred therapist for some 20 years and a member of the Christian Church for more than twice that length of time. For me there is no incompatability in this dual allegiance, but I have frequently been struck by the incredulity expressed by some professional colleagues when they learn of my Christian commitment. They are bewildered, it seems, because they have a view of the Christian understanding of human nature which flatly contradicts the essentially positive and optimistic model that is a basic assumption of the person-centred approach. Their bewilderment is perhaps increased if they are acquainted with the knowledge that Carl Rogers himself had originally intended to become a Christian minister but had, subsequently, renounced theology for psychology and left the Church. It is my impression that Carl himself was also baffled by my Christian involvement and regarded it as some kind of aberration from which I would eventually be released when I no longer had need of external reference points.

There can be no doubt that, as a young man, Carl himself experienced intense feelings of admiration and devotion to the personality of Jesus Christ. This was especially so after his visit to China when he was able, to some extent, to lay aside his earlier religious conditioning and move towards a more personal understanding of his faith. Shortly after his return, when he was 20 years old, he wrote in a letter (quoted by his biographer, Howard Kirschenbaum):

> It is a tremendous relief to quit worrying about whether you believe what you are supposed to believe, and begin actually studying Christ to find out whether he is a personality worth giving your life to. I know that for myself that method of approach has led me to a far deeper and far more enthusiastic allegiance to Him. For the first time in my life, I find myself anxious to tell people what I believe about Him, and about His wonderful Kingdom that He came to establish. I don't wonder that His early disciples simply couldn't keep from teaching the 'good news'. (Kirschenbaum, 1979, p. 25)

From *Person-centred Review*, 5 (4), 1990. Reprinted by permission of Sage Publications, Inc.

It was not long after this, however, that the gradual disenchantment set in that was to lead to his eventual movement away from Christianity and out of the Church. Only in the last 10 years or so of his life did he begin once more to speak and write of experiences to which he would apply such words as 'spiritual' and 'mystical'. He also drew attention to an intuitive faculty of which he was increasingly aware and which he believed gave access to a world behind the face of everyday reality.

The largely autobiographical reflections which follow are prompted in the first place by my desire to continue an unfinished dialogue with Carl. Secondly, however, they serve to reinforce my own conviction that the future of the person-centred approach may well depend on its capacity to embrace the world of spiritual reality and to undertake there the kind of pioneering work which characterised the earlier periods in the domains of psychotherapy and group facilitation. It is my belief that Carl himself might well have been bold enough to blaze this trail, too, if he had not until the end of his life borne the scars of the wounds inflicted upon him by a perverse and primitive theology.

Easter Day in Madrid, 1978

On Easter Day, 1978, in a Madrid hotel I attended a Christian Eucharist presided over jointly by a Presbyterian minister and a Roman Catholic priest. This was in itself remarkable enough, but the members of the congregation made the event even more extraordinary. They were all participants in an international cross-cultural workshop which was taking place in the Spanish capital not long after Franco's death. Between them they represented more than 20 nations and almost every shade of political ideology. They had been brought together thanks to the vision and untiring efforts of Dr Chuck Devonshire and his associates who were convinced that the person-centred approach had a major contribution to make to those who wished to communicate across national, cultural and political boundaries. It was the first large event of its kind and the precursor of many similar workshops in the years that followed.

By no means all the members of this unusual Easter congregation were Christians. Indeed there were some who were avowedly atheistic and many who had certainly not taken part in an act of Christian worship for years if not decades. Among them was Carl Rogers. The afternoon of the same day he and I set off together in a taxi to visit the Prado and, as we bumped along the hot Madrid streets, he told me how moved he had been by the informal service and how strange it was to have experienced a kind of belonging which was never possible for him in a church building. As he was keen to see Goya's paintings, whereas I was set on finding the El Grecos, we agreed on arrival at the famous Art Gallery to go our separate ways. Before we parted company, however, we found ourselves standing in front of a vast painting of the apostle who, down the ages, has been known as doubting Thomas. Carl grinned. 'Ah', he said, 'My patron Saint!'.

The following day, the whole workshop membership moved out of its hotel accommodation and travelled north by coach to the famous hill town of El Escorial, with its royal palace and brooding secular and ecclesiastical buildings dating from the time of Philip II. We took up residence in the enormous modern guest house of the ancient monastery and there continued to struggle (in four languages) towards the creation of a community where each person could find acceptance and understanding. It was in this awesome environment (surrounded by cameras and microphones) that I found myself one morning leaning against a balcony with Carl and discussing with him our respective views of human nature. Unfortunately, I have been unable to track down the film of our conversation and I now retain only the haziest outline of what we said to each other. Friends tell me, however, that Carl often spoke of this conversation which suggests that it touched on issues of importance to him during the last years of his life. One very clear memory I have is that some of our discussion centred on the Christian doctrine of Original Sin.

Rogers and Self-acceptance

In his biography of Rogers, Howard Kirschenbaum tells of events which occurred in 1949 when Carl was Executive Secretary (his own chosen title) of the University of Chicago Counseling Center. By that time his reputation was already considerable. *Counseling and Psychotherapy* had been published 7 years before and *Client-centered Therapy* was only 2 years away. The concepts of acceptance and empathy were firmly established as the therapist's chief tools for helping the client to accept and understand his or her own feelings. To his colleagues Carl was warm, accepting, the attentive listener, the conscientious scholar, the trusting delegator of responsibility. He was, in short, the perfect empathiser who could move around in other people's skins and feel at home there. But who was he? One of his colleagues of those days, T.M. Tomlinson, put it succinctly: 'He is one of the most important people in my life and I hardly know him' (Kirschenbaum, 1979).

It would seem from this revealing comment that, despite his warmth and empathy, Carl was at this time essentially aloof and not much drawn to self-disclosure. This apparent defensiveness seems strangely out of place in a man who was to emphasise the central importance of genuineness and congruence on the part of the therapist. It should be remembered, however, that this concept had received little or no attention in his writings prior to this time. That this was to change was in no small measure the result of a relationship with a female client in which he was now to become deeply embroiled and which nearly destroyed him. He never wrote at length about what was to prove a turning point in his own life, but it is evident that the whole episode was dramatic in the extreme and deeply distressing. It actually resulted in Carl fleeing from Chicago with his wife, Helen, and remaining on the road for some 2 months.

When he eventually returned to the University, Carl was approached by one of his own staff members, Oliver Bown, who had the courage to tell him that it was obvious he was in deep distress and needed help. Bown had the even greater courage to tell Carl that he was in no way afraid of him and that he was willing to offer his therapeutic services if Carl felt able to accept them. Carl, in his own words, 'accepted in desperation and gradually worked through to a point where I could value myself, even like myself, and was much less fearful of receiving or giving love. My own therapy with my clients has become consistently and increasingly free and spontaneous ever since that time' (in Kirschenbaum, 1979, p. 193).

These comments deserve close attention. Here was the therapist who over the years had helped hundreds of clients to a level of self-acceptance from a position where they were deeply self-rejecting. And yet it is clear that at a deep level Carl himself had not come to self-acceptance. The impossible relationship with a disturbed woman had revealed a man who did not consider himself lovable at all. He could imagine that people might like *what he did* but he had no concept of himself as acceptable and worthy of respect at the core of his being. In fact, he later admitted that he felt that in reality he was inferior and simply putting on a contrived front of competence and human effectiveness.

It may perhaps seem remarkable that the founder of an approach to psychotherapy which stresses the innate resourcefulness of the human being and the central importance of self-acceptance, should have been so singularly unconvinced, at the age of 47, of his own value either as a person or as a professional. Indeed, it generates the suspicion that the development of client-centred therapy was perhaps primarily motivated by Carl's own need to escape from deep feelings of unworthiness and inferiority. By 1949, although both theory and practice were to some degree established, it would seem that for their chief exponent they had still, at the deepest level, failed to effect the desired healing.

Early Environment

The irony of this situation is more readily understood when we remember the nature of Carl's own early environment and upbringing. He grew up under the influence of parents who were so deeply devoted to a largely fundamentalist brand of evangelical Christianity that family prayers were said every day and the Bible was the reference book for every occasion – as long as the approved interpretation was provided and accepted. Julia Rogers,

Carl's mother, would herself often conduct family prayers and one of her favourite biblical quotations on these occasions was the scarcely encouraging verse: 'All our righteousness is as filthy rags in thy sight, O Lord' (Isaiah 64:6). The choice of text is revealing for it points to a view of human nature which regards human beings as essentially corrupt. Such a view is commonplace in many Christian circles, but nowhere more so than in strict evangelical churches where the 'fallenness' of man is a central tenet and is accompanied by an emphasis on the judgement of God and the eternal punishment for sinners who do not turn to a personal Saviour by whose sacrificial blood alone they can be saved from damnation. It is perhaps not surprising that, if Carl was subjected to daily doses of theological insights of this kind, he should himself find it somewhat difficult to experience the self-acceptance which, thanks to him, many of his own clients discovered. In short, it seems likely that Carl was the victim for more than half his lifetime of the insidious and damaging power of the doctrine of Original Sin. Reverberations of this psychological captivity remained with him until the end of his life, because only a few months before his death he could write in an article comparing his own work with that of Kohut and Milton Erickson:

> This similarity of views – seeing the human organism as essentially positive in nature, is profoundly radical. It flies in the face of traditional psychoanalysis, runs counter to the Christian tradition, and is opposed to the philosophy of most institutions, including our educational institutions. In psychoanalytic theory our core is seen as untamed, wild, destructive. In Christian theology we are 'conceived in sin', and 'evil by nature'.
> (Rogers, 1986, pp. 2–3)

The Influence of Augustine

St Augustine, reformed libertine and early theologian of the Church, despite much in his work which is of the greatest beauty and wisdom, has much to answer for since it was he who first produced the classic formulation of the disastrous doctrine. In *The City of God* he wrote:

> God indeed created man upright, being Himself the author of natures not of vices. But man, having of his own free will become depraved, and having been justly condemned begat a posterity in the same state of depravity and condemnation. For we all were in that one man (Adam) seeing that we all were that one man who fell into sin through the woman, who was made of him before the sin. (xiii, 14. Quoted in Armstrong, 1986, p. 31)

In another passage from *Enchiridion* he goes one better and states:

> Banished (from Paradise) after his sin, Adam bound his offspring also with the penalty of death and damnation; ... so that whatever progeny was born (through carnal concupiscence, by which a fitting retribution for his disobedience was bestowed upon him) from himself and his spouse – who was the cause of his sin and the companion of his damnation – would drag through the ages the burden of Original Sin, by which it

would itself be dragged through manifold errors and sorrows, down to that final and never ending torment with the rebel angels. (26,27. Quoted in Armstrong, 1986, p. 32)

Leaning on the balcony with Carl at El Escorial, I realised how alive this dark side of St Augustine remains in the psyche of so many twentieth century men and women, religious and non-religious alike. His legacy, it seems, is to have lodged in the collective unconscious of Western men and women the terrifying possibility that they are totally corrupt and altogether unacceptable in the eyes of their Creator. In this Augustine has been supported and buttressed by thousands upon thousands of preachers, fundamentalist biblethumpers and evangelical bullies of all denominations who have attempted to batter souls into submission by the depiction of the human state as foul and utterly self-centred. At El Escorial, as on many occasions before and since, I experienced revulsion at the deep wounds which perverse and judgemental Christian doctrines have inflicted upon humanity. The very buildings which towered over us were the monument of a jealous fanatic who had hounded heretics to death and who had had the audacity to design a palace on the pattern of the grid-iron on which one of the earliest Christian martyrs had been roasted to death. Small wonder in such a setting that we found ourselves talking about Original Sin. In many ways, it was an almost inevitable theme given my own Christian commitment and Carl's early experiences and subsequent struggle with Christian theology. I recall at one point asking him if he felt satisfied with a view of human nature and development which seemed to put the whole weight on environment and social conditioning. I do not remember his answer but it certainly implied that such an understanding was infinitely to be preferred to one which suggested that human nature was by definition corrupt and therefore fundamentally untrustworthy. At the time, I believe I countered this by suggesting that this was a travesty of the Christian viewpoint (although Carl clearly still saw it this way in 1986) and asking him if he had heard of the doctrine of Original Righteousness. Carl had clearly heard of no such doctrine and was immediately riveted by the idea. I only wish that, at that time, I had been able to tell him what I have come subsequently to believe – namely that he himself was one of the chief secular exponents of precisely this doctrine in the twentieth century.

Original Righteousness

In brief, this much neglected doctrine states that humanity is made in God's image and likeness and that we are therefore partakers of the divine nature. Closely allied to this is the doctrine of deification whereby men and women are seen to be created for union with God, capable of being made one with God, called to be the place of God's indwelling. Essential to these doctrines, as indeed to the central doctrine of the Trinity, God as three personed, is the understanding of human and divine nature as relational. For me this is the essential quality of persons as opposed to individuals. When we speak of individuals, we speak of each one in his or her isolation, separate from and in competition with all others, but when we speak of persons we speak of each one in his or her relatedness, in communion with all others. Just as in the paradigm of the Trinity each of the three divine persons lives in and through the others so it is at the human level. We are all members one of another. Donald Allchin, the contemporary Anglican theologian, has claimed in a recent book that, without these doctrines of original righteousness and deification, the doctrine of the incarnation itself in the end becomes meaningless. For how, he asks, can God enter into human form unless men and women were made from the beginning to enter into God (Allchin, 1988)?

The strands of the Christian tradition represented by these doctrines were, it seems, unknown to Carl. In his rebellion against the Augustinian doctrine of Original Sin, reinforced by his experiences in his family and early environment, he moved close, however, to the spirit of those Christians down the ages who have seen the glory of men and women as lying in their capacity to realise their divine potential through their relationship both with God and with each other. The informal Eucharist in a Madrid hotel had about it all the marks of such a co-inherence of the human with the divine. Not only were the barriers between different Christian churches removed but the divisions, too, between those who could claim a belief in God and those who could not. There was at that particular Easter gathering an overwhelming sense both of the uniqueness of persons and also of the corporate membership one of another. As a result there quickly developed a form of communion to which Carl, on his own admission, felt he belonged. This is scarcely surprising for the core conditions of acceptance, empathy and genuineness were present in abundance. In such a group, it was not difficult for every person to experience his or her own essential worth which is perhaps another way of describing the inner experience of original righteousness. Such communion, whenever it occurs, exposes the Augustinian doctrine for the soul-destroying formulation it is.

A Different View of the Garden of Eden

There will be some who will see these reflections on a Spanish Easter as a blatant attempt on my part to claim Carl Rogers for the Christian fold posthumously. I would not be so presumptuous and, as I have shown, there is evidence that in his final months Carl had by no means revised his jaundiced opinion of the Christian view of human nature. It may be, however, that by now, sound empiricist that he is, Carl will have met up with his Patron Saint and, inspired by his example, will be reviewing the evidence at close quarters. Meanwhile, on the terrestrial plain a theologian of striking originality has found in Carl and other humanistic practitioners the inspiration

Carl Rogers and the Doctrine of Original Sin

for an entirely new formulation of the doctrine of Original Sin itself. The Catholic Monk, Sebastian Moore, in his book *Let This Mind be in You* (1985) presents the revolutionary idea that the Garden of Eden myth has been totally misread by most Christian apologists. He points out that the immediate effect of Adam and Eve's eating of the forbidden fruit is their gross discomfort with their bodies and each other's presence. Moore describes this as the story of the beginning of cosmic loneliness for it marks the loss of friendship with (good feelings about) sexual and other desires. In Moore's reading of the biblical text, the original sin is not disobedience but distrust, distrust of God and consequently of ourselves and, more particularly, of our desires. His description of this process and of what he believes to be its universal effect on human nature goes a long way towards explaining why it seems so desperately difficult for most of us to stay in touch with what Carl called our organismic wisdom. In this reading person-centred practitioners, insofar as they are concerned to restore a person's faith in his or her own essential nature, are seen as performing a vital task if paradise is to be regained. Moore's theological analysis of why we behave as if we are essentially untrustworthy in our inmost being offers a fascinating parallel to the psychological analysis of the formation of the negative self-concept in person-centred theory.

> The most radical experience we have of original sin is the memory of beginning to realise that desire could not be trusted. The *reason* desire cannot be trusted is that I am beginning to doubt my desirability. The sense of desirability, that directed me happily through life in infancy, now no longer works for me, for I am no longer just 'this body'. So my sense of being desirable ceases to be trustworthy as a guiding principle. I don't feel good with any conviction and therefore I don't *do* what is good. So not feeling good is the *origin* of the *sin* of not doing what is good. It is the 'original sin', the origin of sin.
>
> But how easy it is to *blame* the sense of being good and desirable that seems to have let us down. So we get the opposite version of what original sin is: original sin is the feeling of being good, it is 'pride', it is 'hedonism'.
>
> It is very easy to make this mistake. It is the easy way out to blame myself for 'coming on too strong', for over-believing in myself.
>
> Because this mistake is so easily made, it has pervaded the Christian moral tradition, which has come to place original sin in feeling good instead of in feeling bad, which is where it should be placed, and the Christian moral tradition has laid itself open to those critics who accuse it of propagating the very disease it claims to be curing.
>
> Thus we get the bad situation that while the best psychologists and counsellors are coming to understand the root of our evil as a bad self-image, Christians tend to say to them, 'You are leaving out original sin' – not realising that these psychologists are, precisely, *pointing* to original sin. (Moore, 1985, p. 83)*

---

* This quotation from Sebastian Moore is take from *Let This Mind be in You*, published and copyrighted 1985 by Darton, Longman & Todd and is reproduced by permission of the publishers.

It is fascinating to speculate what might have happened if Moore's understanding of Original Sin and its genesis had permeated the Rogers' household of Carl's boyhood and adolescence. Certainly Julia Rogers would have been a very different person with a radically different text on her lips. She might well have whispered to the young Carl the words of St Peter: 'You shall come to share in the very being of God' (2 Peter 1:4)

I am inclined to think that if such an environment had existed, we might now be honouring the memory of a much loved pastor and theologian whose life would have transformed the face of the Church. As it is, Carl fled from the Church because he experienced both its doctrine and its corporate life as imprisoning and detrimental to his development. If he had not done so, there might well have been no client-centred therapy and no person-centred approach. God moves in a mysterious way.

References

ALLCHIN, A.M. (1988). *Participation in God*. London: Darton, Longman & Todd.
ARMSTRONG, K. (1986). *The Gospel according to Woman*. London: Elm Tree Books/Hamish Hamilton.
KIRSCHENBAUM, H. (1979). *On becoming Carl Rogers*. New York: Delacorte Press.
MOORE, S. (1985). *Let This Mind be in You*. London: Darton, Longman & Todd.
ROGERS, C.R. (1986). Rogers, Kohut and Erickson: A personal perspective on some similarities and differences. Unpublished manuscript, La Jolla.

Chapter 9
Counselling and the Grocer's Shop on Campus

Escalating Distress

As I write, I am just recovering from perhaps the most demanding academic session that I have experienced in 20 years as a counsellor in higher education. Not that these last 9 months have seen a sudden and unexpected plunge into crisis. They are rather the culmination of a period of escalating clientèle and increasing distress which first began some 5 or 6 years ago. What is more, the university in which I work is in no way exceptional: colleagues in other places paint the same picture and in many instances the increase in clients has been much more spectacular than in my own institution. Thatcher's children (for only a small proportion of student clients have consciously known any other administration) would seem to be finding the going tough in the brave new world of market forces.

It is true that in recent years there has been a marked increase in public awareness of the appropriateness of counselling for relieving personal distress – a crop of national disasters has been tragically instrumental in bringing this about. I do not believe, however, that this heightened awareness accounts for the astonishing rise in client numbers which has produced grotesquely long waiting lists throughout the higher education system and reduced many counsellors to a demoralised state of exhaustion. It is my growing conviction that for many of the young people now entering higher education we have succeeded in creating a world where it is dangerous to fail and where the establishment of a personal value system now requires a degree of mental and emotional courage which it is not easy to sustain. Caught in a complex web of societal pressures and expectations, many students rapidly lose hold of their own precarious sense of identity and make their way in confusion to the counsellor's door.

From *British Journal of Guidance and Counselling*, 18 (1), 1990, with permission.

Ravaged Institutions

It is clear that student distress has been exacerbated, and in some cases directly caused, by the ravages which the institutions themselves have suffered in the last decade. The continuous reduction in government funding, and the consequent re-organisation and 'rationalisation' which has taken place in almost every higher education institution, have had calamitous effects on the lives of many academics and administrators. They have experienced an almost total transformation in the ethos of academic life, and find themselves caught up in a competitive rat-race where not only departments can be locked in internecine strife, but individual worth is construed almost entirely in terms of research output or the ability to attract funds. Many staff who entered upon their careers with a genuine love of scholarship and the pursuit of knowledge find that there is no longer a place for them unless they are prepared to develop the skills and the mentality of the entrepreneur.

Not surprisingly, many have proved unable to adjust themselves to such a shift, while others have done so with great difficulty or with a mounting sense of rage or impotent frustration. A recent survey in the University of Birmingham (Carroll and Fokias, 1989) which attempted to gauge stress and well-being among academic and academic-related staff showed that no fewer than 37 per cent of respondents registered psychoneurotic and psychosomatic symptoms at a level which indicated the need for therapeutic intervention. Women, in particular, recorded high symptomatology in the area of anxiety (especially among research associates and junior administrators), and this is scarcely surprising when one considers that it is frequently women who occupy the more junior and, in many cases, the more uncertain positions in the university establishment. Interestingly, the lowest levels of symptomatology were reported by heads of schools and this provokes the thought that those now assuming leadership roles in higher education may, to some degree at least, be temperamentally responsive to the new ethos and to the 'management' style which goes with it. Nevertheless, even these apparently resilient characters reported a marked discrepancy between the experienced job demand ('very high') and the job demand they would have preferred. They felt, in fact, that they had very little control over the day-to-day experience of their work situations and that they could exercise little personal autonomy in managing their work loads.

The language of the grocer's shop

Against a background of such staff demoralisation and anxiety, the student becomes increasingly vulnerable. One immediate outcome is that staff members are less likely to be available to respond to students in a tutorial or pastoral role: they are too preoccupied with their own concerns or with writing their next research application. It may well be, for example, that some of the current pressure on student counselling services can be traced to the non-availability of tutorial staff or to the perfunctory way in which many academics now feel compelled to carry out their advisory responsibilities.

The malaise, however, goes deeper. For higher education, like so many other areas of our national life, is in the process of losing its soul because it has allowed itself to become infected with what the Catholic Journal *The Tablet* (20 May 1989) recently described as 'the language of the grocer's shop'. Unfortunately, the words we use can quickly change and distort the nature of our experiences and this, I believe, is happening insidiously in higher education. Many students, as a result, no longer experience themselves as people but rather as consumers of knowledge.

What is more, they are concerned to buy the best product available and to show off their new purchases in the most effective way possible. Their teachers, in turn, are no longer educators but the sellers of a product which they must package in such a way as to ensure customer satisfaction.

If we translate this into the experience of the counselling room, we can begin to see why so many students are now obsessively preoccupied with the production of the perfect essay or with obtaining first-class degrees, and why many faculty members are caught up in endlessly designing new and more 'attractive' or 'relevant' courses. They are all the victims of consumerist ideology. Yet so pervasive has been the spread of the new 'faith' that such people have often lost the ability to diagnose the cause of their mounting anxiety or underlying depression. As *The Tablet* pointed out, the hallmark of the consumerist ideology is competition, and its effect as a value system is to alter the thoughts and feelings of people and how they interpret their experiences and relationships. Once the language of the grocer's shop becomes the vernacular of the campus, the whole range of subtle human relationships which can exist between staff and students is reduced to that of buyer and seller. As the terminology of trade gains supremacy, persons disappear from the scene, to be replaced by producers, consumers, commodities and disposable goods. Small wonder that counselling services are besieged by young people in despair because they do not know how to make a success of this academic 'enterprise' or, worse still, because they have lost all sense of personhood and can only weep in bewilderment at the abuse they have received.

It is not, incidentally, without significance that those reporting incidents of sexual abuse have increased in recent years. Here again, I am convinced that the publicity given to such incidents by the mass media does not adequately explain the escalation of such suffering. I am more persuaded that the creeping use of consumerist terminology throughout our culture is leading to a situation where people are no longer perceived and no longer perceive themselves as complex beings with rich inner worlds. Instead they are objects for sale, or abuse, in the market place and are reduced to the crudest and most mechanistic of measures. In such a world one wonders how it can be possible to place a price tag on a person or to calculate the value of love or empathy or compassion.

Counselling Services in a Dark Age

Counselling is concerned with inner worlds, with the validation of subjective reality and with the healing power of relationships. It could not, as an ideology, be further removed from the consumerist ideology which now haunts our society. There is something highly ironic, therefore, about the fact that counselling is booming and that it is often referred to as a 'growth industry'. It is as if the victims of the Thatcherite revolution are seeking refuge with those who are still prepared to receive them as persons and by doing so they are perhaps hastening the demise of the value system of which they themselves have fallen foul. Counselling services are in this sense the monasteries of the new dark age in higher education, for they keep alive the vision of a world where persons matter more than things and where mutuality and understanding are more important than achievement and competition. It is perhaps not surprising therefore that their subversive influence has been detected and that their reformation is already planned in high places.

The attack is subtle in the extreme, for it comes from those who purport to care about 'student services' in higher education and who profess themselves committed to their preservation and enhancement. Such people argue that, if they are to flourish, counselling services must manifestly prove themselves to be efficient and cost-effective and must face squarely the implications of accountability. In other words, counsellors should themselves quickly adjust to the consumerist ideology, ensure that they are offering a good product and learn to serve loyally in the brave new world of the managerial interest. Counsellors in polytechnics and further education are likely to encounter the kindly but zealous reformers first because they are utterly vulnerable to the velvet glove of Her Majesty's Inspectorate. Those of us who work in universities can for the moment cling to the fading image of the community of scholars and the last vestiges of the humane society. For myself, I gain some comfort from the growing army of clients who in the sanctuary of the counselling room discover within themselves a personal language which can challenge the noises from the grocer's shop.

Conclusion

In a dream not long ago, I clutched a newspaper whose headlines ran: 'Counsellors and their clients bring down the government.' It is a consoling thought and the hope that the dream might have predictive power was strengthened by a recent MORI poll commissioned by *The Independent* (2 May 1989) which reported that 70 per cent or more of those sampled believed that during the last 10 years people have become more aggressive, more selfish, less tolerant and less honest. I suppose I am naïve enough to believe that in the end our corporate sense of shame will enable us to shake off the ideology which threatens to destroy what makes the human being most human.

Reference

CARROLL, D. and FOKIAS, D. (1989). Nice work? Stress on campus. *Teaching News*, No. 37, June, University of Birmingham.

Part IV
Papers for Special Occasions

Introduction

For me the invitation to give a lecture to a specially invited audience has always been irresistible. In the first place it is flattering, but secondly it affords an opportunity to be provocative and to take the risk of moving beyond even one's own conventional wisdom. The chapters which follow are all the products of such risk-taking. In them, I chance discovering what I really think and feel and the occasions on which the lectures were originally delivered proved exciting times for me and for at least some of those who formed my audiences.

I have discovered that it is not possible for me to be a person-centred therapist and to remain aloof from the political and social issues of the day. Furthermore, the experiential knowledge gained from intimate therapeutic relationships cannot but generate new criteria against which to evaluate the validity of theological and moral standpoints. In these chapters therefore I elect to stand up and be counted. In so doing, I know I am taking the risk of courting hostility from some and even ostracism by others. It is certainly true that when the lectures were first delivered there were those who refrained from giving me their blessing. More surprising, however, was the discovery that for many I was by no means radical enough. Perhaps this is a reflection of the kind of person I am and I take comfort from the fact that even Carl Rogers described himself as merely a *quiet* revolutionary. If I am honest I suspect that I would not qualify even for that measured title. But I know I can be quite noisy when someone is misguided enough to offer me a public platform and these final chapters may disturb the slumber of some theologians, politicians or guardians of the nation's social mores. The final chapter might even raise the hackles of some person-centred therapists who would prefer to forget that Carl Rogers was still growing when he died with his boots on at the age of 85.

Chapter 10
'Intimacy'

An exploration of human relationships in the light of the incarnational nature of the Christian religion

Father Slade in his book *Contemplative Intimacy* quotes one of William Blake's most tragic poems, 'The Garden of Love':

> I went to the Garden of Love,
> And saw what I never had seen;
> A chapel was built in the midst,
> Where I used to play on the green.
>
> And the gates of the chapel were shut,
> And 'Thou shalt not' writ over the door;
> So I turn'd to the Garden of Love
> That so many sweet flowers bore;
>
> And I saw it was filled with graves,
> And tomb-stones where flowers should be;
> And Priests in black gowns were walking their rounds,
> And binding with briars my joys and desires.

The poem is a fierce condemnation of the Church's attempt to legislate for love as if intimacy could be regulated by a code of moral laws. Father Slade sees it as a grim warning to all those who are inclined through legislation or propaganda to encroach upon man's freedom to express his love (Slade, 1975).

If Blake were to revisit the Garden of Love today he would still find plenty of priests walking their rounds but he would discover, too, that they had been joined by a whole host of contemporary companions. A heterogeneous mob now tramples down the sweet flowers and so powerful are they that they no longer merely bind a man's joys and desires with briars but have well-nigh exterminated them altogether. The chapel is still there with its 'Thou shalt not' plaque but the landscape is further desecrated by a whole

---

A Lecture to the Annual Clergy School of the Norwich Diocese of the Church of England (published by Norvicare Publications, 1982) with permission.

new twentieth century development including a drug factory with 'God is a pill' over the door, a car factory with 'Thou shalt be in affluent perpetual motion' as its motto, a computer centre labelled 'Statistics are power' and a sex shop carrying promises of 'ecstatic orgasm' in neon lights. The squat building bearing the slogan 'Man is a rat' turns out to belong to certain pseudo-scientists called experimental psychologists.

With the garden so monstrously built over, it is scarcely surprising that the experience of intimacy is unknown to many if not to most in our contemporary Western society. Countless thousands are sick for lack of it and do not even know the nature of their sickness. Modern men are dying of loneliness in their urban conurbations and yet are so closed to themselves that often they do not even recognise the symptoms.

The estrangement of man from himself is something which I see in my clients and in others and I have known it in my own life. As a counsellor in a university I spend much time fluctuating between sadness and anger. The sadness is triggered principally by the predicaments in which so many young people I meet find themselves. Experience has badly damaged some of them by undermining almost all faith in the validity of their own thoughts and feelings. They seem to have no knowledge of what they are or of what they could be. For others the predicament is different. They are indeed valued by others and are conscious that they have ability and awareness. And yet they have no taste for living because they are trapped in a cycle of meaninglessness from which they seem powerless to escape. Others, again, are weary of struggling to maintain their own integrity in the face of what they experience as an implacably hostile society where all that counts is materialistic success and competitive achievement. In all these cases, the person is divorced from his experiencing organism although sometimes he will sense its promptings and be fleetingly aware of a meaning in experience, a meaning rejected at once by the conscious self which clings doggedly to another meaning, since that is the way it has previously found approval. There are those moments when we sense what we want to do at the deepest level and yet we refrain from doing it because we cannot trust ourselves enough to cope with rejection or adverse judgement or the likely feelings of guilt which will ensue. Sometimes it is the overwhelming fear of the unknown which forces us to ignore the messages emanating from our total organism and to opt instead for the voice of the conscious self which in such situations invariably adopts the tone of commonsense or eminent reasonableness. And so we remain out of touch with ourselves and therefore incapable of making real contact with another human being. Intimacy is essentially the relationship which occurs at the centre of our own being and, if we cannot trust that relationship and act upon it boldly, our responses to others are likely to be empty gestures. Christians believe that at the centre we find God who is the ground of our being. Intimacy with the centre therefore must always be a relationship of love, a loving self-acceptance born not of complacency or arrogance but from a sense of the presence of God within.

A Story

The new curate had been invited to dinner by the Churchwarden and his wife. He is anxious on arrival for he knows that to some extent he is on trial. Will he make a favourable impression? The Churchwarden is a well-known figure in the town – a solicitor who is well respected and much given to charitable works. His wife is quiet, self-effacing, an attentive hostess. Their two children are also present – a son in his early twenties and a teenage daughter in her last year at school. The atmosphere is a little strained, the conversation pleasant but superficial. Gradually, however, the young priest begins to relax and by the sweet course the good wine has lowered his defences a little and he is more open to his own feelings and perceptions. He is having to acknowledge that he feels oppressed by the Churchwarden, who seems pompous and overbearing. He cannot deny his pleasure in the physical attractiveness of the two women and his desire to know more about them. Above all, though, he is intensely aware of the young man whose eyes seem never to leave his for more than a moment or two. He senses a sadness which is close to the surface and there are moments when the young man's eyes seem to glisten with tears. And yet he is speaking conventionally enough, even if a little softly, and the priest tells himself not to let his imagination run away with him. During coffee the conversation turns to the ordination of women and immediately the curate feels renewed tension in the air. The subject is introduced by the daughter and it is clear that she is in favour of the idea. She asks the curate what he feels and he finds himself responding enthusiastically to her and saying that he sees no theological objections and hopes that acceptance of the ordination of women will come quickly in England. Silence falls and the curate remembers that his vicar does not share his views. Nor, it is clear, does the Churchwarden who seems agitated and makes some remark about horses for courses which the curate does not understand. The curate is aware that his heart is beating faster and senses that he is on dangerous ground. He is more conscious than ever of the young man's eyes focused upon him and he feels impelled to go on. Words come into his head unbidden. 'I feel', he says, 'that the Church has a lot of work to do in sorting out its ideas about the role of women. I fancy that the issue of women priests is only one aspect of a whole area of confusion about sex and sexuality. I don't think the Church's record is very impressive in this area. For centuries we seem to have been pretty twisted up about sex and its place in human relationships. I fancy we need a whole new sexual theology.' At the end of this little speech he feels astonished at his own words. He also knows that in some way he was trying to communicate with the young man whose sadness is now for him an indisputable reality.

He feels exhilarated and experiences a powerful rush of affection for the young people. He wants to say more and feels a great urge to touch them both. Almost instantly, however, he is invaded by a fear which halts him in his tracks. He is aware of the Churchwarden's expression which seems to be a mixture of confusion, disapproval and terror. He feels caught like a rat in a trap and incredibly enough he hears himself talking about the weather. An hour later he takes his leave and as he does so he is poignantly aware that he is exhausted from the effort of checking the flow of feelings which had threatened to control him. He is profuse in his thanks to the Churchwarden and his wife and as he goes out into the night he cannot even remember if he has said goodbye to the young man and his sister.

I am reminded of another dinner party (Luke 7: 36–48):

> One of the Pharisees invited him to dinner; he went to the Pharisee's house and took his place at the table. A woman who was living an immoral life in the town had learned that Jesus was dining in the Pharisee's house and had brought oil of myrrh in a small flask. She took her place behind him, by his feet, weeping. His feet were wetted with her tears and she wiped them with her hair, kissing them and anointing them with the myrrh. When his host the Pharisee saw this he said to himself, 'If this fellow were a real prophet, he would know who this woman is that touches him, and what sort of woman she is, a sinner'. Jesus took him up and said, 'Simon, I have something to say to you.' 'Speak on, Master', said he. 'Two men were in debt to a money-lender; one owed him five hundred silver pieces, the other fifty. As neither had anything to pay with he let them both off. Now, which will love him the most?' Simon replied, 'I should think the one that was let off most.' 'You are right', said Jesus. Then turning to the woman he said to Simon, 'You see this woman? I came to your house: you provided no water for my feet; but this woman has made my feet wet with her tears and wiped them with her hair. You gave me no kiss; but she has been kissing my feet ever since I came in. You did not anoint my head with oil; but she anointed my feet with myrrh. And so I tell you, her great love proves that her many sins have been forgiven; where little has been forgiven, little love is shown.' Then he said to her, 'Your sins are forgiven.' *(The New English Bible*, 1961)

Carl Rogers, the distinguished American psychologist and therapist, tells of an experience in an encounter group.

> The next day some very moving feelings were expressed, and the group paused for quite a time in silence. Sue finally broke into it with some highly intellectual questions – perfectly reasonable, but somehow not at all appropriate to what was going on. I felt, at some intuitive level, that she was not saying what she wanted to say, but she gave no clue as to what her real message might be. I found myself wanting to go over and sit next to her, but it seemed a crazy impulse, she was not in any obvious way asking for help. The impulse was so strong, however, that I took the risk, crossed the room, and asked if I could sit by her on the couch, feeling that there was a large chance I would be rebuffed. She made room for me, and as soon as I sat down she leaped into my lap, threw her head over my shoulder, and burst into sobs. 'How long have you been crying?', I asked her.
> 'I haven't been crying', she responded.
> 'No, I mean how long have you been crying inside?'
> 'Eight months.' (Rogers, 1973)

My purpose in citing these three episodes – the two dinner parties and Carl Rogers' encounter group – is to draw attention to what can happen when we are prepared to stay close to the process of our experiencing and to trust the promptings which originate there. I suggest that when we fearlessly listen to the deepest messages in ourselves and refuse to be deafened by the Babel of other voices which come both from within and without we risk encountering the living God. If that should happen we are faced with the stark choice of loving or withholding love – or moving into intimacy or of backing off from it.

If I am right about this then it follows that listening in depth to ourselves and risk-taking should be the hallmarks of the Christian experience – both activities being central to the practice of love. I want to suggest further that for many Christians the Church's traditional attitudes to relationships, and particularly to sexual relationships, pose immense problems and sometimes render both the fearless listening and the risk-taking well-nigh impossible.

The young curate in our story was momentarily in touch with his loving self and saw clearly what was required of him. And yet he was ensnared in a complex net of fears and prohibitions and could not therefore trust his experiencing and act upon it. He was afraid of his vicar, afraid of the Churchwarden – afraid that they would condemn him for acting impulsively and that he would be unable to cope with the rejection and the possible feelings of guilt. At another level he was afraid of his body and of his own sexuality – enthralled and appalled by the powerful feelings within him and by the desire to make physical contact. He knew beyond all doubt the intensity of the young man's need and sensed there the desperation of a lonely homosexual. He appreciated the women for their physical beauty and longed to know them better. He was overwhelmed with feelings for the future of the human race and had it within his power to confer a blessing on the young people who would help to shape that future. All this he was in touch with – in a very real sense he knew what he had to do. And yet he left them with his love unexpressed and the intimacy evaded. And it was night.

It is perhaps no exaggeration to suggest that for our curate the Christian religion on that evening hindered rather than aided his loving. It did so because there is often, in religious socialisation, a veiled or even manifest message that our sexuality is an impediment to the life with God and that our bodies are corrupt as well as corruptible. It is remarkable and ironic that so profoundly incarnational a religion as Christianity should have communicated so crippling a message. Alienated from the body and deprived of eros, many a Chritian attempts to become a kind of bodyless mind and bodyless minds are severely handicapped in the business of human loving. It is hard furthermore to exonerate the Church from the accusation of sexism throughout most of its history. The separation of soul from body, of reason from emotion, of the 'spiritual' from the 'carnal' life has found much reinforcement from the degradation of women. Indeed, women have often been closely identified with the characteristics of sensuality and emotional instability. There is much to answer for and it is my belief that, as Christians, we have the urgent task of redeeming the body, acknowledging the God-givenness of our sexuality and insisting upon the fundamental equality of the sexes.

In many respects the humanist psychologists have already blazed the trail, although they are often struggling in a darkness which the Christian faith can illuminate. The experience which Carl Rogers records is typical of the quality of the listening and the risk-taking which often occur in small groups where people are committed to the pursuit of empathy and authenticity. There have been occasions during encounter groups when I have come close to understanding the profound significance of St Augustine's words 'Ama et fac quod vis'. Where love is the motive, intimacy can be expressed in whatever way we will and that in no way means an unrestricted permissiveness. Intimacy which wounds the object of love is not true intimacy and such wounds are invariably inflicted where there is exploitation or manipulation for self-satisfaction or self-indulgence.

The account of Simon's dinner party bears many of the marks of humanistic encounter groups as I have experienced and facilitated them. Tears, physical contact, confrontation, shame and guilt, forgiveness, poetic language – here are the ingredients of many a group where people have developed enough trust to disclose themselves and to risk rejection. But there was, of course, a difference. The incarnate God was present at Simon's dinner party.

Jesus's behaviour is by any standard extraordinary and I want to look at it in detail. He is at a dinner party in the house of an eminent Pharisee – we can perhaps conjecture that Simon was liberal in outlook to have invited Jesus at all unless, of course, he was prompted simply by an overwhelming curiosity. Certainly, he does not seem to have been unduly courteous to his guest and has failed to observe some of the customs dictated by social politeness. The arrival of the notorious woman from the town must have been an intense embarrassment to everyone, especially to Simon. But she is weeping and is obviously in great distress: to have thrown her out would seem particularly heartless. She sits herself down as close as she can to Jesus but without interrupting the meal. Her tears fall on to Jesus's feet and it is difficult to imagine that she did not intend this. She wipes his feet with her hair, kisses them continually and rubs them with the oil of myrrh. Perhaps we are so familiar with this story that we no longer wonder at its outrageousness. I suggest that men – especially young ones – might fantasise what it would feel like to have their feet wept over by a prostitute and then rubbed and kissed by her continually (not just once or twice!) – and all the while having supper with an increasingly censorious Archdeacon. But this is what Jesus not only permitted but welcomed for he experienced it as an outpouring of great love. It is difficult to imagine a more striking eruption of the sensual, the sexual and the physical into the world of social convention and legalistic morality. And unless we are prepared to turn Jesus into a bodyless mind, we must acknowledge that as a physical, sexual and sensual being like us he was deeply affected by this extraordinary episode. What is certain is that he felt deeply loved and then poured out his love on the woman who had flouted all the conventions in order to communicate to him the passionate intensity of her devotion.

I am not attempting to elaborate a new morality for sexual and physical behaviour – such a task lies beyond the confines of this present chapter. My intention is to suggest that, if we wish to find intimacy at the centre of our being and to enter into intimate relationships with others, we need to rid ourselves of the deeply rooted fantasy that God is somehow a jealous rival of all that we find sexually attractive or physically pleasurable. He is rather its creator and as such he is present in our feelings of sexual attraction and physical longing and, if we will trust him, he can enable us to use those feelings in the service of his love. Harry Williams in his book *The Joy of God* develops the same theme and quotes an example of a sad parody by Studdart Kennedy which points to a God who disapproves of sexual feeling:

> Pray! Have I prayed – when I've bored the saints with praying
> When I've stunned the blessed angels with my battery of prayer,
> When I've used the time in saying – but it's only saying, saying,
> And I cannot get to Jesus for the Glory of her hair.

On this Geoffrey Beaumont commented: 'Studdart Kennedy knew as well as you and I that in reality it is through the glory of her hair that we come to God, that there we would find Jesus if we would only recognise Him' (Williams, 1979, p. 50).

The late poet laureate is talking about much the same thing in 'Lenten Thoughts'.

> Isn't she lovely, 'the Mistress'?
> With her wide-apart grey-green eyes,
> The droop of her lips and, when she smiles,
> Her glance of amused surprise?
>
> How nonchalantly she wears her clothes,
> How expensive they are as well!
> And the sound of her voice is as soft and deep
> As the Christ Church tenor bell.
>
> But why do I call her 'the Mistress'
> Who know not her way of life?
> Because she has more of a cared-for-air
> Than many a legal wife.
>
> How elegantly she swings along
> In the vapoury incense veil,
> The Angel choir must pause in song
> When she kneels at the altar rail.
>
> The preacher said that we should not stare
> Around when we come to Church,
> Or the Unknown God we are seeking
> May forever elude our search.
>
> And I hope that the preacher will not think
> It unorthodox and odd
> If I add that I catch in 'the Mistress'
> A glimpse of the Unknown God.
>
> Sir John Betjeman, 1979

Harry Williams concludes his chapter with the following reflections on the pernicious outcome of refusing to recognise God in the sexual:

> Blindness is the parent of hypocrisy – 'Thou blind pharisee' as Jesus said. There is something nauseatingly hypocritical in Christians holding up their hands in pious horror at the excesses of what is called the permissive society, when they themselves down the ages have tried so hard and so persistently to keep God out of sex. It is a harvest of their own sowing that they are now reaping, and the hell they abhor is in large part a hell of their own lighting up. (Williams, 1979, p. 49)

I want now to turn to the implications of what I have so far said for a Church which wishes to become a truly caring community. I realise that much of what follows is provocative and may even seem scandalous to some, but I offer it with sincerity and I hope with compassion. I am not at all sure that it enshrines many of the right answers but I am convinced that it at least raises issues which demand urgent and imaginative exploration.

First, I wish to look at ways in which our sexuality for good or ill has shaped our expressions of faith. In this task, as in much else that follows, I am indebted to Professor James Nelson and particularly to his recent book *Embodiment* (Nelson, 1979). The importance of language cannot be overestimated for it constitutes a complex symbolism through which we approach reality. If that symbolism is not adequate to the task then we cannot fully experience the reality. James Nelson reminds us that, when Captain Cook's ship sailed into the harbour of a primitive society, the people of that tribe were unable to see the ship because they had no word or symbol for a vessel of that kind. It may well be that our sense of God is limited because we have been trapped for some time in a theological language which is both sexist and spiritualist – or, to put it more graphically, our theological language has often made it difficult for us to see God as anything other than a powerful if loving disembodied male. God is Father and King and Lord and Judge. He is also spirit (Nelson, 1979). It has not always been so. For those of us who live in Norwich our own Dame Julian speaks thus:

> The human mother may put her child tenderly to her breast, but our tender Mother Jesus simply leads us into his blessed breast through his open side, and there gives us a glimpse of the Godhead and heavenly Joy – the inner certainty of eternal bliss. The tenth revelation showed this, and said as much with that word. 'See how I love you', as looking into his side he rejoiced.
>
> This fine and lovely word 'Mother' is so sweet and so much its own that it cannot properly be used of any but him, and of her who is his true Mother – and ours. In essence *motherhood* means love and kindness, wisdom, knowledge, goodness.
>
> (Julian of Norwich, 1966)

In the Song of Solomon, the lover is a being who comes in many forms, but behind them all is God himself, a God who can be described in these terms:

> My beloved is fair and ruddy,
> A paragon among ten thousand.
> His head is gold finest gold;
> His locks are like palm fronds ...
> His cheeks are like beds of spices or chests full of perfumes,

> His lips are lilies, and drop liquid myrrh;
> His hands are golden rods set in topaz,
> His belly a plaque of ivory overlaid with lapis lazuli.
>
> (Song of Songs 5: 10–11, 13–14)

If we can recapture the symbol of God the Mother who nurses us at her breasts and if we can rejoice in the erotic dimensions of the human–divine relationship then I suggest we might find ourselves able to own and celebrate our sexuality and allow ourselves to feel in love with God. It was Charles Williams who wondered why eros should for ever be on its knees to agape. A concept of God which is big enough to incorporate the feminine and the sexual may actually enable us to affirm love as desire as well as self-giving. What is more a theological language which is neither sexist nor spiritualist may actually make it far less difficult than at present for many women to think of themselves as fully created in the divine image.

If we accept that both masculine and feminine images are necessary symbols of God we are also saying that qualities labelled traditionally as masculine or feminine are both essential for wholeness. In short, for the Christian the personhood to which he or she is called must both incorporate and transcend gender. I would suggest that the Church as a caring community should be committed to a steady and relentless attack on the limiting power of sexual stereotypes and Jesus as always is the exemplar – he is the lover who can weep and embrace, speak in images and stories, debate with scholars and beat the lawyers at their own game, show incredible physical courage and be moved to the tenderest compassion. Jesus transcends the male and female stereotypes and through his personhood invites us to do the same.

The affirmation of the sexuality present in our love for God has perhaps even more far-reaching implications. It invites the Church as a caring community to cherish the deep sexual love of one human being for another and to take its outcomes with great seriousness. Sexual love brings greater openness to life's joys but it also increases the capacity to undergo change and to be sensitive and responsive to pain and suffering. Life is infused with a new energy and there is often a sense of communion not only with the beloved, but also with the whole of creation. To begin to love God like that is to risk being swept up into a cosmic Love which insists that change and openness are necessary, that joy and suffering are to be welcomed and that freedom means a joining with others to a more human future. Such a joining demands a commitment which for some is perhaps only possible if their relationship to God has a sexual dimension that empowers and liberates. The Church needs therefore to find out all it can about the life-enhancing power of sexual love.

So much then for our theological language and the power of symbols to illuminate belief and to change behaviour. It is my belief that the femaleness of God and the sexual dimension in the divine–human relationship are cardinal concepts which once accepted could deeply affect the caring community of the Church and open up many new paths to intimacy.

I want now, as a second major theme, to talk about bodies. I have dwelt earlier on the flesh and bloodness of Jesus in Simon's house. It was that same flesh and blood which our Lord decreed to be our food – food which, to use St Paul's terminology, was to nourish us as members of Christ's body. The image of *the body* is central to Paul and it is a glorious image for, as Paul elaborates it, it enshrines concepts of intimacy, mutuality and inclusiveness. In short, the Body of Christ, the Church, has many ways forward in its primary task of making love a reality in human life or, in James Nelson's phrase, 'incarnating the Incarnate Love' (Nelson, 1979, p. 260). In these final reflections I want to suggest some of those ways forward.

Two essential tasks are to proclaim the wonder of the naked body and the sacramental nature of sexual love. In our day the body is degraded – a thing to be exploited by advertisers and pornographers, a thing of shame and guilt for many. And yet the naked body when uncovered speaks, in Herbert Slade's words, with the 'simplicity of the child, the questing longing of the adolescent, the discovery of old age' (Slade, 1977, p. 119). Adam and Eve when naked could hear the voice of God in the garden but lost it when they grew ashamed of their nakedness. It is not the Church's task to pontificate endlessly against pornography. Much more to the point would be a celebration of the marvel of the human body and an encouragement to Christians to learn how much they possess and how much they have to give through their bodies.

If the naked body is degraded, how much more is sexual intimacy profaned and its significance outrageously distorted by the media of today. All sight has been lost of the fact that a loving act of sexual intercourse is a re-enactment of dying and rising. The self dies in ecstatic surrender to the other but is then received back with new life and replenishment. Of course, sexual intercourse can be misused and abused as indeed can Baptism, the Eucharist and other rituals which we commonly think of as Sacraments. But it is surely the Church's task to proclaim from the rooftops that genital sexual activity can be a royal road to the sacred mysteries. And if that sounds pagan so be it. It is a fact incidentally, that in the mystery of sexual intimacy many of today's young people find their only real sense of the sacred for there they find genuineness, trust, tenderness and surrender (Nelson, 1979, p. 256). It is ironic that when they are nearest to God, and where awe and religious language are appropriate, the most likely reaction of many Christians is to condemn or to be overwhelmed with embarrassment. I sometimes wonder, indeed, if embarrassment is not the besetting sin of the twentieth century Church. It is about time anyway that we overcame our embarrassment about nudity and sexual intercourse and sent the pornographers scurrying to their holes not through the force of our condemnations but by joyful proclamation of the body's true beauty and by the message of God's presence in every act of loving sexual union.

One last thought – a reflection prompted by the inclusiveness of the Body of Christ. With James Nelson I am convinced that as Christians we cannot go on any longer making the nuclear family our unique model for sexual intimacy. We have the possibility of not merely tolerating but positively supporting differing sexual lifestyles as they are lived out with sincerity and love (Nelson, 1979, p. 260). The caring community of the Church can cherish and nourish a diversity of sexual patterns within its own congregations and within society at large. There is room for homosexual and heterosexual couples, for small and large communities, celibate and non-celibate, with children and without. In marriage itself there is much scope for courageous exploration and experiment. Our society desperately needs responsible and committed people to be pioneers in the challenging world of intimacy. If Christians nourished by the love of a God who choses to reveal himself as a fully vibrant human being cannot undertake this work then one may well ask who can.

Acknowledgements

References to and quotations from *Contemplative Intimacy* by Herbert Slade (1975) are used by permission of the publishers. References to *Embodiment: an approach to sexuality and Christian theology* by James B. Nelson are made with the permission of the publishers. Extracts from Carl R. Rogers' *Encounter Groups* (1973) and Julian of Norwich, *Revelations of Divine Love* are reprinted by permission of Penguin Books Limited. Extracts from *The Joy of God* by H.A. Williams (1979) are used with the permission of the author. 'Lenten Thoughts of a High Anglican' by Sir John Betjeman is reprinted from his *Collected Works* (1979) and is used with the permission of the publishers.

References

BETJEMAN, J. (1979). *Collected Works*. London: John Murray.
JULIAN OF NORWICH (1966). *Revelations of Divine Love* (trans. by Clifton Wolters). London: Penguin Books.
NELSON, J.B. (1979). *Embodiment: An Approach to Sexuality and Christian Theology*. London: SPCK.
NEW ENGLISH BIBLE (1961). Oxford: Oxford University Press and Cambridge: Cambridge University Press.
ROGERS, C.R. (1973). *Encounter Groups*. London: Penguin Books.
SLADE, H. (1977). *Contemplative Intimacy*. London: Darton, Longman & Todd.
WILLIAMS, H.A. (1979). *The Joy of God*. London: Mitchell Beazley.

Chapter 11
Counselling and Community Development

I must confess at the outset that I am consumed with a sense of urgency, as I speak to you this evening. I am aware as never before in my life of mighty forces at work in our world and in our society and I believe that the time has come for counsellors and educators who have faith in the human spirit to come out of their consulting rooms and their classrooms and to speak boldly and clearly. They will not be thanked for their pains. They will not be thanked by Government or by those whose task it is to administer ever dwindling budgets. Indeed, I believe it probable that we are only a few years away from the day when those who care deeply about the human spirit will have to do so from the margins of our society and will have to accept the role of the poor scholars and wandering minstrels of the Middle Ages. I do not relish the prospect, but I certainly feel that we need to get into training.

How can counselling hope to permeate our fragmented society or bring to it the vision of a truly human community? Let me make a start by attempting to throw a light on human relating in our contemporary society and more particularly on the issue of discord and reconciliation. Discord is something we hear a lot about from family life to industrial relations. We are constantly reminded that human beings seem poorly equipped to respond harmoniously to each other. Sweet reasonableness is frequently at a premium.

I want to focus for some minutes on some of the major issues which seem to me to colour human relationships and make reconciliation between individuals so difficult and the development of community so painfully slow. Top of my list of obstacles to human relating comes the prevalence of the unexamined life. It still startles me to discover that many people are so frightened of themselves that they never dare to find out who they are. Life, it seems, is lived as a kind of pin ball game, as people bounce off one spring or

---

The first Mary Swainson Lecture given to the Leicestershire Branch of the British Association for Counselling. From *Counselling*, No. 43, 1983, with permission.

another. Blown hither and thither, the individual seems to be at the mercy of things external to himself. There is no sense of an internal resource, let alone a knowledge of what that resource might be. So often when asked, people will say that they do not know what they think or feel. The very question throws them into a blind panic. There is something very terrifying about the prevalence of the unexamined life. Human beings are full of powerful ingredients: anger, grief, love, hate, fear, frustration, desire, violence. We have seen quite a lot of that recently. How dangerous therefore it is for an individual to be so untutored in the art of self-awareness that he or she is a closed book to him- or herself. He is like an unexploded mine who might go off at any minute.

A second prevalent handicap in the business of relating is an undeveloped imagination. We all of us run the danger of existing in a very narrow world which consists entirely of our own thoughts and experiences. But relating requires of us the ability to step into another person's world and to discover what it feels like to view reality through his or her eyes. Such a task I would suggest is beyond the capacity of a man or woman whose imagination has had no opportunity to develop. Unfortunately, our present-day society does little to encourage such development. On the contrary, we live in a world of the explicit, which leaves little work for the imagination. Wasn't it interesting to hear Bernard* saying how nice it was not to have met Mary Swainson† because he was left free to use his imagination and to retain his fantasies? But the world we live in is a world so often of the explicit. Those who sit night by night in front of their televison sets where everything is to be seen in detail and in colour are putting their imaginative faculties in grave jeopardy. The growth of the imagination requires an active and questing involvement with the world about us and with those whom we meet. The passive receptivity of much television viewing saps the energy for such involvement and leaves the imagination undeveloped and lethargic.

Unexamined lives, uncultivated imaginations and then a third stumbling block in the path of relating and reconciliation, and this I call contractual living. Let me explain what I mean by that. Many areas of our lives of necessity revolve around actual or metaphorical contractual agreements. If I do such and such a thing, I shall receive such and such in return. If I pay money, I shall receive goods. If I work consistently, I shall pass my examination. If I behave in a certain way, I shall receive the approval I want. Much of this contractual living is bound up with the notion of rights. If I do such and such, I have the right to expect such and such in return.

Often we are enraged if we feel our rights are being flouted. We are

---

* Dr Bernard Ratigan, Chariman of the meeting and now adult psychotherapist with the Nottingham Health Authority.
† Dr Mary Swainson, Founder of the Counselling Service at Leicester University in whose honour this lecture was given.

permeated by a sense of intolerable injustice. Certainly, the practice of contractual living makes for smooth transactions in life, but when it breaks down, it can cause immense anger or jealousy or fear. What is more, we are not likely to feel forgiving towards someone who has done us out of our rights, someone who has broken the unwritten contract that made us feel safe and protected. And yet forgiveness is often the essence of reconciliation and an essential activity in any community worthy of the name.

You may feel that thus far I have pitched my remarks at a somewhat theoretical level. I will want to refute that accusation. On the contrary I believe with some passion that unexamined lives, impoverished imaginations and contractual strait-jackets are frequently the cause of break-downs in relationships and of hostility between persons and are almost invariably the primary stumbling blocks to the achievement of reconciliation and of that quality of relating which transforms a collectivity into a community. What then is to be done?

First, I would suggest that often when we are in conflict with another person we are actually acting out a conflict within ourselves or a frustration within ourselves. A serious effort to extend our own self-awareness will often reveal this fact. I discover that I am in conflict with someone else because he embodies a part of me that I do not like or will not face. Poor fellow, he is doubling up as my shadow self, but he does not know that and cannot understand my hostility. Or again I choose to fight someone who has developed to a high level a talent or ability which I suspect I possess myself, but not had the opportunity or perhaps the energy to nourish. I am angry or frustrated with myself but he, poor fellow, experiences only that I am angry or frustrated with him.

Secondly, I would suggest that often when another is hostile towards us, we are not the true cause of his or her hostility. A serious attempt to exercise our imagination will sometimes reveal this to us. If I make the effort to identify with the other's life and situation, I may well begin to understand that his hostility springs not from anything I have done but from the frustration in his work or from the fact that I so closely resemble his father whom he detests. So much hostility is directed at people to whom it does not truly belong. The ability to enter another person's world will often prevent us from overreacting when we receive the hostility which we have not really earned.

Thirdly, I would suggest that for many of us unconditionality of relationship is so rare an experience that we are poorly equipped either in the art of forgiving or in the art of accepting forgiveness. As a counsellor, I never cease to be startled when clients say to me things like 'you are the first person who has ever listened to me' or 'I do not feel you are judging me' or 'I can be myself here'. It seems that for many people it is a rare experience indeed to feel acceptance without strings – to be accepted simply by virtue of the fact that they are human beings who merit respect because they exist and not because of what they have done or because of their qualities or abilities. It is when a person feels valued in this way and when such unconditionality of acceptance goes deep that it becomes possible to forgive both others and oneself. Perhaps, even more important, such an experience of unconditional acceptance makes it possible to accept forgiveness when we have wronged someone else. The person who has never felt deeply accepted is often dogged by a sense of unworthiness which makes another person's forgiveness almost unbearable.

The message in all this is clear enough. We need the experience of being unconditionally accepted if we are to embark upon the process of reconciliation with any confidence. Now the counsellors among you will be well aware that, in the last few minutes, I have been drawing upon insights and knowledge which are part of every counsellor's understanding of persons in relationship. I have said absolutely nothing new.

In a sense, I have simply uttered what is to us common knowledge and yet so often it seems that knowledge fails to permeate the life of our society. It fails to nourish; it fails – and here I use a theological concept – to redeem. In all this I see a formidable challenge to counsellors and to the whole counselling movement and not only to counsellors but to every educator who still has hope for our world.

Briefly, the challenge can be summarised as follows. What can counsellors do to influence the society where, for the most part, the unexamined life, the undeveloped imagination and contractual living are the norm? The question as I see it is an urgent one, for the sands are running out. As long ago as 1958 Carl Jung could write in *The Undiscovered Self* these words: 'As in the beginning of the Christian Era, so again today, we are faced with the problem of the moral backwardness which has failed to keep pace with our scientific, technical and social development. So much is at stake and so much depends on the psychological constitution of modern man. Is he capable of resisting the temptation to use his power for the purpose of staging a world conflagration? Is he conscious of the path he is treading and what the conclusions are that must be drawn from the present world situation and his own psychic situation? Does he know he is on the point of losing the life preserving myth of the inner man which Christianity has treasured up for him? Does he realise what lies in store should this catastrophe ever befall him? Is he even capable at all of realising that this would be a catastrophe? And finally, does the individual know that he is the make weight that tips the scales?' That was Carl Jung in 1958.

Counsellors are pre-eminently concerned with the inner life of individuals even when those individuals do not wish to look inside but prefer to keep their eyes firmly focused on the external world. The problem, they say, lies with society, with other people, with the ineptitude of politicians – and perhaps some of it does. But so seldom is that the whole story. For the counsellor, this bridging of the gulf between objective and subjective experience and knowledge is a crucial task in his or her own life and in his or her work with clients. The counsellor whose own life remains unexamined, whose imagination remains starved and who languishes in the chains of contractual living, such a person is unlikely to offer a climate to clients where change and development can take place. Faced with the challenge then, what does the counsellor do?

It can be argued, and indeed often is, that if she or he attends carefully to her or his own development and works conscientiously with those individual clients who seek help then she or he is doing all that can be done. Gradually, it can be argued, a higher level of awareness in individual clients will have a permeating effect on a much wider social circle. There is some truth in this, what I call, contamination theory, but for me it is altogether too slow and too random. I want counsellors to be doing more than sitting in their counselling rooms with individual clients. I want them to acknowledge the awesome responsibility they have for influencing the psychological climate of the world in which we live and to find new ways of fulfilling that responsibility.

The counsellor who has really learned to be in touch with his own thoughts and feelings and to be genuine with his clients, who knows what it is to accept another human being unconditionally and who has developed the empathic skills which enable him to enter the inner world of another, such a person I would claim is in possession of gifts and is embracing a way of being which our world desperately needs to know more about. I do not doubt that some people will accuse me of *folie de grandeur*, but I feel obliged to refute that accusation too and to ask you to reflect with me on the implications of my stance.

I believe that we need to have faith that, despite so many indications to the contrary, we are living in an age where we are poised on the threshold of a momentous phase in our evolution, our evolution as a species. Either we shall take a great leap forward or we shall fall into a ditch of such depth that the days of Noah will be repeated on the face of the earth. I sense this kind of knife edge in my own experience. Despite all the gloom and despondency which lurks around us and to which I have drawn attention this evening, I am also aware of knowing and meeting many extraordinary people. They are committed to trying to live their lives lovingly and authentically and they do all they can to resist the insidious clutches of materialism. Many of these people are also lovers of the earth. They plead for the created world to be honoured and respected and not ravaged. In short, they bear the marks of those who are striving to grasp the tiller of evolution. Such people are the natural allies of those of us who choose to express our concern for life through the practice of counselling. We need to recognise them and to join forces with them. We need, too, to acknowledge that there are countless others who often in confusion and despair long to embrace a way of being which is so often exemplified in the counselling room. In short, we have a treasure and we must not hide it in a therapeutic sanctuary.

Sharing that treasure will mean different things to different people. For some, it will mean a preparedness to let the attitudes and behaviour which characterise their counselling work spill over into their total existence. We must begin to think, not so much of preserving professional boundaries as of transcending them. For others it will mean taking the risk of earning the cynics' ridicule by offering opportunities for personal development and for such things as empathy training. For others again, it will mean being presumptuous enough to offer consultancy to groups and organisations which wish to improve the climate of the human relating within them. Of course, we shall risk doing none of these things unless we believe that there are people out there who are thirsting for such opportunities. If you doubt this, let me bring you a message of reassurance.

After 9 years of taking such risks, both in the University of East Anglia and in the City of Norwich. I no longer question for one moment the existence of such people. Rather my fear is that, as counsellors, we shall lack the faith and the courage to provide the nourishment for which they yearn.

Let me end with a true story. When we founded the Norwich Centre for Personal and Professional Development 2 years ago, we saw ourselves primarily as a counselling service. But we also hesitantly offered ourselves as a training and consultancy resource. We are now faced 2 years later with a situation where we no longer keep pace with the demands that are coming in. Health visitors, teachers, personnel departments, voluntary workers, retirement associations, all of them in different ways are asking to draw on the treasure which we foolishly thought nobody would want. The day when the truth finally dawned on us was when Faith Broadbent, one of the partners, whom some of you know, picked up the phone to hear a rich Irish voice saying: 'Is that the Norwich Centre? I am a Mother Superior of a religious community and we want some help with our group dynamics. Do you do that sort of thing? We are a bit of a challenge, you know. We range from 18 to 81. Well, who could come then? What's your name, dear? Faith! That's what we need! You come yourself, dear! Perhaps we can have a community worthy of the name!'

Reference

JUNG, C.G. (1958). *The Undiscovered Self*. London: Routledge & Kegan Paul.

Chapter 12
Conventional and Unconventional Relationships

My starting point is what seems a kind of contradiction. As a therapist and educator, much of my own life has been spent attempting to understand more about human personality and human relationships. I have read fairly widely and I have tried, sometimes with much pain, to extend my own experience of relating to others in a variety of ways and situations. Twenty years ago, too, I set out on the unpredictable journey of marriage and I am the father of three children. From an early age I was intrigued by language and at school I decided to try to master at least one or two languages other than my own. As a result I have many friends and acquaintances in other European countries and beyond. I simply wish to put on record that I have a fairly extensive track-record on what might be described as the terrain of relating. What is more, during my explorations I have encountered many amazing people who through their acceptance and knowledge have greatly enhanced my own understanding both of myself and of others. Such people are themselves merely representatives of a vast multitude of human beings throughout the world who are wise in self-knowledge and in their understanding of others. In short, there is much evidence to suggest that we are perhaps living in an age where there is available to us a greater *conscious store* of knowledge about ourselves as individuals and as a species than there has ever been before in the history of the world. This is one side of the contradiction.

The other side is all too obvious. It becomes for me increasingly difficult to listen to news bulletins each day. In our own country I am appalled by the startling increase of crimes against the person. The sexual abuse of children, the endless report of rape and murderous assault, the despair which can lead not only to suicide but to the extermination of whole families by a desperate family member – all this and much more suggests that the fabric of personal

---

A lecture given to members of the 'Professional Holiday' Seminar, Great Melton. From *Way of Life*, **19**(3), 1987, with permission.

Conventional and Unconventional Relationships 137

and social relationships is in a state of disintegration. What is more, the economic policies of the present administration have led to an intensification of the divisions within our society: the gap between the 'haves' and the 'have nots' has widened appreciably and the shadow of permanent unemployment has obscured the light for millions. Racism is rampant and it is therefore not surprising that for the majority of our citizens what is currently happening in South Africa, for example, seems of little concern.* On the international scene the picture is no better.

The nuclear threat is as menacing as ever, terrorism proliferates, wars abound often fired by religious or political zeal and prejudice, authoritarian regimes prosper, half the world and more ekes out a miserable existence on the edge of starvation. The nations of the world, it seems, are incapable of meeting in a spirit of understanding and acceptance. Instead they are fired by mistrust, hostility and mutual fear. What is more it would seem that there is often no *will* to understand and to relate, no preparedness to work at the enlargement of the imagination which is the prerequisite for empathy.

Caught in such an apparently contradictory situation I see no alternative to facing with courage the unpalatable probability that our conventional ways of relating to each other, whether as persons, groups or nations, are now proving dangerously bankrupt. At the same time the conscious store of knowledge about ourselves and our relating which undoubtedly exists is lying for the most part unused and unexploited as the world totters towards disaster. We need to wake up to the irresponsibility of permitting such a waste of knowledge and experience.

I do not intend here to explore in any depth the implications of such thinking for nations and the world as a whole, but rather to stay within the narrower arena of our own personal and social relationships. I believe, however, that changes wrought at the first and fundamental level must inevitably affect everything else and that if we do not begin there we shall be building on sand in any case. I wish therefore to look at certain conventional ways of relating which in the light of our increased knowledge and experience can clearly be seen as damaging and can only add to the sum total of human misery. I shall begin with the most fundamental relationship of all, namely that which a person has with him- or herself.

I would suggest that it is scarcely conventional to talk in these terms at all. The relationship I have with myself is not customarily a subject for the dinner table and to talk to oneself is certainly regarded as odd or even mad. Indeed, there is much to indicate that the conventional attitude to self is to avoid contact and to make sure one is never left alone with such an undesirable companion. The fear of silence – so strong among many younger people – is often a sign of the deep reluctance to encounter the self which is seen as

---

* At this time there was brutal repression of black aspirations.

unlikeable, frightening or even unknowable. As a therapist I am repeatedly brought into contact with the attitude to the self which says 'I am not really worth knowing: I am rather stupid and inadequate: I do not like myself very much and I cannot imagine that you would really want to spend time with me'. I would suggest that the conventional relationship with the self is often very much along these lines: it is based upon an attitude of rejection, condemnation or of sheer ignorance which is itself disturbing and unnerving – I am not worth the effort of getting to know. If I am right about this then such a convention is profoundly damaging for all other relationships. If the conventional attitude to self is one of ignorant indifference or worse, then there can be no real prospect of relationship with another person which is qualitatively different. What we actually know about the psychological growth of an individual indicates that a very different attitude to self is required if a person is to experience life as in any way rewarding or fulfilling. It can be summed up in the words self-love and self-acceptance. Such an unconventional attitude to the self will mean a preparedness to treasure and cherish the self with profound implications for such things as the use of time, the balance of work and relaxation, and even the food eaten.

Most importantly, it will determine the emotional, intellectual and spiritual nourishment which is sought. Such an unconventional attitude to the self does not result in arrogance or self-centredness, but in a willingness to acknowledge faults and shortcomings without being burdened with guilt, and in a refusal to be undermined by the adverse judgement of others even if that judgement is sometimes true.

Such self-love and self acceptance will be difficult to attain by the person who constantly seeks approval or direction from external authorities, and yet again, I would suggest that conventionally most people continually seek both affirmation and guidance from experts outside of themselves. It is the unconventional person who relates to himself in such a way that he can say not only. 'I love myself and I accept myself' but also 'The wisdom of which I have greater need is within me'.

The sad, uninformed or rejecting relationships which so many people have with themselves are, of course, in many ways brought about and maintained by the conventional relationships which they experience with others. At this point I wish to stop my rolling prose and to present instead a list of statements which I believe characterise or influence so much conventional relating and which I am convinced from my own knowledge and experience are ultimately damaging to the human person.

1. It is important not to become indebted to another person.
2. It is important to maintain appearances and above all not to show weakness.
3. Men, when they are together, should remain cognitive, discuss external affairs and not be self-disclosing.

4. Intimacy should be confined to one relationship.
5. Physical contact should be reserved for sexual relationships.
6. Parents should be sparing of praise and quick to admonish.
7. Women are emotional and intuitive and men are rational and practical.
8. Wogs begin at Calais.
9. Introspection is unhealthy.
10. It is necessary at all costs to avoid embarrassment.

I should like to elaborate a little on some of these items. My first statement, 'It is important not to become indebted to another person' lies at the back of so much 'contractual living' which I see around us. It is as if the spirit of commerce and barter has entered into many of our personal relationships so that the sense of indebtedness in a relationship becomes intolerable and leads to all kinds of guilt feelings or inappropriate behaviour. Parents expect to be repaid by their children: children feel guilty if they rebel against parental expectations or if they cannot come up to the mark. 'I owe it to them to get a good "A" level etc.' It is as if debts must be paid off – even if the debt is as small as an invitation to a dinner party. They invited us; we *must* invite them back. The outcome of this kind of contractual relating is that there can be no genuine untrammelled giving and no pure receiving. There are always strings attached.

I have become acutely conscious in recent years of the deep loneliness in which so many men pass their days. I am moved by the number of times men say to me. 'I have no real friends' and this often from those who seem to be socially popular and much involved in social and public life. Many years have passed since Ian Suttie wrote about the taboo on tenderness (Suttie, 1935), but much that he wrote then remains true – especially for men. Self-disclosure between men remains rare and they spend their time together discussing business, cars, football, telling dubious jokes or rattling off anecdotes which show themselves up in a good light. It is as if they are intent on appearing coping, competent, tough-skinned, hard. It is the posture of those who never dare to meet: it leads to loneliness and alienation, concealed and somewhat alleviated perhaps by a good marriage or revealed by the desperation and frustration which can lead to sexual promiscuity or worse. The conventional relationship between men is without heart and authenticity and brings no life. Certainly it is never watered by tears.

Intimacy and physicality are in precious short supply within conventional relating. Our society is full of uncherished bodies which have received no human touch for days or weeks or even years. I know of a woman who travelled daily on the underground in the rush hour in order to feel the warmth of other human bodies, but she at least was brave enough to find her own solution, however inadequate and despairing. It is also a standard joke that in a railway carriage people will sometimes open up to total strangers and tell them their most intimate secrets. The reality behind this behaviour is, of course, far from funny. It probably indicates a conventional world where the individual is unable to reveal himself and where there is apparently nobody willing or capable of listening. So often, too, the close relationship whether of marriage or of lovers can be a trap if it is experienced as the *only* arena for intimacy or physical contact. 'They did everything together' or 'They were everything to each other' are for me the saddest of comments on a relationship for they indicate an exclusiveness and a narrowness which is unresponsive to life and which must ultimately leave one member of the relationship bereft, frightened and helpless if the other dies or departs. Intimacy and physical responsiveness are not commodities which should be rationed out with such parsimony. They are the very food of life and we need them in abundance. Convention ensures that many people live their whole lives on a starvation diet.

I wonder why it is that we find it so very difficult to confer praise and approval on others? Working in a university I often feel that I inhabit an institution dedicated to the god of criticism and negative evaluation, but I suppose that this is how the *whole world* appears to many. It is a fact I believe that the vast majority of us go around all the time *expecting* to be criticised, adversely judged, caught out. We live in fear of disapproval and admonition because so often this is what we have experienced. The convention it seems, is to withhold praise or to err very much on the side of laudatory understatement while feeling free to criticise and to pull to pieces even if this is done behind the luckless victim's back. In this way, we create a death-dealing environment in which the human spirit withers and shrinks. Why do we do it? Could it be that for some reason or another we find it embarrassing to give praise or even to receive it? That word 'embarrassment' permeates into so many areas of relating and usually it seems to mean 'Halt! Go no further'. What does the word mean anyway?

Originally to embarrass meant to encumber especially with debts or to perplex or to put into a dilemma, but now it seems to denote making someone feel uncomfortable because we have penetrated into a hidden area of their emotionality or their private world. For my part, I have come to recognise that when I feel embarrassed or when I seem to have caused embarrassment I have moved into greater depth. Embarrassment therefore brings with it the possibility of intimacy and closeness as long as I do not give way to fear or cowardice.

There are many more things I could say in elaboration of my list of ten statements, especially about the stereotyping of the sexes and about the appalling British chauvinism which is still so monstrously alive and well. I should like to conclude, however by listing – again in concise and skeletal form – some of the unconventional relationships which when I see them rejoice my heart. They delight me because I believe they further the development of the human person as I have come to understand that complex and marvellous creature and they delight me because they have within them the seeds of the world's healing.

These are some of the unconventional relationships I like:

1. The loving relationship which a person cultivates with himself or herself. She listens to herself, cares for herself as a body and a mind and a soul. She accepts herself with all her shortcomings and at the end of the day extends to herself a loving and caressing hand and receives her own happiness or unhappiness, her own laughter or tears, her own energy or exhaustion with compassion.
2. The relationship between two men or a group of men which is characterised by the sharing of feeling, by the acknowledgement of vulnerability and by a physical responsiveness. In such relationships men can weep and feel strengthened by the expression and the reception of their tears.
3. The relationship between two people drawn from different backgrounds and different segments of society. Britain remains an appallingly class-conscious society and such relationships can gnaw away at a social structure which alienates and divides us the one from the other.
4. The relationship between two people drawn from different races or cultures. There can be no real hope for the world until millions of us yearn to relate in depth to a person whose language is not our own and whose colour and creed are different from ours. Every such relationship hastens the arrival of such a day.
5. The relationship between a young person and an older person where each delights in the being of the other. Energy, curiosity and physical beauty stretch out to experience and fragility in order to create a partnership of mutual enrichment.
6. The relationship between a parent and child where both are open to learning and where the parent recognises that his or her own development depends on a commitment to the child which is continually informed by the child's need both for holding and challenging. Most relationships between parents and children fall far short of this unconventional ideal.
7. The relationship between a man and woman or a man and man or a woman and woman which is committed and secure but which turns its back on exclusiveness and enables each partner to extend to others warmth, understanding, physical cherishing and space for private sharing. I am describing a love relationship which makes possible and encourages other love relationships and does not hug its loving to itself. Sexual consummation in such instances belongs to the primary relationship, but sexuality has its place in all the others and is acknowledged, welcomed and integrated in a way which is satisfying to both persons.
8. The relationship between two souls where bodies, feelings and thoughts meet in the knowledge that they know only a fragment of life and of reality and are therefore free to live in the worlds of the invisible and of eternity. These are the relationships where both beings know that they are only a little lower than the angels. Such unconventional relationships are blissful because they refuse to be earth-bound.

Let me summarise. I believe that we now know a great deal about what, as human beings, we need from our relationships if we are to grow to the fullness of our stature. And yet I see our world on the edge of an abyss. Such a state of affairs is fuelled and exacerbated by much that goes on in our own conventional ways of relating to each other. I have tried to indicate some of the more maladaptive behaviours which I see around us and, finally, I have attempted to give at least a glimpse of those unconventional relationships which I believe are more in accord with the needs and desires of our true natures and certainly with the needs of our bruised and ravaged world.

In conclusion, now that we have mentioned the angels, a few words about relating to God. I am not bold enough to attempt a definition of a conventional relationship with God, but I suspect that if such a definition were possible it would include substantial elements of the contractual living which I have described earlier. As a therapist I have often shared the pain of clients whose relationship with God has involved them in a deep sense of unworthiness, of having failed to come up to the mark, of not having earned the reward of divine favour. They go in fear of judgement and burdened with guilt. What is more, they are often further undermined by what they sense to be the condemnation or disapproval of their fellow Christians. The unconventional relationship with God for which I myself yearn is totally devoid of such judgemental dimensions. Just now and again I allow myself to know that I am loved because I am me and for no other reason. With that kind of knowledge I am free to return that love and to make all the mistakes that are necessary if I am to grow in love. Conventional relationships with God are, I suspect, permeated by the guilt of having sinned or the fear of sinning. The unconventional relationship of which I speak allows me to acknowledge that I have sinned and that I shall sin and that nothing can alter the fact that I am most deeply loved. As in all good relationships, I can relax and breathe and smile at the one who loves me.

Reference

SUTTIE, I.D. (1935). *The Origins of Love and Hate*. London: Kegan Paul, Trench, Trubner.

Chapter 13
Who Hates the Counsellor?

The notion of the counsellor as a figure of hate or fear is at first a strange and unlikely idea. After all, counsellors are usually perceived as benevolent and kindly persons concerned that their clients shall develop in creative and constructive ways. True, there are those who believe that counsellors are molly-coddlers and that they pander to dependency and a lack of moral fibre but such people, too, are scarcely likely to be afraid of the counsellor. Their attitude will probably be one of indifference or, at worst, of scarcely veiled contempt. Others again will be influenced in their judgement by equally false or partial understandings of the counsellor's work. The counsellor in such cases may be seen as essentially an advice-giver or a purveyor of information about personal or vocational matters and as such is perceived as 'useful' or 'useless' depending on the perceiver's experience of those who have given him advice or information in the past.

It is intriguing that, in the case of many professions and occupations, they often arouse fear precisely because they are imperfectly understood. With understanding, suspicion frequently evaporates and is replaced by a realistic and more accurate perception of the person and of the work with which he or she is concerned. It is my contention in this paper that with counsellors the situation is often the exact opposite. As long as counsellors are poorly understood, they do not constitute much of a threat. They can be dismissed as vaguely useful or comfortingly benevolent or, at worst, pathetically ineffective. In this respect, incidentally, they have much in common with the clergy.

In order that nobody in this audience this evening is in ignorance of what *I* mean by counselling or of what it involves to be a counsellor, I shall now embark upon a somewhat lengthy parenthesis. I intend to describe in some

---

The Fifth Ben Hartop Memorial Lecture, University of Durham (published by Durham University School of Education, 1988). Reproduced with permission.

detail my understanding of the work of the counsellor as I have experienced it for the last 20 years working in the person-centred tradition among university students and in private practice (Mearns and Thorne, 1988). As I do so you might care to focus your attention on the question: 'Who would be afraid of a person who acts on beliefs such as these?'

My distrust of experts runs deep. In some ways it is fair to state that the person-centred counsellor must learn to wear his expertise as an invisible garment if he is to become an effective counsellor. Experts are expected to dispense their expertise, to recommend what should be done, to offer authoritative guidance or even to issue orders. Clearly there are some areas of human experience where such expertise is essential and appropriate. Unfortunately, all too many of those who have sought my help over the years have spent much of their lives surrounded by people who, with devastating inappropriateness, have appointed themselves experts in the conduct of other people's lives. As a result, such clients are in despair at their inability to fulfil the expectations of others, whether parents, teachers, colleagues or so-called friends, and have no sense of self-respect or personal worth. And yet, despite the damage they have already suffered at the hands of those who have tried to direct their lives for them, such people will often come to me searching for yet another expert to tell them what to do. As a person-centred counsellor, while accepting and understanding this desperate need for external authority, I do all I can to avoid falling into the trap of fulfilling such a role. To do so would be to deny a central assumption of the approach, namely that the client can be trusted to find his own way forward if only the counsellor can be the kind of companion who is capable of encouraging a relationship where the client can begin, however tentatively, to feel safe and to experience the first intimations of self-acceptance. The odds against this happening are sometimes formidable because the view the client has of himself is so low and the judgemental 'experts' in his life, both past and present, have been so powerfully destructive. The gradual revelation of a client's *self-concept*, that is the person's conceptual construction of himself (however poorly expressed), can be harrowing in the extreme for the listener. The full extent of an individual's self-rejection often proves a stern challenge to the counsellor's faith both in the client and in his or her own capacity to become a reliable companion in the therapeutic process.

Listen to this exchange taken verbatim from an interview with a mature student at the University of East Anglia:

Client: I don't remember my parents ever praising me for anything. They always had something critical to say. My mother was always on about my untidiness, my lack of thought about everything. My father was always calling me stupid. When I got six 'A' passes at 'O' level he said it was typical that I had done well in the wrong subjects.

Counsellor: It seems you could never do anything right in their eyes no matter how hard you tried or how successful you were.

Client: My friends were just as bad. They kept on at me about my appearance and told me that I was a pimply swot. I just wanted to creep around without being seen by anyone.
Counsellor: You felt so awful about yourself that you would like to have been invisible.
Client: It's not all in the past. It's just the same now. My husband never approves of anything I do and now my daughter says she's ashamed to bring her friends home in case I upset them. It seems I'm no use to anyone. It would be better if I just disappeared

This brief extract captures the sad and almost inexorable development of a self-concept which then undermines everything that a person does or tries to be. There is a sense of worthlessness and of being doomed to rejection and disapproval. Once such a self-concept has been internalised the person tends to reinforce it, for it is a fundamental tenet of the person-centred viewpoint that our behaviour is to a large extent an acting-out of the way we actually feel about ourselves and the world we inhabit. In essence, what we do is often a reflection of how we evaluate ourselves and, if we have come to the conclusion that we are inept, worthless and unacceptable, it is more than likely that we shall behave in a way which demonstrates the validity of such an assessment. The chances therefore of winning esteem or approval become more and more remote as time goes on. As a person-centred counsellor, however, I believe that all clients, even the most self-rejecting with the direst of self-concepts, have within themselves vast resources for development. They have the capacity to grow towards the fulfilment of their unique identities which means that self-concepts are *not* unalterable and attitudes and behaviours *can* be modified or transformed. Where development is blocked or distorted, this is the outcome of relationships which have trampled upon the individual's innate and basic need for positive regard and which have led to the creation of a self-concept and accompanying behaviour which serve as a defence against attack and disapproval. The counsellor's task is to create new conditions of relationship where the growth process can be encouraged and the stunting or warping remedied. In a sense, the counsellor attempts to provide different soil and a different climate in which the client can recover from past deprivation or maltreatment and begin to flourish as the unique individual he or she actually is. It is the nature of this new relationship environment and the counsellor's ability to create it that are central to the whole therapeutic enterprise.

It is possible to describe the nature of the growth-producing climate briefly and clearly and many of you here will be familiar with it. Carl Rogers believed, and after 20 years I continue to agree with him, that it is characterised by three conditions. The first element focuses on the realness or genuineness or *congruence* of the counsellor. The more the counsellor is able to be himself in the relationship without putting up a professional front or a personal façade the greater will be the chance of the client changing and developing in a positive and constructive manner. The counsellor who is congruent conveys the message that it is not only permissible but desirable to be yourself. He also presents himself as transparent to the client and thus refuses to encourage an image of himself as superior, expert, omniscient. In such a relationship the client is more likely to find resources within himself and will not cling to the expectations that the counsellor will provide the answers for him. The second requirement in creating a climate for change and growth is the counsellor's ability to offer the client a total acceptance, a cherishing, an *unconditional positive regard*. When the counsellor is able to embrace this attitude of acceptance and non-judgementalism, then therapeutic movement is much more likely. The client is more able to feel safe to explore negative feelings and to move into the core of his anxiety or depression. He is also more likely to face himself honestly without the ever-present fear of rejection or condemnation. What is more, the intensive experience of the counsellor's acceptance is the context in which he is most likely to sense the first momentary feelings of self-acceptance. The third element which is necessary in the therapeutic relationship is *empathic understanding*. When this is present, the counsellor demonstrates a capacity to track and sense accurately the feelings and personal meanings of the client; he is able to learn what it feels like to be in the client's skin and to perceive the world as the client perceives it. And what is more, he develops the ability to communicate to the client this sensitive and acceptant understanding. To be understood in this way is for many clients a rare or even a unique experience. It indicates to them a preparedness on the part of the counsellor to offer attention and a level of caring which undeniably endows them with value. Furthermore, when a person is deeply understood in this way, it is difficult to maintain for long a stance of alienation and separation. Empathic understanding restores to the lonely and alienated individual a sense of belonging to the human race.

It is tempting to stop with this clear exposition of the person-centred approach and in a sense all that is most important has been said once attention has been focused on the hypothesis of the inherent growth principle and on the theory of the core conditions for therapeutic movement.

In a recent paper two American colleagues, Jerold Bozarth and Barbara Temaner Brodley (1986), have attempted, however, to explore what they see as a number of supporting assertions which follow from Rogers' central propositions and which are likely therefore to feature in the underlying belief system of the person-centred counsellor's credo and throw an illuminating light on both the theory and the practice of person-centred counselling.

The first series of assertions which Bozarth and Temaner Brodley advance is concerned with the essential nature of human beings. The belief that all human beings have within them the innate capacity to grow towards their own unique fulfilment (or to move towards self-actualisation as it is sometimes expressed) is buttressed by four further propositions. *Human nature*, it is postulated, *is essentially constructive* and not destructive. It is indeed this belief which frequently draws the criticism that the person-centred approach is over-optimistic or naïve and does less than justice to the 'shadow' or 'dark' side of the human psyche. The person-centred counsellor, however, sees destructive behaviour and feelings simply as manifestations of the person who is essentially constructive and self-preserving when that person is functioning *under unfavourable conditions*. Aggression and destructiveness are interpreted as resources which the person brings into play when his desire to grow is thwarted or threatened or when, in potentially terrible circumstances, his very existence is at stake. Secondly, *human nature* is seen as *basically social* so that human beings are by nature protective, caring, compassionate and understanding towards each other. It is argued that the dependence of human infants and the interdependence of adults points in this direction as does the innate capacity to infer imaginatively the experience of others. The third proposition asserts that *self-regard is a basic human need* and this is linked to an extreme position of respect for persons so that every effort is made by person-centred practitioners not to violate a person's sense of autonomy, resourcefulness and self-respect. The final proposition in this first series of supporting assertions is that human beings are basically motivated to pursue the truth; that they have, in effect, a scientific nature which wants to tease out the reality of situations and does not wish to seek refuge in deception or half-truth.

The second series of assertions presented by Bozarth and Temaner Brodley is more concerned with the beliefs that directly influence the counsellor's behaviour and attitude towards his clients. The first is a kind of rationale for the importance of empathy. It follows from the 'scientific' nature of human beings that what a person perceives is a major determinant of personal experience and of behaviour. Logically, therefore, it is clear that *to understand a person one must attempt to grasp his or her way of perceiving reality* or, in short, one must understand empathically. The second assertion underscores the person-centred counsellor's *commitment to the individual* as at all times *the primary reference point* even if the context is the facilitation of a group or the fostering of improvement in a family or an organisation. So-called 'group realities' are therefore treated with scepticism and what may be regarded as extreme measures are taken to ensure that individuals are not sacrificed on the altar of group goals. The third assertion commits the person-centred counsellor to a belief in the *concept of the whole person*. Such a belief will enable the counsellor to avoid the danger of relating only to a fragment of his client and his client's experience. It will underline too, the awareness that people grow and change and continually discover and reveal more of themselves. Such a belief will enable the counsellor to be patient and tolerant and even hopeful in the face of despair. It will also lead to moments of joy and awe when further facets of the unique person are revealed. It emphasises, too, that to relate to a person in the present means by definition relating to his past and his future. The fourth assertion in this second series proposes that *persons are trying their best to grow and to protect themselves* in the light of the internal and external circumstances that exist at that time. In short, the counsellor is invited to trust the client's real desire to do the best he can even if the resulting behaviour is felt to be from some perspectives bad, wrong or misguided. Persons are neither totally in control of themselves nor totally self-determining. They do what they can and it is therefore appropriate neither to blame nor to give excessive merit to people for their actions. This does not mean that we are not responsible for what we do. We remain responsible even when we cannot help our actions and we exercise responsibility by pursuing self-awareness as the means of effecting change both within ourselves and within our circumstances.

The final assertion offered by Bozarth and Temaner Brodley is of such central importance to the whole practice of person-centred counselling that it requires separate discussion. Its implications furthermore go far beyond the therapeutic arena and extend into almost all domains of social and political life. They point to the person-centred counsellor's belief in the *importance of rejecting the pursuit of control or authority* over other persons. Alongside this there is the corresponding commitment to share power and to exercise control cooperatively. In the counselling relationship this implies an ever-watchful attentiveness to any imbalance in power between counsellor and client and a constant seeking to equalise power through any procedures, whether verbal or otherwise, which remedy a power imbalance. This emphasis on the abdication from power seeking reinforces even more vigorously the person-centred value that authority about the client lies in the client and not in an outside expert. Bozarth and Temaner Brodley mention with much justification that this value is insufficiently internalised by many therapists who lay claim to be person-centred in their practices. As a result such people do not understand the implication of the value – namely that they are not free to intervene unilaterally or to direct when they are acting as counsellors. Furthermore, they cannot expect to escape feelings of conflict or tension if they are obliged or drawn to adopt therapeutic procedures culled from other schools of thought where the belief in *abdicating power in order to empower* is not a central tenet.

The inherent growth principle, the conditions for therapeutic movement and the supporting assertions offered by Bozarth and Temaner Brodley together constitute a powerful statement of belief for the person-centred counsellor and this I now summarise.

The person-centred counsellor believes:

- That every individual has the internal resources for growth.
- That when a counsellor offers the core conditions of congruence, unconditional positive regard and empathy, therapeutic movement will take place.
- That human nature is essentially constructive.

- That human nature is essentially social.
- That self-regard is a basic human need.
- That persons are motivated to seek the truth.
- That perceptions determine experience and behaviour.
- That the individual should be the primary reference point in any helping activity.
- That individuals should be related to as whole persons who are in the process of becoming.
- That persons should be treated as doing their best to grow and to preserve themselves given their current internal and external circumstances.
- That it is important to reject the pursuit of authority or control over others and to seek to share power.*

Let me now return to the question which I left in your minds before I began on this lengthy but central digression. 'Who would be afraid of a person who acts on beliefs such as these?' The first answer is, assuredly, many clients – at least initially. Those who come seeking an expert who will tell them all they need to know or advise them authoritatively what to do will be disturbed or even infuriated by a counsellor who treats them with respect as a repository of their own wisdom. They may well be frightened by the challenge to confront their own confusion and pain, to acknowledge their own thoughts and feelings. They will see the task as too daunting and may well run away – with those who are particularly well defended cursing the counsellor into the bargain as inept and incompetent or unwilling to help them in their need. Over the years, I have come to recognise that these clients who curse me and leave hating me in this way are often the most terrified of all. Fortunately, some return at a later stage to acknowledge their fear and to try once more to relate to the counsellor who had so frightened them by refusing to exercise the domination they craved.

My second answer is more contentious. I believe that there are often practitioners in the helping professions – and reluctantly I must include some counsellors among them – who are threatened by the kind of counsellor I have described. Helping is now a massive personal service industry and there are many in our society whose professional existence and financial security are invested in a mode of helping which depends on a complete theoretical understanding of human development and/or the acquisition and deployment of a whole armamentarium of techniques and skills. I am not attempting to deny the immense value of other therapeutic approaches. As a person-centred counsellor, I do not have exaggerated claims for my approach. I readily accept that other ways of working are shown by research and in experience to achieve successful outcomes and I do not wish to present my

---

* For a much fuller discussion of the issues raised here and elsewhere in this chapter see Mearns and Thorne (1988). Much of this lecture was subsequently incorporated into the book.

way as a universal panacea. At the same time, however, I am aware that the person-centred approach to counselling does not commend itself readily to, for example, most intellectuals. There are at least two powerful reasons for this. In the first place, the approach lays primary stress on the quality of the relationship between counsellor and client and, secondly, it travels light as far as theoretical concepts are concerned. Intellectuals, however, usually delight in theoretical complexity and also tend to be somewhat apprehensive about relationships which demand a depth of involvement. It is therefore not surprising that both in academic and professional circles the person-centred approach is sometimes dismissed as facile or superficial or is even castigated by some as naïve and misguidedly optimistic. Another common or patronising response is to regard person-centred counselling as simply embodying what all good counsellors do anyway at the beginning of a therapeutic relationship – before, that is, they pass on to deploy much more sophisticated techniques which can *really* deal with the client's problems.

There can be little doubt that in many ways the person-centred approach is strikingly out of alignment with much that characterises the current culture of the Western World. Carl Rogers often used to comment that his way of being and working ran counter to the mechanistic ethos of a technological society which thrives on efficiency, quick answers and the role of the expert. In Rogers' view such an ethos has the effect of reducing human beings to the level of objects and of placing disproportionate power in the hands of a few. What is more, it gives ample opportunity to those who seem only too willing to hand over responsibility for their lives to others. Clients who run away from the person-centred counsellor may find themselves only too happy to place themselves in the care of a practitioner who will do things to them and tell them, be it ever so gently, how to behave. In this way they are spared the pain of seeking self-awareness and self-knowledge. I am suggesting here that there is in some clients and in some caring professionals a basic fear of both self-awareness and of relating in depth. In the case of certain professionals this is compounded by a strong desire, often unacknowledged, to hang on to power and to the role of the expert. The outcome of all this is a reinforcing in our own culture of the prevalence of the unexamined life.

A prevailing ethos where the unexamined life is coupled with a failure to exercise empathy is intolerable for the person-centred counsellor. He has no option but to declare war upon it and every time he sits down with a client he is indirectly engaged in such a battle. In the last year or two, however, it has become increasingly clear to me that simply by attempting to do my job I am becoming a threat to those whose aim it seems is to inhibit the self-awareness of the individual and to discourage imaginative identification with the lives of others. I speak, of course, of those who are currently charged with the government of our nation.

The third answer therefore to my question 'Who would be afraid of a person who acts on such beliefs?' can be summarised thus: 'Those who trade on certainties, who encourage individuals to focus on external gain and achievement by assuring them that society does not exist but only the individuals who constitute it, who induce guilt and a downward spiralling self-concept in those many people who find themselves marginalised and humiliated by a competitive and entrepreneurial ethos where dog eats dog and where the level of stress accelerates uncontrollably in the fight for supremacy and survival.' In higher education, counsellors in the last 12 months have been all but overwhelmed by the alarming escalation in the numbers of those, both students and staff, seeking their help. The stress in individuals is without parallel in recent years and it is nationwide. It is a scandal that in this country we now inhabit a psychological environment which is about as detrimental to personal and interpersonal development as could be conceived and where even high-flying male Yuppies are succumbing to anorexia.

Materialism has most of us firmly in its sway and the poor, the suffering, the alienated, the insane are embarrassing marginalia who must not be allowed to disturb our world. Indeed, to exercise imaginative compassion is to threaten a way of being where the attitudes and activities which are highly valued include material acquisition, competitiveness and the obsession with so-called hard technology and hard science. It is not, I believe, overstating the case to suggest that we live in a society whose values encourage the pursuit of aims that are well-nigh immoral and that has actually institutionalised several of the sins known to traditional Christianity as mortal or deadly – gluttony, envy, pride, covetousness, jealousy. The appalling nature of the trap into which we have fallen is even more starkly revealed when we realise that if our present economic system is to survive we must actually consume more and more in order to keep in work those whose task it is to produce more and more. The vicious circle of materialism dictates that we must go on growing materially for ever.

Those of us who are counsellors also value growth enormously, but when we speak of it we are using a very different language to that of politicians. We are talking of the development of persons, the realisation of human potential, the emotional, intellectual and spiritual growth of men and women. For us growth focuses on the inner world of the mind and spirit: growth is internal. Such growth is not possible, however, in isolation. We depend on each other for our nourishment and the personal freedom which we cherish depends, not on self-assertiveness, but on the ability to relate without fear to others. We value personal growth but we also value the human relating which is the necessary context for such growth. These are the values that underpin the roles we have chosen to play out in society even if, as is frequently the case, we prove unworthy of them. Of course, we are often hypocrites and there is no doubt that professional altruism looks pretty questionable when, for example, a professional association of 'carers' is shamelessly bargaining for financial advantages for its members. And yet it would be a gross misrepresentation of the facts to be so caught up in cynicism that we lose sight of the fact that many of those in the helping professions derive genuine satisfaction from seeking other people's advantage and good. Indeed, if there was not a powerful altruistic motivation at work in the personal service professions, then many of the tasks could never be accomplished at all. I cannot escape the feeling that many of those working in the caring professions would still want to do the work even if the financial and material rewards were even less than they are. The values of growth and human relating are such that in a powerful sense the carer embodies a moral idealism even if at times he or she is a somewhat grey and uninspiring embodiment.

I do not intend to imply that the Prime Minister or the members of her cabinet and administration are consciously malevolent.* The evil springs not from conscious will but from blindness, from a lack of awareness, from an inability to embrace the values of growth and human relating which I have suggested are the very corner-stones of person-centred counselling. Such blindness is evil because it seeks to avoid the pain of self-awareness. It is essentially the outcome of spiritual laziness and its characteristics are an unwillingness to self-examine, a constant abuse of power, and an almost total inability to empathise with others. In a remarkable book which has become a best-seller entitled *The Road Less Travelled* (1978) the author, Dr Scott Peck, an American psychiatrist, writes as follows:

> I define evil as the exercise of political power – that is the imposition of one's will upon others by overt or covert coercion – in order to avoid extending one's self for the purpose of nurturing spiritual growth.

I see in those compelling words a peculiarly apt description of our present administration. Behind the philistinism, the cutting and scrimping of the cost accountants, the build-up of nuclear armaments, the growing conflict with the churches, the hostility towards liberal education, there lurks a profound desire to avoid awareness of inner realities and a determination to crush any signs of spiritual health which may appear. As I watch the Prime Minister* on the television or read her speeches and those of many of her ministers I am conscious of an active avoidance of that kind of feeling and thinking which lead to empathy and the increase of self and other awareness. Such behaviour is not the outcome of non-love, it is the acting out of antilove. And antilove is evil.

Antilove seeks to destroy compassion whenever it appears and its most insidious weapon is to use the very language of compassion in order to do its destructive work. Latterly, our present government has even ceased to camouflage its intentions in this way and has preferred to use the language of rationalisation and efficiency, but we may be sure that from time to time

---

* Mrs Thatcher was at this time leading a Conservative administration.

there will be a re-emergence of the words of concern. When this happens, when the voice of compassion is heard from Whitehall once more, then I suggest that those of us in the helping professions need to be doubly on our guard. We may be tempted to believe that we can relax and take comfort in the belief that ultimately human evolution is on our side and that the evolutionary flow of love will in the end win out over the forces of evil and entropy. It is imperative that we do not succumb to such false comfort. Evolution *is* on our side but only if we fulfil our responsibilities in hastening the process. I fear the time has come when those of us who have been presumptuous enough to accept and embrace the role of counsellors and carers must leave the relatively protected environment of our professional circles and descend into the market place. To do that creatively without ourselves falling victim to the very blindness which we abhor will require a humility of staggering proportions. Whatever happens we are bound to be called arrogant, power-seeking, naïve or mad. I tremble, but in this City and University I take courage, for after all you have a Bishop* who has recently been called all these things. And what is more it is clear that he has attracted such opposition because he induces fear and hate in those who have set their faces against empathy and who have no intention of sharing power. May his example be increasingly contagious.

References

BOZARTH, J. and TEMANER BRODLEY, B. (1986). The Core Values and Theory of the Person-Centered Approach. Paper prepared for the First Annual Meeting of the Association for the Development of the Person-Centered Approach, Chicago.

MEARNS, D. and THORNE, B.J. (1988). *Person-centred Counselling in Action*. London: Sage.

PECK, M.S. (1978). *The Road Less Travelled*. New York: Simon & Schuster.

---

* The Right Reverend David Jenkins, the controversial Bishop of Durham and an outspoken critic of the Thatcher government's economic policies.

Chapter 14
Carl Rogers: The Legacy and the Challenge

A Personal View from a Reluctant Prophet

It was one of Carl Rogers' powerful insights that what is most personal is most universal. Emboldened by this assertion, I set out to explore my own indebtedness to Carl Rogers and to the client-centred/person-centred approach to therapy whose fiftieth birthday we celebrate at this time. Indebtedness, however, suggests a fixed and somewhat passive state whilst I am currently aware of an inner restlessness in my own life which is not unconnected to my professional activity. More than 20 years as a person-centred practitioner have brought me to a point where I feel increasingly compelled to re-examine the boundaries of both theory and practice and to assess the challenge of the years ahead. The role of prophet is not one that I assume with any great enthusiasm for prophets seldom receive a warm reception – especially, I suspect, in their own professional country. I am fearful that some of my friends and colleagues in the person-centred world may not take too kindly to some of the things I have to say and, for this reason, I wish at the outset to make it clear that I do not regard myself as some kind of representative spokesperson for the client-centred tradition. What follows are simply the personal reflections of one person-centred therapist who has spent most of his professional life in a provincial city in eastern England.

A Formidable Legacy

Howard Kirschenbaum and Valerie Henderson in their introduction to the recently published *The Carl Rogers Reader* (1990) state categorically in their

---

A lecture to celebrate the fiftieth anniversary of the founding of client-centred therapy, given in Paris, Norwich and Vienna, 1990. Subsequently published in German in *Perspektiven Rogerianischer Psychotherapie* (eds R. Stipsits and R. Hutterer), WUV Universitätsverlag, Vienna, 1992.

opening sentence: 'Carl Ransom Rogers ... was the most influential psychologist in American history.'* Most people, I believe would agree with that judgement and it is not difficult to accumulate evidence in support of it. Carl was professionally active for 59 years and was prodigiously conscientious and productive. His achievements are not easily summarised but they include not only the founding of a new approach to psychotherapy, but such pioneering work as recording and publishing complete cases of psychotherapy, carrying out and encouraging more scientific research on counselling and psychotherapy than had ever before been undertaken, developing the intensive therapeutic group experience usually known as the 'encounter group', spreading the principles of therapy into almost all areas of the helping professions, and adapting discoveries made initially in the counselling room to the resolution of intergroup and international tension and conflict. Such astonishing activity was accompanied by prolific writing: Carl wrote 16 books and more than 200 professional articles and research studies. By any criteria this was a giant of a man and his legacy is formidable.

Confirming Personal Knowledge

In the light of such a catalogue of achievements, it seems churlish of me to reflect that I sometimes wonder whether Carl Rogers actually taught me anything that I did not already know. And yet, as I ponder on this seemingly ungrateful and somewhat arrogant reflection, I sense that Carl would be amused. After all, he maintained that the best facilitator was the one who left others believing that they had done it all by themselves. For me, Carl was more than an influential teacher could ever have been for he gave me the courage to discover what I already knew and to know it fully for the first time. He endowed my own experience with authority and at the same time supplied the concepts and the words with which to articulate with clarity what before I had only dimly sensed and confusedly attempted to put into practice.

When I began training as a client-centred therapist in 1967 it felt like coming home. It was, for example, immensely liberating to read of Carl's trust in the human organism and of his deep respect for an individual's capacity, given certain conditions, to discover his or her own resources for facing life's challenges. Instinctively, I had always shared this faith and had clung on to it in the face of religious and philosophical theories which often reflected a very different evaluation of human nature. It was as if Carl validated my own stubborn idealism by giving credibility through his own painstaking experience as a therapist and researcher to my seemingly over-

---

* All quotations from *The Carl Rogers Reader* are reproduced with the permission of the publishers, Constable Publishers, London.

optimistic view of human potential. It was not a question of my falling into line with the great man's discoveries: it was rather a sense of being called in from the cold and endowed with a new respectability. I suppose another way of putting it is to say that Carl enabled me to feel that I might really be quite wise and not seriously deluded as I had often secretly feared. Such affirmation did my self-regard a power of good.

As I came to understand the core therapeutic attitudes of acceptance, empathy and congruence, the same awareness of familiar ground amazed and delighted me. This recognition came at a time when I was depressed by the death of my mother (whose pain I had always experienced more deeply than was good for me) and the suicide of a much loved Sixth Form student. My capacity to understand the inner world of others seemed in such a situation more of a curse than a blessing and I must have been close to abandoning a way of being which often seemed to render me more vulnerable than was tolerable. I suppose Carl's exposition of the core conditions had the effect both of clarifying how it was I wanted to be in relation to those who sought my help and of releasing me from the sense of apartness which was threatening to induce in me a kind of therapeutic masochism. Since that time, I have met many others, both in the therapy professions and outside of them, who owe to Carl the powerful reassurance that it is not foolhardy to want to accept and to understand other people and to be honest with oneself and with them. What is more, Carl's work suggested that to embrace such a way of being need not lead necessarily to a kind of emotional martyrdom.

Legitimating Love

Some 20 year ago the British sociologist, Paul Halmos, wrote a provocative book entitled *The Faith of the Counsellors* (1969). A central theme of the book is that the social work and therapy professions have elaborated complex theories of human personality and interaction in order to make it respectable, legitimate and practical for them to love their clients and to receive love in return. For me, the initial impact of Carl's work was to illuminate the truth of Halmos's proposition. I had reached a point, I believe, where I was painfully confused about what it might mean to love another human being; furthermore when I tried to do so I often felt naïve or sensed that I had illicitly moved across sacrosanct boundaries. As I devoured Carl's words in *On Becoming a Person* (1961) and *Client-centered Therapy* (1951) my confusion evaporated. I recognised instantly that to offer clients the kind of relationship characterised by the presence of the core conditions was, in practice, to love them. The clarity of this realisation was liberating to an unimaginable degree. Not only was it apparently legitimate to love one's clients, but here was an eminent therapist who insisted that it was both necessary to do so and sufficient. What is more, he did not confine himself to vague and general precepts but spelt out in detail the nature and process of such loving. In short, Carl – gently, authoritatively and without a trace of sentimentality – both validated my previously confused efforts and gave them new illumination and direction. This was life transforming because it enabled me to see that my professional responsibility required me to be myself with confidence.

Quiet Miracles

If I were to attempt to summarise in one sentence Carl Rogers' principal legacy to humanity I think I would express it thus: *he enabled countless people throughout the world to be themselves with confidence*. Client-centred therapy has made it possible over the years for thousands of human beings to discover that if they can begin to trust themselves they will discover that they are wise and not crazy, lovable and not despicable. This process of personal transformation is so simply stated that it is easy to forget that we are talking about something which in former times might well have been called miraculous. I should like, therefore, to put an extended proposition in somewhat dramatic terms: *'The legacy of Carl Rogers is that he enabled countless people to be themselves with confidence. He achieved this by illuminating through his life and work a way of relating to others which permits miracles to occur.'*

The miracle, as I have come to experience it, has many facets. Most obviously, it concerns the client. In a typical case the person who comes for help is self-rejecting, has low self-esteem, feels ashamed and has little confidence in his or her ability to relate to others. If client-centred therapy goes well, it is likely that at a future point (be it measured in weeks, months or years) this same person will have attained a large measure of self-acceptance, will think well of himself or herself and will be relating to others without fear. It is also probable that guilt feelings will be much reduced and the sense of shame largely diminished. I sometimes think that we client-centred therapists have become so accustomed to this process that we are in danger of taking the miracle for granted. We have ceased to be awe-struck by the relationships in which we are involved day by day and week by week. And yet it is clear that we are an essential part of the miracle. Because of the way we are with our clients, we make a significant contribution to the process of transformation which they undergo. In short we are agents (perhaps in many cases the primary agent) of an internal movement within the other person which enables a passage from self-hate to self-love, from shame and guilt to openness of being, from isolation to connectedness. Such a process does not leave us unaffected, for it demands a commitment to a disciplined life where our clients provide a constant challenge to our capacity to extend to them our acceptance and empathic understanding and to our preparedness to be honest with ourselves and with them. Clearly, we do not always succeed and our failures, if we do not take care, will threaten to undermine us. The loving in which we are engaged is no task for the faint-hearted for it cannot depend on immediate attraction or reciprocity. It is my own experience, furthermore, that as the years go by the task becomes more difficult: the clients, it seems, are more severely damaged and the movement from self-hate to self-love becomes for them more arduous and more unpredictable. If we lose heart and cease to display the commitment and the discipline which our work requires, we are likely to become ineffectual and even injurious to our clients. If, however, we acknowledge our own centrality in the working of miracles, then we shall be concerned to know how we can continue in such a profession when it seems that, contrary to most human tasks, experience leads to our work becoming not easier but more complex and demanding.

New Terrain

In an article published in 1986, the year before his death, Carl provided, I believe, the beginning of an answer to this dilemma. He wrote that his view had broadened into a new arena that could not as yet be studied empirically. He continued:

> When I am at my best, as a group facilitator or a therapist, I discover another characteristic. I find that when I am closest to my inner, intuitive self, when I am somehow in touch with the unknown in me, when perhaps I am in a slightly altered state of consciousness in the relationship, then whatever I do seems to be full of healing. Then simply my presence is releasing and helpful. There is nothing I can do to force this experience, but when I can relax and be close to the transcendental core of me, then I may behave in strange and impulsive ways in the relationship, ways which I cannot justify rationally, which have nothing to do with my thought processes. But these strange behaviours turn out to be *right*, in some odd way. At these moments it seems that my inner spirit has reached out and touched the inner spirit of the other. Our relationship transcends itself and becomes a part of something larger. Profound growth and healing and energy are present. (Kirschenbaum and Henderson, 1990)

As I read these words for the first time, I had the experience once more of becoming aware of something that I already knew. Indeed, in this instance, I had the excitement of realising that I had the year previously myself written in somewhat similar terms in a short, essay entitled 'The quality of tenderness' (Thorne, 1985) (see Chapter 5). Carl had observed a fourth and powerful characteristic in a growth-promoting relationship and called it 'presence'. I, for my part, had become increasingly conscious of a quality of relating which I chose to call 'tenderness'. As I read again what I had written in 1985, I concluded that we were talking about the same thing.

> Inwardly I feel a sense of heightened awareness and this can happen even if I am near exhaustion at the end of a gruelling day. I feel in touch with myself to the extent that it is not an effort to think or to know what I am feeling. It is as if energy is flowing through me and I am simply allowing it free passage. I feel a physical vibrancy and this

often has a sexual component and a stirring in the genitals. I feel powerful and yet at the same time almost irrelevant. My client seems more accurately in focus: he or she stands out in sharp relief from the surrounding decor. When he or she speaks, the words belong uniquely to him or her. Physical movements are a further confirmation of uniqueness. If seems as if for a space, however brief, two human beings are fully alive because they have given themselves and each other permission to risk being fully alive. At such a moment I have no hesitation in saying that my client and I are caught up in a stream of love. Within this stream there comes an effortless or intuitive understanding and what is astonishing is how complex this understanding can be.... Always there is a sense of well-being, of it being good to be alive and this in spite of the fact that problems or difficulties which confront the client remain apparently unchanged and as intractable as ever. Life is good and life is impossible, long live life. (Thorne, 1985)

The two descriptions are strikingly parallel in a number of important respects. In the first place they speak of a high level of consciousness in the therapist, of a 'heightened awareness' or 'a slightly altered state of consciousness', of 'being in touch with the unknown'. Secondly, there is a sense of the therapist being responsive to the intuitive rather than to the powerful rational part of his or her being and as a result being endowed with new and often complex understanding. Thirdly, there is a powerful experience of relating at a new and deeper level: Carl speaks of 'inner spirit' reaching out to 'inner spirit' while I speak of two persons giving themselves and each other permission 'to risk being fully alive'. Fourthly, there is the experience of the transcendent, that is to say of two people being linked into something greater than themselves: Carl states explicitly 'Our relationship transcends itself and becomes a part of something larger' while I speak of being 'caught up in a stream of love'. Fifthly, in this transcendent state there is an overpowering sense of energy, well-being and healing.

Later in the same article Carl, as he reflects on the experience he has attempted to describe, wrote: 'I realize that this account partakes of the mystical. Our experiences, it is clear, involve the transcendent, the indescribable, the spiritual. I am compelled to believe that I, like many others, have underestimated the importance of this mystical, spiritual dimension' (Kirschenbaum and Henderson, 1990). It is my conviction, buttressed by experience, that those of us who are concerned to ensure the vitality and the development of the client-centred tradition need to take these words of Carl's with the utmost seriousness. In short, what would it mean if we began to acknowledge and even to emphasise the importance of the mystical, spiritual dimension and then to face the implications of such an emphasis for our work as client-centred practitioners?

Suspicion of the Spiritual

Before attempting a response to that question, it is worth noting that Carl did not himself live long enough to pursue the path into this new terrain. In his account of the interview with a client called Jan, which concludes the same article quoted above, he dwells with obvious pleasure on those responses which he calls 'intuitive'. He is particularly delighted to have captured one such response on a recording for the first time. But there is no further discussion of the 'mystical, spiritual dimension' and no further reference to the transcendent. What is more, in the final posthumously published presentation of 'Client-centred psychotherapy' which Carl co-authored with Ruth Sanford and which appeared in 1988, this 'new characteristic' of the therapeutic relationship receives no mention. Perhaps for a chapter which was to appear in a comprehensive textbook of psychiatry, Carl believed it inappropriate or premature to give weight to an element which could not yet be studied empirically. The scientist and researcher may have rebelled against the inclusion of such clearly 'spiritual' material. There is, however, another possible explanation which I hope is untrue. It could be that Carl came to feel that he had strayed into dangerous territory and that it would be unwise to risk his reputation by developing his exploration of such controversial ideas. Such fears would certainly be given substance by an article which has recently appeared by Harry Van Belle from Redeemer College in Ontario, Canada (1990). Van Belle* is acutely uncomfortable with Carl's late move to mysticism although he believes that it was prefigured in many of his earlier writings. Almost despairingly he writes:

> In them [his earlier writings] a preference for attitude rather than technique, for being and becoming rather than doing is already evident. This preference comes to its fullest expression in his latest publications. By moving from a way of doing to a way of being Rogers may have exceeded the bounds of therapeutic thought and may have given us a philosophy of life, a world view or even a religion instead.

A few lines later Van Belle can contain himself no longer and observes:

> Personally I find Rogers' latest view rather esoteric and otherworldly. I wonder whether in essence it differs all that much from the world avoiding fundamentalistic view of his parents which he abandoned as a youth. (Van Belle, 1990)

Van Belle at least is honest and states with clarity what I suspect is privately felt if not expressed by many other client-centred practitioners. For them, as for Van Belle, Carl's pioneering work embodies a profound respect for individual persons and for the development of their unique identities. The move towards a transcendental dimension seems to put this validation of the individual at risk. It smacks of a 'mystical universalism' and raises fears of a view of reality where the individual counts for little and is merely an insignificant part of a greater whole. Its distinctly 'religious' flavour also engenders anxiety in the hearts of those who have suffered and escaped from

---

* The quotes from Van Belle (1990) are published with the permission of the Leuven University Press.

the bruising impact of dogmatic creeds and doctrinal rigidity. At the very least it suggests that at the end of his life Carl may have betrayed the 'third force' of humanistic psychology and aligned himself in spirit with the 'fourth force' of the transpersonal psychologists. For those client-centred practitioners who have devoted their energies to the faithful accompaniment of their clients, to the creation of the climate for growth and to the understanding and validating of subjective reality, such an invitation to enter into the cosmic dance is inevitably viewed with suspicion if not alarm.

Implications for Therapeutic Practice

At a more pragmatic level, the notion of a transcendent reality creates what could be termed 'operational difficulties'. What are the implications for therapeutic practice if a client-centred therapist determines to take seriously Carl's contention that he or she should attach importance to the mystical, spiritual dimension? What might it mean to create a climate of relationship characterised by the qualities, not only of acceptance, empathy and congruence, but also of presence? As it is my own belief that Carl's upholding of the spiritual dimension constitutes not a deviation from his former work but the crowning of it, it is clearly incumbent upon me to address this issue. Indeed, I believe that the future of client-centred therapy may well depend upon whether this issue is confronted or avoided.

What is an Individual?

Two of the most common criticisms of the client-centred tradition concern ego inflation. It is often argued that the strong emphasis on the unique value of the individual and of his or her subjective reality can lead clients to disregard the needs of others and to enshrine selfishness as a philosophy of life. Others have argued, from a different but related angle, that client-centred therapy grew out of midwestern middle-class values with its emphasis on self-sufficient individualism and is therefore of limited relevance in a culture which emphasises a view of the person that sees him or her as essentially related to the larger society, both human and non-human. This view has been forcefully presented in a recent article by Len Holdstock (1990) who argues that black African culture, for example, is renowned for its emphasis on groupness and interdependence. In such a culture the notion that the locus of control is to be found inside the individual person gives way to the much more complex idea that the individual can only find true identity insofar as he or she participates in the surrounding world of interpersonal relationships and of the rest of the created order. Holdstock has no hesitation in stating that such an understanding 'reaches into the realm of the spiritual' and he embraces the concept, first introduced by E.E. Sampson (1983) of 'ensembled individualism', that is an individualism which is defined by its participatory involvement in the surrounding field and not by its separateness from it.

It is possible, I believe, to see Carl's work with encounter groups and then with cross-cultural communities and the peace movement as his gradual discovery of the glory of human beings when they are truly interconnected and find their fulfilment in participation which enhances rather than denies their uniqueness. To those critics who accused him of encouraging and promoting selfishness and self-centredness through his powerful validation of individual experience, he pointed to the evidence provided by such groups of the essentially social nature of men and women when they are truly heard and valued. It would seem, too, that it was through his own participation in groups that Carl became profoundly aware of deeper levels in his own being and was able to become increasingly open in his response to others. In the closing stages of many an encounter group or cross-cultural workshop, he would certainly have subscribed to the African saying quoted by Holdstock: 'I am because we are. We are because I am.'

Client-centred Therapy and the Spiritual Dimension

This discussion of 'ensembled individualism' is not a diversion from the issue of the client-centred therapist and the spiritual dimension. On the contrary, it goes to the heart of it for it confronts the therapist with an understanding both of himself and his client which has profound implications for the therapeutic undertaking. In brief, it postulates that neither the therapist nor the client can fully own and embrace their identities in isolation from each other and from the created order of which they are both a part. The therapeutic relationship thus becomes an undertaking in which, the more the participants can be present to each other, the more they will be confirmed in their ensembled individualism and in their shared belongingness to a transcendent order. In such a conceptualisation of the therapeutic relationship, much will therefore hinge on the therapist's capacity to be present to his or her client. We return now to the issue of what it would mean actively to cultivate Carl's fourth characteristic of the therapeutic relationship.

My answer to the question may seem like the ultimate anticlimax but I believe it to be nothing of the kind; it is rather a statement having profound implications for the future of the client-centred tradition. The therapist who wishes to cultivate presence needs only to trust the authority of the client's unique way of being and to offer a relationship characterised by acceptance, empathy and congruence. Carl did not set out in any conscious and deliberate way to give his presence to clients, any more than I strive to achieve what I have come to recognise in my own terminology as tenderness.

This fourth quality, however we define it, is the outcome of the therapist's trust in the client's actualising tendency and in the commitment to the offering of the core conditions. And yet it is utterly transforming: it is like the sudden coming into full bloom of a flower which previously had revealed only a hint of its splendour. I do not believe its emergence can be forced and yet at the same time I sense that *the more congruent I am, the more likely it is that such transformation will come about.* If I am right about this, then it suggests that the future of the client-centred approach will depend neither on the development of new client-centred skills and theories nor on the integration of techniques and insights culled from different traditions. It will rest rather on the ability of client-centred therapists to be congruent in ways which give access to the fullness of being where language is inadequate and where we must make do with such words as mystical, spiritual and transcendent. I wish, finally, therefore to examine what it might mean for client-centred therapists to discover ways of being more transparent to their clients, more open to the feelings and attitudes flowing within them in the moment of relating.

Congruence

In the final exposition of client-centred therapy referred to above, although he does not refer to the transcendental, Carl states unequivocally of congruence: 'This is the most basic of the attitudinal conditions that foster therapeutic growth.' He goes on to describe congruence as a condition where 'what the therapist is feeling at an experimental or visceral level is clearly present in awareness and is available for direct communication to the client when appropriate'. Later he acknowledges that achieving this condition is certainly not simple. 'Being real involves being thoroughly acquainted with the flow of experiencing going on within, a complex and continuing flow' (Rogers and Sanford, 1988). It follows from these observations that the therapist who wishes to be maximally congruent will be able to face his or her own inner world without fear: he or she will not cut off if the going gets tough or if strongly positive or negative thoughts and feelings surge into consciousness. Indeed, such occurrences will be welcomed for they are the stuff of direct personal encounter where the therapist's daring to be real assumes a new potency which can dissolve barriers at a stroke and establish a new level of intimacy. This does not mean that the therapist imposes upon the client or burdens the client with all his or her feelings and problems. It does mean, however, that the therapist is prepared to face the complexity of his or her own being in the knowledge that to do so is vital to the client's well-being.

Old and Growing

It is my own belief that Carl in the closing decade of his life faced the mystery of his own being in ways which would have previously been unthinkable. We have glimpses of this in some of the things he wrote during those years. He speaks of his increasing openness to the physical and sensuous sides of his nature and of his pleasure in touching, hugging and kissing. He describes with great honesty the difficulties surrounding his wife's long illness and the powerfully psychic events at the time of her death which led him to be open to the possibility of a continuation of the individual human spirit. In 1980, he reports an increasing awareness of his capacity for love and of his sexuality and rejoices in the fact that he has built relationships where these needs can find expression. Shortly before his death, he writes with awe of his involvement in three of the world's 'hottest' areas of tension – Northern Ireland, Central America and South Africa – and of the wonder at realising that through his writings he is in personal touch with many hundreds of thousands of people. There is a sense that his life is growing more and more adventurous. He concludes the article written to celebrate his eighty-fifth birthday with the words: 'I hope it is clear that my life at eight-five is better than anything I could have planned, dreamed of or expected. And I cannot close without at least mentioning the love relationships that nurture me, enrich my being and invigorate my life. I do not know when I will die, but I do know that I will have had a full and exciting eight-five years' (Kirschenbaum and Henderson, 1990).

This, then, is the man who discovered that there were times when simply his presence in a relationship seemed full of healing and when he and his client moved into the realm of the transcendent. It is scarcely surprising that this should have occurred, for it is evident that Carl had reached the point where he loved and trusted himself with such assurance that he was in no way afraid of his own being and could therefore 'be thoroughly acquainted with the flow of experiencing going on within, a complex and continuing flow'.

Spirituality and the Task Ahead

Once more Carl Rogers tells me – and I suspect countless others – what I already know. He tells me that I am trustworthy and desirable, despite my many imperfections, and that the more I can risk being fully alive the more I will be a transforming companion for my clients and for all those whose lives I touch. In short, he assures me that to be human is to be endowed with the spirit of life and to enjoy a uniqueness which paradoxically links me to my fellow human beings, my ancestors and the whole of the created order. As a client-centred therapist, I have the privilege and the responsibility of accepting and cherishing my own being in the service of those who seek my company and I know that if I can really do that we shall both discover that our spirituality and our humanity are indivisible.

I have said little that is new and perhaps I know nothing now that I did not know before I started. And yet for me there is a sense of a firmer and fresher conviction. Once again I feel affirmed in my personal knowledge and I can sense Carl smiling somewhere in the background. I am sorry that, while I have perhaps extended somewhat the notion of the individual in client-centred therapy, I have not proposed new and exciting strategies or interventions for jaded client-centred practitioners. To do so, however, would, I believe, have been to dodge the issue. The challenge of the 1990s, as I experience it, is to be a client-centred therapist in a world which requires urgently that we recognise that we are members one of another and that we depend for survival on the only earth that we have. Being congruent in such a context demands that we lose our fear of our own natures and take the risk of being fully alive. If we succeed in this task we should not then be surprised if we become agents of transformation and find ourselves in a transcendent reality. Acceptance, empathy and congruence – these three, as always, but the greatest and the most difficult and the most exciting and the most challenging is congruence.

References

KIRSCHENBAUM, H. and HENDERSON, V. (Eds) (1990). *The Carl Rogers Reader*. London: Constable Publishers.
HALMOS, P. (1969). *The Faith of the Counsellors*. London: Constable.
HOLDSTOCK, L. (1990). Can client-centred therapy transcend its monocultural roots? In: G. Lietaer, J. Rombauts and R. Von Balen (Eds), *Client-centred and Experiential Psychotherapy in the Nineties*. Leuven: University of Leuven Press.
ROGERS, C.R. (1957). *Client-centered Therapy*. Boston: Houghton Mifflin.
ROGERS, C.R. (1961). *On Becoming a Person*. Boston: Houghton Mifflin.
ROGERS, C.R. (1980). *A Way of Being*. Boston: Houghton Mifflin.
ROGERS, C.R. (1986). A client-centred/person-centred approach to therapy. In: I. Kutash and A. Wolf (Eds), *Psychotherapist's Casebook*. New York: Jossey-Bass.
ROGERS, C.R. (1987). On reaching 85. *Person-Centered Review*, vol. 2 (2). Beverly Hills: Sage.
ROGERS, C.R. and SANFORD, R. (1988). Client-centred psychotherapy. In: H.I. Kaplan and B.J. Sadock (Eds), *Comprehensive Textbook of Psychiatry*, vol V. Baltimore: Williams & Wilkins.
SAMPSON, E.E. (1985) The decentralization of identity. Toward a revised concept of personal and social order. *American Psychologist* 40.
THORNE, B.J. (1985). *The Quality of Tenderness*. Norwich: Norwich Centre Publications.
VAN BELLE, H.A. (1990). Rogers' later move towards mysticism. Implications for client-centred therapy. In: G. Lietaer, J. Rombauts and R. Van Balen (Eds), *Client-centred and Experiential Pychotherapy in the Nineties*. Leuven: University of Leuven Press.

Postscript

The experience of compiling the material for this book has been both satisfying and unnerving. I have enjoyed going through my own archives and meeting there an array of former selves most of whom do not cause me too much embarrassment even if I might, in some instances, choose to express myself somewhat differently today. What is unnerving, however, is the feeling that the production of 'anthologies' of this kind is usually reserved for those whose creative life is all but over and who are no longer expected to set the world alight.

It may be, of course, that this is a wholly accurate reflection of the actual situation and that time will show only too clearly that I have now shot my bolt. It would be dishonest of me, however, to conclude on so pessimistic a note. Whatever my own future contribution may turn out to be or not to be, I have a quiet conviction that person-centred therapy is here to stay and that its transforming effect on human relationships in general, and on helping relationships in particular, has only just begun. Much, however, will depend on the present generation of person-centred practitioners and on their commitment to a way of working which demands nothing less than the involvement of their whole persons with their vulnerability and their brokenness as well as their strengths and skills. Such commitment and involvement cannot be undertaken without the most rigorous self-discipline and without the nurturing support of a community worthy of the name. The person-centred therapist who wishes to be a part of that empire of paid carers who function exclusively within the bureaucratic pattern of the 9-to-5 day has not begun to understand the discipline of which I speak. What is more he or she will have no vision of the community without which even the most intrepid person-centred therapist must ultimately fail for lack of the self-same intimacy which is the gift beyond all price.

Author Index

Allchin, A.M., 108
Armstrong, K., 107
Arrowsmith, W., 89
Association for Student Counselling, 85

Beaumont, Geoffrey, 125
Betjeman, Sir John, 125
Bown, Oliver, 105
Boy, A.V., 35
Bozarth, Jerold, 146
Broadbent, Faith, 135
Burn, M., 32

Carroll, D., 112
Chadwick, Owen, 88

Devonshire, C.M., 28, 53, 67, 69, 103
Dewey, John, 25
Dryden, Windy, 1
Dymond, R.F., 43

Eyre, Richard, 5

Fokias, D., 112
Frankl, Viktor, 90–91
Freud, S., 98
Frick, W.B., 35, 87

Halmos, Paul, 156
Henderson, Valerie, 154, 158, 159
Hoffmann, John, 99, 101
Holdstock, Len, 161

Irvine, Gerard, 5

Julian of Norwich, 119, 126

Jung, Carl, 7–8, 10, 18, 79, 133

Kilpatrick, William Heard, 25
Kirschenbaum, H., 26, 102, 104, 154, 158, 159
Kremer, J.W., 67, 69

Lambers, Elke, 53, 55
Lao-Tse, 27
Lyward, George, 6, 12, 31–32

McLeod, John, 56, 63
Maslow, Abraham, 87
Mearns, Dave, 28, 42, 53, 55, 56, 144, 149
Montefiore, Hugh, 5
Moore, Sebastian, 21, 79, 109–110
Moustakas, Clark, 86, 92

Nelson, J.B., 126, 128, 129
Nelson-Jones, R., 29
Newman, J.H., 88

Oatley, K., 25

Peck, M.S., 152
Pine, G.J., 35
Polanyi, Michael, 27

Rogers, Carl, 8–10 *passim*, 28, 44, 76, 117, 122, 150, 154–165
 and Christianity, 102–103, 105–110 *passim*
 on client choice, 98
 on client selection criteria, 36
 on congruence, 163

on the core conditions, 41, 50–51,
  74, 156
development of person-centred
  therapy, 25–27
on empathy, 40
and groupwork, 51–53, 57, 63–64,
  162
legacy of, 154–155
on loving the client, 156–157
on Mrs Oak, 43–44
on presence, 158, 162–163
self-acceptance of, 104–105

Sampson, E.E., 162
Sanford, Ruth, 160, 163
Shertzer, Bruce, 9, 10–11
Slade, H., 119, 128

Spurling, Laurence, 1
Suttie, I.D., 139

Tausch, R., 35
Tayler, Stuart, 5
Temaner Brodley, Barbara, 146
Teresa, Mother, 80
Thorne, B., 1, 16, 28, 41, 42, 45, 73,
  144, 149, 158–159
Tomlinson, T.M., 104

Van Belle, Harry, 160
Villas-Boas Bowen, M., 58

Williams, H.A., 125, 126
Wood, J.K., 57, 65

Subject Index

Entries followed by '(BT)' refer specifically to discussions of the author's personal experience in relation to the indexed subject.

acceptance (unconditional), 39–40, 95–96 (BT), 98–99 (BT), 132–133
  see also self-acceptance
Association for Humanistic Psychology, 28, 54

case examples, see clinical case experience
Centre for Cross-Cultural Communication, 69
change, see therapeutic change
childhood experience (BT), 3–4
Christian belief (BT), 9–10, 16
  and Carl Rogers, 102–103, 105–110 passim,
  doctrine of Original Righteousness, 107–108
  doctrine of Original Sin, 106–110 passim
  the human body and 128
  intimacy and, 119–129 passim
  relationship with God (BT), 142
  sexuality and, 126–129
  tenderness and, 75–76
  see also Church (the); mystical experience
Church (the), viii, 5
client-centred counselling/therapy, see person-centred counselling/therapy
clinical case experience (BT), 13–14, 45–49, 93–94
community development: counselling and 130–135
conditions of worth, 31–32, 39
congruence, 10 (BT), 39, 98–100 (BT), 145–146, 163, 165
conscience, 90–91, 94–96 passim
consumerist ideology, 113–114
core conditions (Rogerian), viii, 50–51, 156 (BT)
  see also acceptance, congruence, empathic understanding, presence
creativity, 31
  in large groups, 62

defences, 33–34
denial (as a defence), 33–34
distortion, perceptual (as a defence), 33–34
disturbance, see psychological disturbance

embarrassment
  and intimacy, 140
  in sexual matters, 128
empathic understanding, 40–41, 146, 147
  in childhood (BT), 4, 9
encounter groups, 51–52
'ensembled individualism', 161–162
ethical issues
  ethical confrontation in counselling, 93–101
  see also value

existential issues, 85–92

Facilitator Development Institute (Britain), 28
   large group experience, 53–72 *passim*
Finchden Manor (Tenterden), 6, 11–12
fully functioning persons, 31

genuineness, *see* congruence
government policy, critique of, 152–153
   see also consumerist ideology; materialistic culture
Group Relations Training Association, 54
groupwork, 36–37, 50–72 (large group)
   beginning stages of, 58–60
   development of large group, 60–64
   developments in Britain, 53–54
   effective leadership in 66–67
   FDI Workshops, 54–72 *passim*
   La Jolla Programme, 52
   modes of learning in, 64–66
   mutuality/intimacy in, 61–63 *passim*
   prepatory stages for, 57–58
   Rogers' move into, 51–53, 162
   societal/cross-cultural implications, 69–70
   as a training experience, 67–68
guilt, 73, 79
   (in)appropriate, 90, 94–96 *passim*

human nature, 146–147

I-Thou relationship, 27
intimacy, 42
   and Christian belief, 119–129
   paucity of, 139–140
   see also love; mutuality
introjection, 32
intuition, 158–160 *passim*

love, 19, 156 (BT)
   in counselling, 15, 16, 18, 77, 156
   sexual, 127
   see also intimacy

materialistic culture, 89, 90, 111–115 *passim*, 120, 150–1
meaning, *see* value

mutuaility, 42
   in large groups, 61–63 *passim*
mystical experience (BT), vii–viii, 4, 19–22
   see also transcendent state in counselling

Norwich Centre, 28

organismic self, 29–31 *passim*
Original Righteousness, doctrine of, 107–108
Original Sin, doctrine of, 106–110 *passim*

Person-Centred Approach Institute International, 28
person-centred counselling/therapy, viii–ix
   change in, 34, 43–44
   and community development, 130–135
   development in Britain, 27–28
   ethical confrontation in, 93–101
   goals of, 34–35
   groupwork in, 36–37, 50–72
   historical context of, 25–27
   human nature in, 146–147
   image of the person in, 28–29
   limitations of, 44–45
   love in 15, 16, 18, 77, 156
   psychological disturbance in, 29–30, 31–34
   psychological health in, 30–31
   selection criteria for, 35–37
   spiritual dimension in, 159–165 *passim*
   stages in, 42
   theoretical assumptions of, 28–34
   therapeutic style in, 38–41
   therapist qualities in, 37–38
   threatening principles of, 150–151
   the transcendent in (BT), 158–159
   underlying belief system of, 146–149
   in a university setting (BT), 111–115 *passim*
   value and meaning in 85–92 *passim*
   see also core conditions; Rogers, Carl (*Author Index*)

Subject Index

Person-Centred Network, 54
physicality (body)
   in Christian belief, 128
   paucity of, 139–140
power
   in group learning, 64
   personal (BT), 10
   in person-centred counselling, 148
presence, 158, 162–163
psychological disturbance
   acquisition of, 31–33
   conceptualisation of, 29–30
   perpetuation of, 33–34

relationships, 136–142
   with God (BT), 142
   with self, 137–138, 141
   unconventional, 140–141

self-acceptance, 9–10 (BT), 138, 146
self-concept
   negative, 29–30, 32–33, 144–145
   and therapeutic change, 43, 145
self-disclosure: men and, 138–139

sexuality, 79
   and (Christian) faith, 126–127
spiritual dimension, *see* Christian belief; mystical experience; person-centred counselling, spiritual dimension in; transcendent state in counselling

tenderness, 41–42, 73–81, 158–159
   defined, 76
therapeutic change, 34, 43–44
training (counsellor) (BT), 8–12 *passim*
transcendent state in counselling (BT), 158–159

unconditional positive regard, *see* acceptance
university setting for counselling (BT), 88–89, 111–115 *passim*

value: search for, 85–92

wartime memories (BT), 3–4

Zen, 27